MW00998871

Praise for *En Comunidad*

Here's our book, at last! España and Herrera's engaging narrative, and the voices of teachers and students, remind us that we are en comunidad when we express our care, love, and understanding for emergent bilingual learners of Spanish, English, and all world languages. *En Comunidad* confirms that students possess intellect, creativity, and imagination across their language assets and repertoires. We educators have been waiting for España and Herrera as our colleagues, guides, and seers, and they're here at last. Thank you for guiding us further in our journeys toward literacy, libertad, and equity through your humane work, vision, and practices.

—R. Joseph Rodríguez, teacher and author of *Enacting Adolescent Literacies Across Communities: Latino/a Scribes and Their Rites*

It shouldn't be a mystery or a chore to educate secondary Latinx bilingual learners. To this end, teachers need to learn how to center their students' voices and experiences in their classrooms, and in so doing, make education meaningful to them. Kudos to Carla España and Luz Yadira Herrera for this conceptually rich, beautifully written, and highly accessible text that indeed charts a new way forward.

—Angela Valenzuela, Professor, Department of Educational Leadership and Policy at the University of Texas at Austin

This book centers around how to empower minoritized Latinx students as learners by helping them value their own language, their own history, their own community, and themselves in a system that has marginalized them for centuries. *En Comunidad* is not only for Latinx students or teachers who teach Latinx students, but for all American students and teachers who desire to bring real democracy to this country and make this world just for all people. This is indeed a wonderful book.

—Danling Fu, Professor, College of Education at the University of Florida

Somehow this book manages to be at once deeply personal and profoundly practical at the same time. Carla and Luz weave their own stories as Latinx educators and students with concrete, transformative suggestions for making all students feel welcome, honored, and supported in our schools. Each year there is one book that comes out that makes me wish I could go back to my first year of teaching and do it all over again—to do it better. This is the book for me this year. How I wish I had had Carla and Luz in my ear, and how glad I am they are here for you now.

—Kate Roberts, author of *A Novel Approach*

In this incredible book, Carla and Luz remind us that, like in all good teaching, the most effective classrooms place students at the center of teaching and learning. In a mix of critical pedagogy and inspirational practice, they demonstrate ways to build curriculum around students' lives, to avoid the trap of monolithic thinking, and to trust—truly trust—students to fill in knowledge gaps (including our own) through shared discussion and inquiry. Carla and Luz guide us to consider: when classrooms are shared spaces, when children teach as much as they learn, we, as a community, can thrive.

—Christopher Lehman, Founding Director of the Educator Collaborative and coauthor of *Falling in Love with Close Reading*

This book is a radical departure from every other professional development book I've read about teaching emergent bilinguals. Carla and Luz's embrace of each student they work with and their staunch belief that every child brings an abundance of value to our classrooms—not in spite of, but because of their linguistic heritage—feels revolutionary in this day and age. Then they went one step further and made those ideals tangible by providing engaging, practical lessons about language, identity, and literacy. Every educator who reads this book will be changed by it. And perhaps most importantly, so will our students.

—M. Colleen Cruz, author of *The Unstoppable Writing Teacher*

Dr. España and Dr. Herrera hit a home run. Together, they beautifully bridge the gaps among theory, policy, practice, and personal experience. Their work evokes untold Latinx histories and offers culturally sustaining pedagogical approaches to classroom practice. It's clear this work is not only about sustaining Latinx raciolinguistic ways of being; it's also about sustaining researchers and classroom practitioners. This work reminds us that we are here and we belong.

—Steven Arenas, English teacher and recipient of the NCTE Early Career Educator of Color Leadership Award

In this book, grounded in research and lifted by story, Carla and Luz provide compelling rationales and practical ideas for valuing students' and colleagues' linguistic repertoires and identities. As a monolingual teacher, this book exponentially expanded my growing understanding of best practices for teaching all children and for building inclusive and appreciative learning communities in which everyone is seen, heard, and valued.

—Kathy Collins, coauthor of *I Am Reading: Nurturing Young Children's Meaning Making and Joyful Engagement with Any Book*

As a scholar who seeks to challenge racial and linguistic hierarchies in the education of Latinx children, the most common question that I receive from teachers and administrators is how they can work to dismantle these hierarchies in their day-to-day practice. Now the answer has become more simple: *En Comunidad*. In this book, España and Herrera treat seriously the idea that the cultural and linguistic practices of Latinx children are legitimate and should be made central to their educational experiences. It is a must-read for all educators who work with Latinx students.

—Nelson Flores, Associate Professor of Educational Linguistics, Penn Graduate School of Education

En Comunidad pushes beyond the common notions of learning language, using language, or having language. Authors España and Herrera send the invitation to *live* language. When we are safe to live our languages inside classroom spaces, we can live a more represented, connected, and liberated life. And I can't imagine a greater gift to give students. Thank you, Carla and Luz, for writing a book that not only offers an insightful course on language but also helps us take the power off the page and into the classroom with a series of researched, dynamic lessons.

—Maggie Beattie Roberts, coauthor of *DIY Literacy*

Have you ever wondered what bilingual education would look like if it were intentionally designed to sustain the rich practices and identities of Latinx children, families, and communities? If so, you will definitely want to read *En Comunidad*. In this engaging book, you will be introduced to a critical bilingual literacies approach to curriculum and teaching. Intentionally centering bilingual Latinx voices, values, practices, and experiences, this approach invites us to consider robust pathways for engaging in teaching that honors bilingual Latinx students' full identities. *En Comunidad* offers us powerful lessons for transforming the education of bilingual Latinx students in the pursuit of justice.

—Mariana Souto-Manning, Professor of Early Childhood Education and Teacher Education, Teachers College, Columbia University

Carla España · Luz Yadira Herrera

Foreword by **Ofelia García**

En Comunidad

Lessons for Centering the
Voices and Experiences of
Bilingual Latinx Students

Heinemann
Portsmouth, NH

Heinemann
145 Maplewood Ave., Suite 300
Portsmouth, NH 03801
www.heinemann.com

Offices and agents throughout the world

© 2020 by Carla España and Luz Yadira Herrera

All rights reserved. No part of this book may be reproduced in any form or by any electronic or mechanical means, including information storage and retrieval systems, without permission in writing from the publisher, except by a reviewer, who may quote brief passages in a review, and with the exception of reproducibles (identified by the *En Comunidad* copyright line), which may be photocopied for classroom use.

Heinemann's authors have devoted their entire careers to developing the unique content in their works, and their written expression is protected by copyright law. We respectfully ask that you do not adapt, reuse, or copy anything on third-party (whether for-profit or not-for-profit) lesson-sharing websites.
—Heinemann Publishers

"Dedicated to Teachers" is a trademark of Greenwood Publishing Group, Inc.

The authors and publisher wish to thank those who have generously given permission to reprint borrowed material:

List in "Teaching Within a Close Reading Ritual to Build Independence" from *Falling in Love with Close Reading: Lessons for Analyzing Texts—and Life* by Christopher Lehman and Kate Roberts. Copyright © 2014 by Christopher Lehman and Kate Roberts. Published by Heinemann. Reprinted by permission of the publisher.

Poem from *The Moon Within* by Aida Salazar. Copyright © 2019 by Aida Salazar. Reprinted by permission of Scholastic and Gallt & Zacker Literary Agency.

Library of Congress Cataloging-in-Publication Data
Names: España, Carla, author. | Herrera, Luz Yadira, author.
Title: En comunidad : lessons for centering the voices and experiences of bilingual Latinx students / Carla España and Luz Yadira Herrera.
Description: Portsmouth, NH : Heinemann, 2020. | Includes bibliographical references and index.
Identifiers: LCCN 2019047574 | ISBN 9780325112480
Subjects: LCSH: Hispanic Americans—Education. | Hispanic American students—Psychology. | Education, Bilingual—United States. | Culturally relevant pedagogy—United States.
Classification: LCC LC2669 .E76 2020 | DDC 370.117—dc23
LC record available at https://lccn.loc.gov/2019047574

Editor: Tobey Antao
Production: Victoria Merecki
Front cover ilustration: Nathalie G. Cruz
Cover and text designs: Suzanne Heiser
Typesetter: Gina Poirier Design
Manufacturing: Steve Bernier

Printed in the United States of America on acid-free paper
6 7 BB 25 24 23
October 2023 Printing / PO# 4500878386

A papá y mamá por animarme y criarme
"más Chilena que los porotos."
A mi pareja en la vida, Angel, por darme
el espacio para crecer en mi profesión
y en mis sueños.

—C. E.

To my Remi, mi amorcito.
You teach me how to be a better mami,
teacher, and scholar.
Y a mi familia. Los adoro.

—L. Y. H.

Contents

Foreword

Latinx temas, textos y translanguaging en comunidad

In *En Comunidad*, España and Herrera have succeeded in doing what most books for teachers of emergent bilingual students fail to do—view Latinx children holistically, from *inside* the comunidad, and not simply from outside. With a lens that centers Latinx voices and experiences, the book does not simply offer guidance as to how to best teach English, or even how to best teach Spanish, which many books for teachers of Latinx students attempt. Instead, this book offers teachers a systematic approach to teach Latinx bilinguals with temas that interest them, textos that tell their stories and historias, and a translanguaging approach that encourages the literacy actions of Latinx bilinguals without paying heed to the linguistic borders that have restricted their own voices.

This book is unlike any other. From the very beginning España and Herrera share their own stories and experiences as immigrants from Chile and Mexico and what that has meant for their own work as educators of Latinx children. Their method, which they call a *critical bilingual literacies approach*, emerges from their own experiences, their own traditions, their own texts, their own questions. But España and Herrera extend their experience with that of the Latinx comunidad, nourishing their perspective not only with the experience of Latinx bilinguals entre mundos but also reserving a place for the America that is often left out of the conversation—the one often referred to as Latin America.

What makes this book so important for teachers is the encyclopedic knowledge that the authors have about temas of importance to the Latinx community, the textos that are appropriate to be informed about those temas, as well as how to put to work translanguaging pedagogical practices to ensure an inclusive and just education for the Latinx comunidad. This book is not a simple guide. Centered on texts to educate children in elementary and middle schools, it offers profound knowledge of *temas*, *textos*, and translanguaging practices important for the many teachers of Latinx students in the U.S. Here, the word *texts* does not just refer to rich children's literature—narrative fiction, nonfiction, and poetry—but also history, scholarship, music, digital texts, music trailers, interviews with authors, speeches by historical figures, documents such as those related to DACA, social media, spoken word performances, and other texts. Whereas the knowledge systems of Latinx comunidades are often presented elsewhere in truncated fashion as of de aquí or de allá, España and Herrera bring all of it together, thereby forming a newly integrated knowledge system that is of and for *all* Latinx comunidades.

Juntos, in comunidad, the authors present resources for the education of Latinx children regardless of language or genre of text, or the national identity of the author, or even the national scenario in which the action took place. For example, the book includes work by Chicana activists such as Gloria Anzaldúa and Cherríe Moraga, and the Puerto Rican Sonia Nieto; but it also introduces teachers to Latin American cantantes de protesta like Violeta Parra, Victor Jara, and Mercedes Sosa. It does so to integrate Latinx students' lives not only linguistically and culturally, but also historically, geographically, and in terms of identity. In claiming this space of intersections in which Latinx children perform their lives and their literacies, the authors appeal to Crenshaw's scholarly concept of intersectionality. This time, however, the intersectionality takes shape in actual lives, and not simply in scholarly perspectives or legal manuals.

It is this intersectionality that also enables the authors to present textos that are categorized not by language, as is often the case in bilingual classrooms, but by temas that the textos represent. In presenting the textos in this way, España and Herrera are making a statement. The literacies of Latinx students are not static and are never monolingual, even when the text is in one language or another. There are no monolingual texts if bilingual children are engaged in reading, listening to stories, speaking about them, or writing about them. By leveraging the bilingual students' translanguaging through pedagogical practices that enable it, rather than restrict it, the critical bilingual literacies approach that España and Herrera introduce helps teachers and students unlearn ideas about the supremacy of the English language that continues to restrict Latinx children's opportunities to do literacies. The Latinx children's language practices and voices are centered, and not the language of nation-states, whether English or Spanish.

The critical bilingual literacies approach is developed step by step by drawing from different genres. The authors know that it is not enough to tell our stories; it is also important to know our histories, stand against injustice, be sustained with poetry, and become not simply researchers but also advocates of our community. These are the larger themes that structure the book. Each chapter starts with a description of a momento de aprendizaje for the authors, and a reflection on those moments of learning. The lessons then are grounded on a personal learning moment, a moment that has opened up alternative understandings to the truncated knowledge and segregated dual cultural/linguistic systems that the authors themselves faced in schools as both students and teachers.

Every lesson in this book is richly populated with textos and pedagogical steps that can be taken. What is surprising to me about the outlined steps is that they do not in any way dismember language into bits and pieces of structure, as is often the case in outlining lessons for Latinx bilinguals. Instead, the authors reintegrate the language repertoire of Latinx bilinguals and use it fully to engage students with relevant temas and textos. To do that, they leverage not only the language practices of students and authors but also those of families and friends.

The stories of the comunidad are then put in relationship with those in the past that have been relegated to something called "history" that is often presented as separate from lives in the present. But continuing with the intersectional lens, the authors make clear that the present Latinx stories are grounded in our histories, and that Latinx history helps us understand the present moment.

Although the critical bilingual literacies approach taken in this book is steeped in a workshop approach to literacies, the focus is not on the types of reading and writing that often characterize workshop literacy models. Read-alouds, shared reading, guided reading, and independent reading are included throughout, as are predrafting, drafting, and editing final writing products. But these types of literacy activities are not presented in mechanical, segregated ways. Instead, they are integrated in the lessons so that children and their teachers are taking true action, not simply going through the motions of each of the components of the reading and writing workshop.

Another reason why this book is different from others is that even though it focuses on decolonizing language and knowledge systems, it is a text written by teachers, for teachers in schools. Teachers in this book are guided to perform critical practices and enact critical ideologies within the school itself. The dismantling of the coloniality of knowledge that España and Herrera do in this book is done with courage and simplicity and always thinking of the education of the Latinx comunidad. The authors, for example, introduce the terms related to colonization with which students should be familiar. But they do so as they build a multilingual vocabulary chart. The lessons also help teachers deconstruct master narratives and learn about the history of Latinx oppression and resistance in the United States. They do so while helping teachers understand how students can take notes with purpose. And while providing teachers with many counternarratives, histories of activists from an integrated aquí y allá are introduced, which is important for the background knowledge of teachers who have been educated either in the U.S. or in Latin America with little study of Spanish or Latin American history, stories, literature, and songs. The book, for example, introduces teachers to Dolores Huerta, the labor leader and civil rights activist of the mid-twentieth century, but also to José Martí, the Cuban revolutionary philosopher and literary figure of the late nineteenth century. And alongside Oscar Arnulfo Romero, the Salvadoran bishop who spoke out against poverty and social injustice and was assassinated in 1980 while saying Mass, the authors introduce Arturo Schomburg, the Afro-Puerto Rican historian and writer who raised awareness about the contributions of AfroAmericans and AfroLatinos in the early twentieth century, as well as Sonia Sotomayor, named to the Supreme Court in 2009 and the first Latina Justice. Keeping with the tema of comunidad, the authors also consider the history of social movements, such as United Farm Workers, as well as the Young Lords, but also of liberation theology in Latin America.

The action of Latinx students as they do literacies through temas that are of the comunidad and not through dominant narratives often evoke strong emotions. España and Herrera do not shy away from evoking students' intense emotions as they develop a critical consciousness. But they show teachers how to prepare for those moments and protect students from their reactions and feelings. In many ways, the textos that the authors introduce act as sources of resistance as well as healing. Here, educators are called to be more than providers of education. Teachers are redefined as edu-activists who see their role as taking strong actions in support of Latinx comunidades to bring about social change.

In a more just society, the transformation of the Latinx community has to start by changing the stories and lenses with which education scholars view the comunidad. España and Herrera enter into the comunidad with the stories of their own and others' journeys, but also with the myths, poetry, songs and social protest that have nurtured that comunidad for years. The book makes visible the knowledge of the Latinx comunidad that is hidden when our lens as educators opens only to English and U.S. linguistic and cultural practices and their knowledge system. This book makes the Latinx community visible in all its complexity: its linguistic and cultural practices, its histories of oppression, and its activism and resistance. By offering textos that raise not only the teachers' and children's social consciousness but also their imagination and creativity, this book offers ways of reconstituting the literacy education of a comunidad as it learns about its Latinidad. España and Herrera take us on a journey in a camino well-traveled and yet, not made visible for U.S. educators until now.

Ofelia García
The Graduate Center, City University of New York

Acknowledgments

"Caminante no hay camino, se hace camino al andar," says Antonio Machado in one of our favorite lines of poetry. In our lives, we've crafted our paths as bilingual Latinx students, teachers, and now teacher-educators. The experiences that have shaped our identities and approach to teaching have informed this book—a book that combines our love for bilingual education, culturally and linguistically sustaining children's literature, social justice, and activism. We hope that this will be an important contribution to educators and teacher-educators who advocate with and for bilingual Latinx children in a world that often dehumanizes the experiences of minoritized children inside and outside of schools.

Our deepest gratitude to all of our mentors who have contributed to our growth and continue to inspire us. We've had many throughout our journey, but for both of us, there is the one and only Ofelia García, who was the chispa for this book project, recognizing the threads in our life's work and calling us to share it through this book. You have been more than a mentor to us, and for and to you, estaremos eternamente agradecidas. Another mentor helped us reimagine what education could look like and our role in it: Profesora Yvonne De Gaetano, who has been a part of Carla's teaching journey up to the present moment.

We thank the many bilingual educators and bilingual programs that have created liberating spaces for all of us, students and teacher-educators: teachers and administrators at PS MS 161 Don Pedro Albizu Campos School in New York City, where it all began for Carla, and schools across the United States, Chile, Colombia, and Mexico that have opened their doors for professional growth together; the students at CS 200 in Harlem, whose stories and multilingualism inspired Luz to rethink her role in the classroom and in education; the teacher candidates in our respective teacher education programs, who we continue to learn so much from; and our K–8 students, who made us teachers at the beginning of our journey. You belong, and deserve the world.

Thank you to our stellar editor Tobey Antao, whose curiosity, openness, and unending support of all our ideas made it possible to create something we truly believe in. Your brilliant suggestions and editing made us better writers in the process. And a big shout-out to Victoria Merecki, Suzanne Heiser, Kim Cahill, Catrina Marshall and the rest of our Heinemann team for their collaborative effort in helping this project come into fruition.

And finally, we thank our families for their unconditional love and support. Honramos su sacrificio. We thank you for giving us the time and space to engage with this work. And to our dearest friends, thank you for rooting us on throughout this entire process.

Love,
Carla and Luz

A Note About the Language in This Book

In this book, we focus on school as an institution with the potential to carve out spaces where bilingual Latinx students can fully exist and be a part of the learning and teaching experience. For many U.S. Latinxs, this has not been a reality in our school experiences. Instead, we've navigated through society on the margins, felt the oppression of colonization, and internalized harmful messages about ourselves.

One way we can make school a more liberating place for bilingual Latinx students is to embrace their full linguistic repertoire: rather than privileging English, we can give students the opportunity to use features of both English and Spanish freely. Although not all Latinx students use features of Spanish—some may use Indigenous languages—this book focuses on using features of Spanish and English. You'll notice as you read that Spanish words are not italicized and that we do not consistently provide English translations. These are intentional choices: we are not working from the assumption that English is the default language. We do not want to "otherize" Spanish words and features that naturally occur in our writing. This approach—called translanguaging—is not new. Latinx children's book authors, our bilingual and multilingual K–12 students, and many bilingual educators commonly use translanguaging. Our intent in using translanguaging in this book is to convey to multilingual readers that their language practices are welcomed and accepted, to illustrate for monolingual English readers that texts that embrace bilingual language practices don't exclude them, and to encourage *all* readers to ensure that their bilingual students have this same freedom in their own writing at school.

As Newbery medalist and *New York Times* best-selling author Meg Medina explained during the 2018 National Council of Teachers of English (NCTE) Annual Meeting, using language features of both English and Spanish shows trust in our readers: we trust that you will use your linguistic resources to navigate through the text and make meaning (Medina 2018). Acompáñennos en este camino, together in community, as we grow in our knowledge of our Latinx students' lives, languages, and learning experiences.

Centering the Voices and Experiences of Bilingual Latinx Students

◇◇◇◇◇

What does it mean to teach students who engage in language practices that reflect the fluid use of English and Spanish? Let's take a look at a few examples.

- A teacher for over ten years, Yaritza García teaches a classroom of bilingual and multilingual learners in Harlem, New York. Her students speak English, Spanish, and Arabic. Some are from Yemen and others are from the Dominican Republic. Some are in her Bilingual Dual Language class and others are in her monolingual classroom. She plans bilingual read-alouds and engages her middle school students with the use of iPads, accessing translation applications and creating presentations with their bilingual voices that get recorded and shared with the classroom community.

- A teacher candidate from Honduras in a New York City bilingual teacher preparation program, Carolina McCarthy, meets with a small group of students, in the first-grade Bilingual Dual Language Spanish classroom where she is conducting her student teaching placement. The classroom teacher, a former monolingual white woman who studied in Spain and continues to build on her bilingual journey, has just corrected the Central American and South American students and Carolina on their pronunciation of certain words in Spanish, along with the way they call certain items in Spanish as compared with her way. The classroom teacher has shared that her way of calling things is the "correct" way. Students are confused and Carolina is thinking of ways to affirm the students' language practices while being confident in her own language journey and Afro-Latina identity that have been shamed by the classroom teacher.

- Jane Barnes, a lead teacher for her third-grade classroom, is a white woman teaching in a culturally and linguistically diverse urban setting. She has studied Spanish enough to be able to teach her fourth-grade Bilingual Dual Language class but not enough to make her confident in reading the academic articles assigned to her in graduate coursework. She welcomes teacher candidate Marlena Miranda, who has been speaking Spanish and Italian since her childhood with her Mexican-Italian family. During the "English day" when the Bilingual Dual Language upper grades instruct in English, Ms. Barnes previews her reading workshop lesson in Spanish, has a chart up with the vocabulary terms in Spanish and in English, and while students read independently, she facilitates one small group in Spanish.

- Marlena takes note of her observations and compares these with her experience in another bilingual classroom she observed where there was a strict language separation. If students were lost, shut down, or apprehensive on either of the "Spanish-only" or "English-only" days, they did not receive the kind of support she witnessed in this class with Ms. Barnes. Carlos, another student teacher in the room next door where the third-grade Bilingual Dual Language class is held, also takes notes. In his experience, the classroom teacher is from Puerto Rico and has studied Spanish in schools in Puerto Rico, in New York City, and in Spain. This classroom teacher also makes sure that all students have access to books in both Spanish and English. Carlos feels challenged by this use of Spanish, since his own schooling experience growing up was mostly in English.

• Valerie, a monolingual white woman, teaches bilingual and multilingual students in monolingual middle school classrooms. Valerie has just finished her first year at a middle school in a neighborhood that was quite different from where she taught for five years prior to her change of school. Previously, most students came from the Dominican Republic, and Valerie got to know the families and students really well. This time, Valerie is learning more about different cultural and linguistic practices along with policies that directly impact her students. Valerie finds refuge in poetry and writing; she engages in these herself while also sharing with her students.

These stories reveal how educators either welcome students' experiences and shape schooling to be a liberating journey or struggle to create a positive experience for all students.

We, Carla and Luz, have been some of these teachers. Before that, we were the students: both those who have been shamed, and those who have been welcomed and motivated to learn because our teachers acknowledged who we are and how we learn. We have been those teachers who at times are faced with the question, What do I do now? when a challenge arises. We have also been those teachers who seek the help of our community, colleagues, and mentors when planning instruction. Now, as bilingual teacher-educators, we join with teacher candidates in advocating with and for our bilingual Latinx students. Our experiences have been the driving force that led us to collaborate in this book, bringing together our journeys as bilingual students, teachers, and teacher-educators. We hope that this book can inspire all educators, teachers, and teacher-educators to be thoughtful in creating a welcoming, liberating, and transformative learning environment for all Latinx students.

We use the term "Latinx" as a more inclusive, gender-neutral alternative to "Latina" or "Latino." Our use of terms should be full of thoughtfulness, not for what is trending but for what looks out for the most marginalized/racialized populations. Afro-Indigenous poet and artist Alan Pelaez Lopez encourages us to ask the following questions as we use the term Latinx: "'what have I done to show up for Black, Indigenous, women and femmes of the Latin American diaspora today?' and 'why?'" (2018).

How Can We Center the Voices and Experiences of the Latinx Students in Our Classrooms?

From our work with a wide range of bilingual Latinx students, our research and scholarship, our mentorship from luminaries in the field, and our own experiences, we have identified six essential practices for teachers who center the voices and experiences of Latinx students:

Practice #1: Get to know our students' journeys.

We use *journeys* to describe those experiences that continuously shape and influence our students' realities. It may mean navigating identities that do not fit neatly into boxes that students check off on a form or questioning how others define them versus how they self-identify. Some students have had varied immigration experiences and may be growing up as the first generation in the United States. Perhaps it is a combination of experiences that include the ways their language practices have been interpreted, and other aspects of who they are, all of which impact their lives in various ways. These also reveal how students respond to issues of marginalization. As educators, we have to create meaningful spaces for the sharing and learning of all of our journeys.

Carla's story

I was about to turn five years old when I stepped foot for the first time in a school in the United States. I had just left my family in Chile and traveled with my mother so we could join my father who had been in New York for a year. That transition, as undocumented immigrants, brought out many tears and fears throughout my childhood. The rejection at times was palpable, as was the resilience I witnessed in my parents. I remember getting lost with mamá once in Queens, New York, right in the middle of winter. This was before smartphones, and mamá feared asking for help as it could've resulted in being deported. Eventually we made our way back home, but to this day, every time I pass the street where this happened, I feel the fear and pain and can never hold back the tears.

Toward the latter part of my elementary school years, my abuelita from my dad's side joined us from Chile. This was the first time we had someone from our family back in Chile live with us in New York. It made a huge difference as the transition leaving our entire family behind was a very lonely one. Papá was super happy to have his mom in our midst, but worked so hard that only mamá and abuelita were able to attend my school events.

Luz's story

My father first arrived in San Jose, California, on his own, while my mom and I stayed in Mexico. He started out as a custodian at an office building and cleaned offices after hours, late into the night. He arrived with ten dollars in his pocket, and since it took several weeks for him to get his first paycheck, he would eat leftovers he would find from office meetings and parties earlier that day. Later, when I asked him about that experience when he first moved to San Jose, I will never forget how I felt when he told me about the time that he was so hungry that he picked up a half-eaten apple from the garbage bin in an office he was cleaning. My mother and I joined him before my first birthday. Sometimes my mother went to help him clean so that he could finish faster, and on those days, they left me in the care of a neighbor. We shared an apartment with others, and when my father had some of his savings stolen from a jacket pocket (he didn't have a bank account then), my mother told him that she was going back to Mexico and taking me with her. We had been together in San Jose for less than a year. For the next several years, my father went back and forth from California to Mexico to see us at least once a year.

> In discussing these stories from our lives, we must acknowledge our privilege in being reunited with our family and in eventually becoming documented. There are many children who experience extended or permanent family separation, and the trauma that ensues must not be ignored throughout their schooling.

What this means in our work

Teaching approaches for bilingual or multilingual Latinx students that focus on strategies often fail to contextualize the students' experiences. Even the terms used to label our students exemplify this practice, for example, *English Language Learner* (ELL). In this text, in our research, and in our work with schools we use the term *Emergent Bilingual Learner* (EBL) to describe those students who are at the beginning of the bilingual journey or bilingual continuum (García 2009). Although our stories are not representative of *all* Latinx students, we share these as examples of our own lived experiences and their impact on our school life. Family relationships, documentation, and socioemotional factors are just a few, but important, aspects of our students' multifaceted journeys. Consider these questions both from your own and your students' perspectives. These can help you develop your knowledge of yourself and possibly your students.

- How would you describe your journey through schooling?

- How would you describe your relationships with family and community?

- How would you describe the way you navigate the many aspects of your identities?

- Where are the areas of privilege in your journey? Where are the areas where you've been disadvantaged?

Practice #2: Understand our students' language practices.

We use the phrase *language practices* to highlight how we engage with language and how languaging is a process that is performed differently depending on context. This helps us describe how we use language to communicate, convey emotions, and create or support relationships. Our language practices reflect our linguistic resources, some of which may be nurtured in our schooling or suppressed. A bilingual child, for instance, may have language features categorized as Spanish or English in their repertoire, and thus their language practices often involve the use of all of those features as they seek to communicate, make connections, and negotiate relationships.

Carla's story

I remember leaving my elementary school classroom and joining other kids for a few minutes a day and sitting in a small room that looked like a closet. There, we would use our Spanish as we translated words. At La Escuela Argentina, a Saturday program in Spanish that was held in my neighborhood, I learned Argentinian songs, learned words from their regional varieties of Spanish, performed traditional folklore dances, learned their history, and participated in class. From middle school through high school, I developed my linguistic repertoire and my confidence when translating workshops, classes, and sermons at our local church. I also helped my parents in conversations with doctors, bank representatives, computer companies, and employers. Whether it was about bills, their jobs, or advocating for our rights, I translated and conveyed information. I was the family's interpreter, and I was learning a lot about the world very fast. Later in graduate school I learned about this being called "language and cultural brokering" and it is a common practice with children of immigrants (Orellana 2009). It was tough for me to read this as a researcher and an adult, noticing how common it is, how researchers interpret these practices as a skill, and how growing up it was rare to feel as if my schooling embraced this at all.

Now as a teacher-educator, I hear the common stories from bilingual Latinx teacher candidates and inservice teachers who feel like something was lost as their schooling developed their English but not their Spanish. Bilingual programs were either nonexistent in their schools or, if they existed, families were not informed about their benefits and feared their children falling behind, placing them in monolingual programs. Now in a graduate program, reading and writing in Spanish is not only a challenge for these teachers but also an emotional point as they realize the impact that monolingual schooling had on their identity and drive to become bilingual educators, especially when the ways they speak Spanish are questioned or shamed in their schools. They sit in the same classrooms as white teacher candidates and inservice teachers who took courses in Spanish in high school and/or college, and several had opportunities to travel to Spanish-speaking countries for study abroad. White teacher candidates are more comfortable writing papers for graduate courses in Spanish, and their ways of speaking Spanish are welcomed in their schools.

Luz's story

When I was seven years old, we finally joined my father in Los Angeles in a tiny studio apartment. By this time, I had two brothers, and we were a family of five. My father was no longer cleaning office buildings in Los Angeles, he was now an auto electrician, a skill he learned from my grandfather. "Tienes que escribir una oración," said Harvey, my classmate at my new local elementary school in Los Angeles. It was my first day of school. "¿Oración?" I thought it was an odd request from the teacher to ask me to write a "prayer," but I began writing the "Our Father" prayer in my notebook: "Padre Nuestro, que estás en el cielo . . ." "¡No, eso no! ¡Una oración usando estas palabras!" Harvey exclaimed and pointed to some foreign list of words. I was embarrassed. I had no idea what those words meant that I was supposed to be using in a sentence. I don't think I had even heard of the word *oración* in Spanish before; I knew how to write sentences well, but I just had not heard that word *oración* in that context before. In Mexico, I started school at three years old, so I learned to read and write early. My third-grade teacher was a monolingual English speaker but knew to sit me next to Harvey, my bilingual buddy. I was fortunate to have arrived several years before Californians voted for Proposition 227, which placed heavy restrictions on bilingual education and virtually eliminated these programs in the state. (CA Proposition 58 was passed in 2016, which lifted the ban on bilingual education and reversed Proposition 227.) Still, my elementary school's version of a bilingual program was getting pulled out of class several times a week for Spanish literacy. It was not the most supportive system, but it allowed me a space to be myself, to amplify my voice, and to show what I could do.

Even from a young age, as the oldest of four children (my sister was born soon after we reunited with my dad), I was the family's official interpreter. I was given the task to answer phone calls from utility companies, speak to my dad's clients on the phone, read correspondence from creditors, and talk to cashiers at stores, among many other types of language brokering (Orellana 2009) that needed to be done.

What this means in our work

Too often, bilingual students are viewed as "lacking," as needing to "develop academic vocabulary," as "English Language Learners," and not as sophisticated speakers and interpreters of complex language practices. Understanding *all* of the ways that our students engage in multiple literacies across language practices means validating the varied experiences and funds of knowledge (Moll et al. 1992) of bilingual students. We need spaces that center our language practices, which in turn can enable us to experience success in these same spaces. Marjorie Faulstich Orellana's (2009) research on the role of children of immigrant parents as language and cultural brokers also shows the complex language practices of children and how these practices build empathy for diverse experiences. We must listen to the language experiences of bilingual Latinx students, including those who do not consider themselves bilingual or have felt stifled in their bilingual journey. Whether it is due to assimilationist survival tactics from generations of discrimination experienced by loved ones or formal schooling that did not provide support in the development of their bilingual identities, it is important that they, too, are acknowledged.

Consider these questions:

- What are your language practices? What languages make up your linguistic repertoire?

- Has your schooling supported or silenced your language practices? Why?

- How do your language practices inform your teaching?

- How would you describe your beliefs about teaching (your pedagogical stance) when it comes to working with emergent bilingual children?

Practice #3: Understand our students' (and their families') traditions of literacies.

In this book, we take a broad view of literacy, following the legacies of sociocultural approaches. These approaches consider that literacies happen in context, for example, the various practices that families engage in, such as oral traditions, including storytelling, proverbs, and elder and community wisdom that have been passed down through generations. These also include digital literacies as well as literacies most commonly associated with youth culture: you may have students who can fully explain the use of social media platforms, online gaming communities, music-related literacies (hip-hop, K-pop), and the informational how-to videos they watch repeatedly to learn more about their interests.

Carla's story

During the school week, I would try my best to make something out of what I heard and read in school. "Hi, Dad!" came really quickly when I was five. Papá would sit with me every day and help me with math homework after he got home from his job at a local restaurant. From the second I walked into our home, I did not feel behind. I did not feel like I struggled or lacked anything as I was made to feel during the school day. "¿Vamos a comer charquicán?" I'd ask my parents or abuelita. "¿Mi hijita cómo le fue en el colegio? ¿Tiene muchas tareas? ¡Cuéntenos!" They would ask me to tell them about my day in school. I would listen to mamá's stories and impersonations. I would tell stories about my school day, follow papá's instructions on cooking a Chilean meal, and listen to music. Sometimes, papá would show us a Bible study he was working on or how translations differed. At other times, we would listen to a sermon or a song and write out notes or the lyrics because I would practice these in Spanish and English in preparation for rehearsals with the church choir. My favorite activity (after singing) was walking over to the movie rental store and looking for films that had subtitles in Spanish. We would watch these films in English and read the subtitles. In other words, before I did my homework—or sometimes afterward on movie nights—I was already engaged in multiple literacy practices.

I will forever be grateful to Professor Anaida Pascual-Morán, who came from Puerto Rico to Princeton, New Jersey, to teach a liberating pedagogies course. And Professor Ernest Morrell, who at Teachers College engaged graduate students in a course on critical literacies. As an adult, I have been able to witness educators who are aware of students' multiple literacies and create curricula with this awareness. As a student in their classrooms, I have experienced how transformative it can be for instructors to really see our full humanity.

Luz's story

As a mother of a Black biracial son, one of my main priorities has been to build a library for him with rich bilingual children's literature. At minimum, we read one book in Spanish and one book in English before bedtime. Of course, he always pushes for more, partly also because he wants to delay bedtime as much as possible, and I usually oblige. When I insist on turning off the lights, he usually has one more request that I similarly can never deny, "Can you tell me a story? ¡Un cuento!" And I make up a cuento bilingually on the spot, "Había una vez . . ." Remi is usually the protagonist and hero. This always brings me back to my own mother's stories. We didn't have books for bedtime stories. Some may believe our family was literacy-deprived since we didn't really have books, except for my mom's romance novels. But our mother always told us cuentos. And we would always beg for more traditional folktales, but our favorite was our family's oral history. She told us stories of her and my father's childhood in Mexico, cuentos of that time that her mamá Lupe, her grandmother, was kidnapped by a young man (my great-grandfather) who liked her, "se la robó," she would say, and she was later forced to marry him and give up the love of her life to preserve her integrity, as the old ways demanded. I have come to see just how rich my family was in literacy, even though we didn't have many books.

What this means in our work

Too often, emergent bilingual or multilingual students and their families are considered—and even labeled—illiterate. Sometimes, speakers who engage in using features of Spanish and English are even deemed to be "semilingual." This kind of language does not validate the many literacies with which our students engage at home and in their communities. In addition to our experiences shared here, we can see our students engaged in multiple literacies when they navigate across social media and digital media and know how to use these and other ways of communication across different contexts. For example, when taking students on a trip to a museum or to see a play or musical, we all are engaging in multiple literacies.

Worse, this notion of emergent bilinguals or multilinguals as "semilingual" reflects a perspective that views bilingualism as a deficit. Although our individual experiences are not representative of all kinds of literacy experiences, they can give an idea of how bilingual students' literacy practices can, in fact, be far more complex than those students are asked to show in English-only settings.

Consider these questions:

- What are some of the multiple literacy practices you grew up with in your home and community?

- Were any of your own literacy practices present in your schooling? If so, why do you think these were welcomed? If not, why do you think these were not integrated in your school experiences?

- What do you know of your students' multiple literacy practices? How can you learn even more about these practices?

- How do you consider your students' multiple literacy practices in your planning and teaching?

Practice #4: Affirm, be in solidarity with, and help create awareness of our students' language practices.

Sonia Nieto, one of the key figures in the field of equity in schooling, has encouraged educators to seek beyond "tolerance" in our work with children, especially language-minoritized students. Affirming our students' language practices means that we must get to know and validate their backgrounds and journeys and, most importantly in our work with Latinx students, learn about the varied experiences. In other words, in both of the following examples from our stories, language is intimately connected to place. Although this has been central to our understanding of ourselves, language practices, and family identities, it is also a privilege that we have had to be able to travel back and forth. We must be thoughtful in learning about different experiences so that we can be in full solidarity with students who may not have the same privileges or opportunities. Also, as thoughtful, critical thinkers, we can and should consider the reasons why we may have had opportunities our students have not.

Carla's story

My family is always thankful that I can return to Chile on visits and participate in gatherings. They love that I got to sit with abuelito and listen to him describe how he created his model wooden boats. They love that I got to sit with abuelita and learn how to make "calzones rotos," fried "broken underwear" (goodies with sugar). They love that I got to sing at events and heal through music in Spanish and in English. It never fails that when I hear Violeta Parra's, Víctor Jara's, or Mercedes Sosa's songs in Spanish, something within me is called back. I feel a profound connection, one that takes me to memories of family gatherings around a guitar, one that stops me in my tracks and reminds me of my raíces, my roots. Being able to have these moments with my family and engage thoughtfully using my full linguistic repertoire has been life-altering. I understand more of where I come from and have a better sense of what motivates me in my life.

I remember my elementary school choir instructor, who welcomed these language practices. My high school Advanced Placement Spanish teacher, Ms. Lo, was another adult in a school setting who helped me develop my bilingual identity. In my graduate school experience in a teacher preparation program, my instructors in a Multicultural Education course and in a course that was fully taught in Spanish, encouraged me to write my stories, lesson plans, and papers in Spanish. Taking courses in Spanish, having assignments that encouraged me to write in Spanish, and teaching in Spanish all validated a more expansive view of my identity and my role not only in the field of education, but also in this country.

Luz's story

Language was and continues to be a large part of my identity, as it is for many of us. My family was instrumental in developing in my siblings and me a strong cultural identity, and one of the most significant ways this happened was through our annual trips to Mexico. My favorite part was spending time with my cousins, and to connect and communicate with them, we needed to speak Spanish. That was reason enough to sustain and take pride in my language. Our yearly road trips are part of my fondest childhood memories. I looked forward to it all year. And when we arrived after two days on the road, we were free. Although schooling for me did not provide spaces that engaged me in conversations with my home language and cultural practices, I felt that the support from my family and close connection to Mexico filled that void. Yet, I recognize that this is not the case for all students. Schools should be a place where all kids can feel validated, one that does not feel widely separated from home, and where children can choose to be their fullest selves.

What this means in our work

Angela Valenzuela's (1999) pivotal research on subtractive schooling sheds light on how experiences that fail to honor students' cultural and linguistic practices have lasting effects, both academically and emotionally. In moving beyond respect for language practices, we can help students think about the role of language and power in our lives, how they connect to who they are, their past, their present, and their future. This helps us all process not only what we do with our language practices but also how we feel. In the words of scholar, author, poet, and activist Gloria Anzaldúa (1987):

> So, if you want to really hurt me, talk badly about my language. Ethnic identity is twin skin to linguistic identity—I am my language. Until I can take pride in my language, I cannot take pride in myself... Until I am free to write bilingually and to switch codes without having always to translate, while I still have to speak English or Spanish when I would rather speak

Spanglish, and as long as I have to accommodate the English speakers rather than having them accommodate me, my tongue will be illegitimate. (59)

Consider these questions:

- What are some of the connections between your language practices and your cultural practices?

- What are your students' language practices?

- What cultural practices are accepted, validated, and celebrated in your school? What examples show what is accepted compared with what is silenced?

- How can you engage students in a discussion on the important links between language and culture?

Practice #5: See the connections between school and government policies and their direct effects on our students' lives.

Educators have to be aware of the policies, political climate, and national narratives that impact our students. Figure 1.1 (page 19) identifies some policies that have negatively impacted Latinx students' lives.

Carla's story

I was not in a bilingual program growing up. There were no Bilingual Dual Language or Transitional Bilingual programs in my schools (I went to two different elementary schools). Although my formal schooling was structured by very fixed and separate language use (English during the week, Spanish on Saturdays), my daily life and informal schooling reflected a different reality. My language practices were much more fluid. My experiences outside of the classroom reflected multiple literacies (I could read and interpret songs, religious texts, credit card bills, computer manuals, stories) where my bilingual practices were central to my identity, relationships, and understanding of the world. I love that I can be my full self and express myself in settings that reflect this reality. Unfortunately, this kind of freedom to be your full self is not allowed for all children in educational spaces. As a bilingual speaker, this meant that growing up, I moved fluidly using features of Spanish and English. There was no distinct "Spanish" or "English." In other words, I pulled from a language repertoire that had regional varieties of Spanish (from Valparaíso and Viña del Mar, Chile to Queens and El Barrio in New York City) and English (from Queens to Harlem and the Bronx in New York City).

Luz's story

My family's ability to move freely back and forth from Mexico to the United States was critical in developing a positive cultural self-identity. It is a right that many people do not get to exercise. I grew up in a time before the extensive militarization of the border. My dad had a green card that he was able to attain through the Immigration Reform and Control Act of 1986 ("Amnesty Act") during the Reagan era. My mom had a Mexican passport with a visa, and although one of my brothers and I were undocumented, we simply said, "American citizen" to the border agent as we crossed the border. That was enough to get us through back then; kids didn't have to show any documentation. Nevertheless, I grew up being hyperaware of my undocumented status. I remember feeling nervous even as a third grader when my mother filled in a random string of nine numbers in school documents and other official paperwork that asked for a social security number. It took years for my father to become an American citizen, and eventually that facilitated our pathway to citizenship. The fears that came along with my undocumented status were never acknowledged in school, despite serving a largely immigrant population.

What this means in our work

Maybe your story has some similarities to our experiences or maybe our stories remind you of one of your students' journeys. Or maybe this was a unique experience to you but now you are starting to understand the complexity of Latinx students' experiences. Every experience is unique, and we share ours in this chapter to highlight how these experiences are impacted by policies. We must acknowledge that for many, there is no pathway to citizenship. There is no "line" for our students and families to join to seek authorization. Also, decades-long U.S. intervention in many of our Latinx students and families' home countries has caused long-lasting political and economic destabilization. As educators in the United States, we must recognize the impact that U.S. policies have had and continue to have on our students' lives.

Teaching is not a neutral act. Our words, our actions, and even our silence on issues that matter to our students and families reveal our beliefs about humanity and teaching.

Consider these questions:

- How have you been personally affected by broader sociopolitical policies?

- How have your students been affected by current policies?

- How have you been affected by some of the same policies that impact your students? Why might these policies target you and/or your students?

- How is your teaching impacted by these policies?

Practice #6: Understand that our students live in the intersections of many cultural practices and identities.

Our understanding of our students' identities and systems of oppression are informed by the foundational work of Kimberlé Crenshaw, professor at UCLA and Columbia Law School. Crenshaw uses the term *intersectionality* to "denote the various ways in which race and gender interact to shape the multiple dimensions of Black women's employment experiences" (Crenshaw 1991, 1244). We consider the intersection of race, gender, class, sexuality, ability, language practices, and documented status—among other ways of self-identifying—as we learn about the marginalization of Latinx students in both bilingual/multilingual and monolingual classrooms.

Carla's story

My favorite moments with my sixth graders were the times we read poetry together and wrote our own. I'll never forget the time we read "Soy como soy y qué" by Raquel Valle Sentíes (2005) along with other poems in our poetry packets on the topic of identities, immigration, migration, and growing up. The line "dos culturas que chocan entre sí/two cultures that come up against one another" from Sentíes' poem deeply resonated with our classroom community. I shared with students the strong connection I felt to my homeland in Chile and to my community in New York. I also shared how I felt when I returned to Chile and how there was something that was pulling me back to New York even though I loved my family and missed them very much. In their poems, students expressed their own forging of their hybrid identities, creating bilingual anthologies with poems on the topics of growing up and being bilingual, along with family, community, home, and other topics of their choice. Through our classroom community conversations, reading poetry, writing poetry, and reading memoirs of experiences like ours, we were able to process what were sometimes revealed to be traumatic experiences. Although there was beauty in how we helped one another and how we became aware of the different factors that contributed to our healing and self-defining approach, there was tension. We acknowledged the pain, the changes, the tension, and the beauty.

Luz's story

My upbringing, alongside my constant connection to my homeland, as well as having learned in college the rich history of Mexico, has helped me make sense of the world and helped ground me in who I am. Schooling, as it is for so many youth of color, has brought both enriching as well as oppressive experiences. I have been fortunate to mostly have had teachers who knew how to make me feel like my voice mattered. Although I didn't really learn the history of my people until college, it was not too late. I learned about the complex societies in ancient Mexico, the connections between globalization and the mass migration to the United States from Mexico and other parts of Latin America during much of the twentieth century, and the Chicano movement and struggle that began in the 1960s and continues today.

Learning this changed my perspective of the world and brought so much clarity into my life, and because of this I can be more grounded into who I am and be in connection with my community. As Blackstock (2011) and Cross (2007) explain, this community actualization leads to cultural perpetuity. In other words, self-actualization is not the end goal. We must listen to the wisdom of our elders, to indigenous epistemologies, or other ways of knowing. This framework allows children and youth to feel safe, respected, and loved and sustains their deep connections with their raíces.

What this means in our work

U.S. Latinxs do not have to entirely identify with Chilean culture, Mexican culture, or other cultures, with limited definitions of what it means to be an "American." As Anzaldúa (1987) reminds us, U.S. Latinxs are a "borderlands" people, not entirely one or the other, but a hybrid of both, with a unique and powerful identity.

Consider these questions:

- How do you self-identify (race, ethnicity, language, sexuality, ability, religion, etc.)? How do these identities intersect?

- Were your identities sustained in school? If yes, how do you think schools sustained these identities? If not, why not?

- How do your students self-identify? How do their identities intersect?

- How does your school perceive students' identities?

- How do your identities impact your teaching practice?

A New Way Forward: A Critical Bilingual Literacies Approach

To honor the voices and experiences of our bilingual Latinx students, we must approach bilingual curriculum and pedagogy with a critical lens. This approach is akin to culturally sustaining pedagogies, critical pedagogy, antiracist pedagogy, and decolonizing pedagogy, but we want to be intentional about the focus on critical lenses, bilingualism, and multiple literacies. We use the term *critical* because of the urgency to contextualize bilingual education within historical moments, particularly colonizing measures that erase the land ownership, histories, language practices, and identities of language-minoritized communities. We need to consider the very real and visceral policies and practices implemented in and outside of schools impacting bilingual students. With the phrase *critical bilingual literacies*, we seek to *de*center Eurocentric practices in education—teaching Latinx students how to read in Spanish using methods translated from English (Escamilla, Hopewell, and Butvilofsky 2013), using children's literature that is not culturally and linguistically authentic (Riojas Clark et al. 2015), implementing strict language separation in Bilingual Dual Language programs (Palmer et al. 2014), and interpreting Latinx students' families participation in school through a deficit perspective (Valenzuela 1999)—and instead *re*center our bilingual Latinx students' knowledge and ways of being. A critical bilingual literacies approach is consistently vigilant of ways that Latinx voices are silenced, recognizes students' bilingualism, and acknowledges that there isn't just one literacy practice but many literacies with which bilingual Latinx students navigate their lives. A critical bilingual literacies approach is characterized by four guiding principles that provide a more humanizing pedagogy and help us actively resist the problems mentioned previously:

Four Guiding Principles for Teaching Bilingual Latinx Students

1. **Constantly self-reflect** on language ideologies while engaging with texts, classroom experiences, and research on bilingual practices.

2. **Practice a pedagogy that focuses on all participants' "unlearning"** the notions of *linguistic supremacy* that uphold Eurocentric notions/racialized language hierarchies (Alim and Smitherman 2012).

3. **Analyze linguistic practices, literacies, and power.**

4. **Celebrate bilingual Latinx linguistic practices** and plan content (curriculum, texts) and methods from the perspective of the bilingual learner.

If we want to provide learning experiences that will help our bilingual Latinx children to thrive, we must construct an educational narrative that places the lives and experiences of these children at the forefront of curriculum design and implementation. These are necessary for classrooms that are made up entirely of bilingual Latinx students as well as for the monolingual spaces with only a handful of bilingual Latinx students. In other words, it is imperative that schooling experiences are liberating and transformative across contexts.

This approach builds on the work of leading educators, scholars, and activists, and of the Latinx students we have learned from throughout the years. These include Gloria Anzaldúa's (1987) concept of *hybridity*; *critical pedagogy* mentors Paulo

Freire (1970), Ernest Morrell (2007), David Kirkland (2008), and Wayne Au (2011); *culturally sustaining pedagogies* as theorized by Gloria Ladson-Billings (1995), Geneva Gay (2000), and Django Paris and H. Samy Alim (2017); *raciolinguistic ideologies*, or the study of how language is racialized, as studied by Nelson Flores and Jonathan Rosa (2015); and *translanguaging* as conceptualized by our mentor, Ofelia García (2009). Translanguaging decenters white, middle-class norms of speaking, listening, reading, writing, and knowing. This goes beyond modifications of curriculum. As Ofelia García (2018) has said, "Translanguaging is not modifying linguistic behavior, but to dismantle monolingual supremacy." See pages 20–21 for more about translanguaging.

This critical bilingual literacies approach builds on the work of Paris and Alim (2017), who call for "schooling to be a site for sustaining the cultural ways of being of communities of color" (5). Figure 1.1 describes some of these practices compared with examples of oppressive education approaches.

How This Book Can Help

In this book, we provide sample sequences of lessons that are designed by and for a bilingual Latinx community. These lessons help us implement a critical bilingual literacies approach by including diverse texts and experiences that engage families, communities, and social issues and validating bilingual Latinx language practices. These lessons are held together by an investigation of linguistic practices, literacies, and power. This is done across 3–5 and 6–8 grade bands. Each sequence of lessons includes the following:

1. An organizing **topic** or theme that sustains "the cultural ways of being" (Paris and Alim 2017) and knowing of our Latinx students around issues of language practices, literacies, and power.

2. Bilingual **texts** that go beyond tolerance and toward affirming and being in solidarity with our Latinx community (Nieto 1994).

3. **Translanguaging**—defined as the linguistic practices of bilinguals, a pedagogical approach, and a means for social justice as students' language practices are honored (García and Leiva 2014).

Figure 1.1 Oppressive vs. Transformative Education Approaches

Oppressive Education Approaches	Transformative Education Approaches
English-only legislation (which eliminates bilingual education) • California Proposition 227 (1998) • Arizona Proposition 203 (2000) • Massachusetts Question 2 (2002)	Bilingual legislation • Title VII Bilingual Education Act (1968) • Aspira Consent Decree (1974) • California Proposition 58 (2016) reversing Proposition 227 (1998) • Massachusetts Language Opportunity for Our Kids (LOOK) Bill (2017) reversing Question 2 (2002)
Legislation that bans ethnic studies • Arizona HB2281	Legislation that permits or requires ethnic studies • HB2281 being struck down by a federal judge (2017) • AB2016 ethnic studies curriculum being implemented for all public high schools by 2019 (2016)
Insisting on English in school • Telling students "No Spanish allowed here" • Telling students to "speak American" • Telling students "It's English time now" in Bilingual Dual Language programs when students speak in Spanish	Honoring students' languages in school • Students engaging in conversations using their full language repertoire • Students' writing representative of their varied language practices (i.e., translations, Spanish use across drafts)
Using monolingual, monocultural/white-normative texts • Texts not representative of students' experiences • Texts not representative of students' identities • Texts not representative of students' language practices	Using diverse texts • Texts representing multilayered experiences • Texts representing hybrid identities • Texts representing fluid language practices (translanguaging in texts)
Viewing Latinx families from a deficit perspective • Considering "Spanglish" an inferior practice • Assuming that Spanish-speaking families are not interested in their children's education • Not seeing the value of family and community partnerships, especially when these are language-minoritized families of Latinx students • Implementing family separation policies for asylum-seeking families	Validating and welcoming Latinx families • Highlighting Latinx families' language practices • Asking families for their input through meaningful participation • Valuing family and community partnerships across the school year, in classrooms and school-wide events • Implementing a humanizing approach to welcoming asylum seekers

Translanguaging

Translanguaging is when a multilingual person's full linguistic repertoire is used and honored, instead of trying to keep narrowly focused on a single language.

One aspect of translanguaging has already been described in our personal stories, where our language practices are much more fluid than that of the strict separation of languages that is often demanded in schools. Yet that only addresses translanguaging as the linguistic practices of bilinguals. Translanguaging is also the way a teacher teaches. In other words, as a pedagogical approach, translanguaging describes the method of an interactive read-aloud that is read in one language while the conversations, prompts, notes, and responses are in more than one language. For example, when Yaritza, the teacher from the beginning of our chapter, reads Duncan Tonatiuh's *Separate Is Never Equal: Sylvia Mendez and Her Family's Fight for Desegregation* (2014) to her bilingual and monolingual sixth-grade students, she creates a space for students to respond to the reading using their full linguistic repertoire. Bilingual students' notes are in Spanish and in English. Also, Yaritza's vocabulary chart with visuals is in both Spanish and English.

When translanguaging is embedded throughout schooling, it is a means for social justice: it validates and humanizes bilingual students' learning processes (García and Leiva 2014). For example, making sure that texts are available in Spanish and English is one way we can do this in our reading workshop; another is creating spaces in our writing workshop and writing celebrations for students to create bilingual and multilingual texts. What message does it send to students when they are "allowed" to speak and read in Spanish during short conversations about texts in our classes, but when it comes to published writing or mentor texts that are read, these students are only "allowed" to use English? How do students and adults (families, administration, teachers, and other school staff) interpret literacy practices when only writing and texts in English are posted on bulletin boards and celebrated? Translanguaging disrupts this practice, decentering whiteness and monolingualism that continue to be the norm in school settings.

Translanguaging disrupts the belief that nation-states were constructed around "named" languages and instead focuses on the people who are enacting their various language practices (García 2016). Colonialism has "invented" or created these superficial boundaries around the way we language, calling them "languages," and as such, it is our role as educators of all students to acknowledge these boundaries to undo them. The lessons in this book provide examples on using translanguaging as a method of teaching, as communicative practice, and as a means for social justice so that all educators—bilingual, multilingual, or monolingual—can still disrupt monolingual norms in schools.

Yes, you can use translanguaging in your classroom even if you don't speak Spanish.

Throughout our schooling experiences and many teacher preparation programs, teachers are often considered the sole bearers of knowledge, transmitting content to students who are viewed as empty vessels. Paulo Freire (1970) called this the "banking model of education." Although this model likely is not taught explicitly, vestiges of it persist in classrooms that prioritize a set agenda over individual students' strengths and areas of growth. Although schools might not use the term *empty vessel* when describing students, we often hear "Those kids don't know," "Their families don't care," "English language learners need to develop academic language," "Those newcomers don't have vocabulary," and similar phrases that permeate faculty meetings, caregiver-teacher meetings, and instruction. Translanguaging disrupts this. Creating translanguaging spaces calls for teachers to consider students' ways of knowing and their use of their entire linguistic repertoire as valid contributions to the classroom learning community. We know from experience that there can be some discomfort in launching this work. Here are some ways to make this transition:

- Have bilingual glossaries readily accessible in the classroom.
- Use mobile applications and translation software that can dictate text.
- Pair students strategically to create bilingual texts.

continues

- Use bilingual texts for read-alouds and independent reading and practice.
- Welcome family and community members as language partners.
- Collaborate with colleagues and friends who can help in your own language learning journey.
- Extend your learning through various online outlets, including podcasts and classes, to gain a deeper insight on how your students communicate and learn.

The sequence of lessons is designed within the contexts of our particular students' experiences and realities. They contextualize the learning experiences within the broader sociopolitical climate so that we, their teachers, can understand the humanity of the children we teach and develop lessons that are specifically tailored to them. Although the sample sequence of lessons is to be considered simply a guide, the core of these lessons follows a critical bilingual literacies approach—consideration of topic, texts, and translanguaging—which is a structure that can be used universally with bilingual students. Many of these lessons can be done with a study group with your colleagues, as well as with your students. For example, teachers on a grade team can each select a lesson to read and share at a grade team meeting, or subject-area teachers at the upper grades can select different lesson sequences to read, implement, and reflect on together at faculty meetings. The book can be read as a book club text where teachers bring student work from the lessons to discuss and plan together. We recommend that you engage with this text in collaboration for two major reasons. First, the lessons in this book build on and expand our knowledge of the complexity and variety of Latinx bilingual students' experiences through meaningful topics, texts, and translanguaging. Second, all of the lessons result in writing products. These call for reflection, analysis, and planning in collaborative spaces that meet consistently and offer ongoing support.

In Chapter 2, "Examining Language Practices and Identities," we work with our students to explore our language ideologies, as well as consider the role that these have in the classroom. Chapter 3, "Telling Our Stories," describes a sequence of lessons on storytelling anchored in our ancestors. Chapter 4, "Knowing Our Histories to Understand the Present Moment," focuses on connecting historical moments with current events. Chapter 5, "Taking an Informed Stance Against Injustice," outlines lessons for the bilingual student as a reader, writer, researcher, and advocate.

In Chapter 6, "Sustaining the Community Across the Year with Poetry," the lessons focus on ways to help make space for students' processing of trauma and sharing their resilience through poetry. Finally, Chapter 7 provides a blueprint on how to engage in this work, asserting our roles as readers, writers, researchers, and advocates. Across all of the following chapters, we center the voices of bilingual Latinx students. As this book collaboration shows, we believe in the power of community, and we hope you engage with thought partners so that we, along with Paris and Alim (2017), can get to know the language practices of communities of color as we "resist, revitalize, and reimagine" (12).

As we embark on this work, let us consider the words of Cherríe L. Moraga, Chicana writer, essayist, and playwright. To the two of us, she is one of the inspirational figures in our journeys.

> I write to remember. I make rite (ceremony) to remember.
> It is my right to remember.
>
> —*Cherríe L. Moraga, 2011*

In one way, this work is a way for the two of us—Carla and Luz—to "write to remember," as we share our favorite lessons and moments from the classroom. In another way, this work conveys the ways we all, as educators, "make rite to remember," as we go through the moves or rituals we rely on in building community and learning together with our students. Most importantly, this work reminds us of our and our bilingual Latinx students' "right to remember." When we remember and reflect on transformative moments, we continue to learn, revisit, and revitalize our personal and teaching journeys.

Examining Language Practices and Identities

◇◇◇◇◇

Momento de aprendizaje

"¡Me acuerdo de usted! ¡Pero se me olvidó su nombre!" yelled Felipe when Carla walked into their classroom. Carla was setting up for a bilingual demonstration literacy lesson on character analysis using *El color de mis palabras* (2004) (in Spanish) and *The Color of My Words* (2001) (in English) by Lynn Joseph in this classroom in the Washington Heights neighborhood of New York City. Felipe had come up to Carla after class the year before to share how his mother was learning English along with them and how they would read books together. This time, classmates helped Felipe remember Carla's name, and the student excitedly said, "Buenos días, Sra. España." Immediately, the administrator in the room said, "No, we don't speak Spanish in this classroom. It's an intermediate English class."

Reflecting on That Moment

As we reflect on this moment, we have wondered what contributes to the language practices, language ideologies, and teaching philosophies of both teachers and administrators. In this case, this same administrator had commented to Carla about the students in this school, saying that "those kids have no culture." Carla, an educator of color, and the principal, a white woman, had different journeys leading up to that reading lesson and their interpretations of the children in the school. For Carla, it was a really emotional moment to hear these comments about both the class and the students. Given Carla's teacher preparation journey in a bilingual program and personal experience as a bilingual speaker, she responded:

> *Que lindo que se acuerdan de mi. Yo también tengo lindos recuerdos de ustedes. Ahora, durante esta lección vamos a escribir y hablar en español y en inglés ya que ser bilingüe es muy lindo. During this lesson you can speak and write in both Spanish and English, using your discussion and the bilingual glossaries to help you translate your notes.*

The lessons in this chapter consider how a school community can address discrepancies on beliefs about language practices, allowing room for students and teachers to be listened to and the freedom to teach on these topics of language, power, and cultural histories.

First, we do this by helping educators understand our bilingual students' experiences. In other words, we begin by acknowledging that we can always learn more about the varied experiences of our Latinx students. This means unpacking and calling to task comments like "those children have no culture" or "those kids lack . . ." because when we look beneath the surface of this deficit narrative, we find a discrepancy between how Black and Brown, Indigenous, undocumented, and other minoritized communities' practices are interpreted and how those of white children are interpreted.

Second, these lessons help us understand and implement teaching methods that provide bilingual Latinx students with a more humanizing way to learn. We reflect, discuss, revisit, and rethink beliefs about language practices and how these are connected to our identity. For all children, and bilingual children specifically, these lessons help them see the connections between how we communicate with our varied language practices and how we view ourselves. Do children feel confident when speaking in Spanish? If yes, why? If not, what contributes to feelings of shame or discomfort? We advise that you engage with the texts and reflection protocol in community with other educators during a study group, grade team meeting, or faculty meeting first, before implementing in the classroom. This is crucial given that the transformative topics and texts presented in these paired lessons require critical thinking around issues of language and power, help us question which practices and people are privileged, and challenge us to unpack and reveal our own teaching stance. Hundreds of educators (and students) have already embarked on this journey of reflection and practice with us through these lessons. It is with urgency, hope, and joy that we share these lessons with you.

Introducing the Paired Lessons

Figure 2.1 Steps for a Close Reading on Language Practices and Identities

These lessons give us opportunities to reflect on our ideas about language through multiple readings of transformative texts. As educators and authors Chris Lehman and Kate Roberts (2014) note, "Powerful literacy strategies tend to be powerful life strategies" (6). The first lesson focuses on bilingual language practices and identity. The second addresses the tension between bilingual language practices, identity, and pressures in society. Both lessons begin with an initial reading and use Lehman and Roberts' three steps for close reading. These are followed by a process that guides us to consider bilingual practices and issues of identity in our classrooms. Finally, the lessons culminate by considering actions we might take to improve our students' experiences in our classroom and school (see Figure 2.1). Although each lesson is built around a specific text for the purpose of explanation, the lessons also include recommendations for alternate texts. All of the texts have to do with bilingual language practices and identity and include translanguaging in some way, helping us consider how our experiences shape the way we understand bilingual language practices, as well as how our language practices shape the way we think. As of the printing of this book, all of the texts mentioned in the lessons are available online or in print.

Supporting Translanguaging in Paired Lessons

- Deliver the lesson in English, in Spanish, or using features of both.

- Use the text(s) recommended to allow students to either hear one language and read the words in another or hear more than one language in one text. Both of the recommended introductory texts provide these opportunities and have an English translation.

- Encourage students to:

    - *Discuss (in small groups and as a whole class) the texts using their entire linguistic repertoire.*

    - *Take notes on the text using their entire linguistic repertoire.*

- Accept and celebrate students' discussions and writing of their ideas as they use all the features of their language repertoire.

Connecting Our Language Practices to Our Identities

This lesson is an introduction to bilingual language practices and identity: family, culture, and place/land as connected to identity.

Preparing to Teach: Considering the Texts

Because this will be the students' first experience with the lesson protocol, we recommend a highly accessible form of text, such as videos or picture books. Selecting such a text—one that represents a practice of some language-minoritized communities—both validates the practice and provides much-needed representation.

In modeling the lesson, we use a short clip from "Earthworks: Miguel Chapter 1" (Pimentel 2017a), which includes a family speaking in both Spanish and English. In this series of six chapters or mini-episodes (from six to under fifteen minutes each), singer-songwriter and producer Miguel travels through Michoacán, Mexico, with his father and brother, visiting family, getting to know the land, and connecting through music. In these six minutes, we are introduced to Miguel, his family, the purpose of their trip, and the role of music in their lives. We also get to know about Miguel's connection to Mexico. The clip begins with images of Mexico and moves to a scene when Miguel and his father and brother all visit a family radio station where Miguel speaks in Spanish and they sing together. Other excerpts from subsequent chapters in this series elaborate on this with connections to land, learning from the land, and living in a way that this relationship is nurtured.

Although the lesson is modeled using the short clip from "Earthworks: Miguel Chapter 1," this lesson can also be used with the alternate texts listed. Middle-grade teachers can use the text in this lesson or may choose alternate texts from the lists below. Grades 3–5 teachers can use the digital text or picture books suggested in the following lists.

Alternate Digital Text Options for Grades 6–8

- "Earthworks: Miguel Chapter 3" (Pimentel 2017b) (video in English with conversations in Spanish)

- Ana Tijoux's "Antipatriarca" (2015) (song or music video in Spanish)

- Calle 13's "Latinoamérica" (elvecindariocalle13 2011) (song or music video in Spanish)

- Episode 11: "The Paper Menagerie" by Ken Liu in *LeVar Burton Reads* podcast (Burton 2017) (clip from podcast in English)

- *Radio Ambulante* episode "Recién llegados" (NPR 2017) (clip from podcast in Spanish)

Alternate Digital Text Options for Grades 3–5

- Clip from a *Victor and Valentino* episode (multilingual animated Cartoon Network program)

- Clip from a *Nina's World* episode (multilingual animated YouTube video)

- Clip from a *Maya & Miguel* episode (multilingual animated PBS Kids program)

- *Immersion* (2009) short film by Richard Levien (Media That Matters)

Alternate Texts for Grades 3–5

- *Marisol McDonald and the Clash Bash/Marisol McDonald y la fiesta sin igual* (2013) by Monica Brown

- *Mama's Nightingale: A Story of Immigration and Separation* (2015) by Edwidge Danticat

- *Juana & Lucas* (2016) by Juana Medina

- *Mango, abuela y yo* (2015) and *Mango, Abuela, and Me* (2015) by Meg Medina

- *Martí's Song for Freedom/Martí y sus versos por la libertad* (2017) by Emma Otheguy

Step 1: Initial Viewing

Set up the context and purpose of the activity first. Share with students that you will use the text to have a discussion on bilingual language practices and identities, focusing on the factors that contribute to learning about where they come from, their stories, their identities, and their language practices. Next, watch the video clip without any interruptions (if you are using "Earthworks," show Chapter 1 from minute 1:55 through 7:43). Immediately after this first viewing, ask students to discuss their observations in small groups (keeping the groups to two to four students encourages all members to share) for about five minutes. Make sure one person in each group is documenting the observations, because these will be compared with what students share *after* they return to the text several times. You can ask students some guiding questions to get them thinking about the content of the video: *Why did Miguel go on this trip? Why did he ask his father and brother to join him? What are they learning in this scene?*

Step 2: Use a Close Reading Lens

Now, tell students that you will watch again, this time focusing on the words that Miguel uses, and pausing to note them. You can access a transcript of this clip on the video's YouTube page. Prompt students to look for words that evoke strong emotions, words that evoke strong images, and words that convey a clear idea (Lehman and Roberts 2014). Each group will note down the words, or you can give them a copy of the partial transcript in Figure 2.2 for them to follow along as they watch the video clip from minute 1:55 to 3:47.

> Music is in my blood. Growing up, music was always in my family. Most people think of me solely as a Black artist but there's a reason why my name is Miguel. My father is from Mexico and in search for a better life, he and his family came to the U.S., so until now, I haven't been able to come back. That's why I took my dad and my brother with me: to find the Mexico we've been missing, to see the challenges it's facing, the people that are affected, and the cultures some people are fighting to preserve. We are here to find their stories, as well as my family's [story], and my own.
>
> —*Singer, songwriter, producer Miguel in "Earthworks: Chapter 1" (Pimentel 2017a)*

Figure 2.2 Miguel's Introduction to Michoacán Visit

Once you pause at the end of this introduction, have groups briefly discuss the words/phrases that they wrote down. You might choose to first explain how you would take down some phrases. At this point, you might pick one group or lens to highlight and give some examples. Then, have the class follow your lead. See Figure 2.3 for an example of what groups might gather.

Figure 2.3 Sample Observations Using Close Reading Lenses

Words That Evoke Strong Emotions	Words That Evoke Strong Images	Words That Convey a Clear Idea
"Music is in my blood" "solely as a Black artist" "search for a better life" "I haven't been able to come back" "cultures some people are fighting to preserve"	"music was always in my family" "the people that are affected"	"[music is] where it all started for me" "My father is from Mexico and in search for a better life, he and his family came to the U.S." "We are here to find their stories, as well as my family's [story], and my own"

Step 3: Identify Patterns

For the next step, ask students to consider noticing what the words they've noted have in common. They can use highlighters or write these on sticky notes and sort. Another option is to have them use the class chart with the three lenses/columns and look across to move the words/phrases into other boxes (for those with interactive SMARTBoard capabilities) to label with a category or pattern. If students took notes digitally and you projected them to the class so all could see (or if they all have devices where they can see other groups' observations), then students can highlight the patterns they notice, assigning a different color to each observation. Some teachers have done this by writing the phrases on sentence strips and having students participate by moving them around. See Figure 2.4 as an example of what it might look like if students identified patterns such as family, Mexico, music, and identity. Students often notice the emerging themes in this text even after watching for only a few minutes. However, if you feel that students need more practice, then you can view other video clips from the series.

Figure 2.4 Sample Patterns

Family	Mexico	Music	Identity
"music was always in my family" "That's why I took my dad and my brother with me: to find the Mexico we've been missing"	"I haven't been able to come back" "cultures some people are fighting to preserve"	"music was always in my family" "Music is in my blood"	"[music is] where it all started for me" "solely as a Black artist" "We are here to find their stories, as well as my family's [story], and my own"

Step 4: Develop Statements

Provide some guiding questions to help students put together their patterns of obser-vations (such as language, family, music, identity, or Mexico) into developed state-ments. For example, you might ask: *What is Miguel saying about family, Mexico, music, and the connections to who he is—to his identity?* Let students continue discussing in groups for a few minutes before bringing the whole class together and have represen-tatives share out the groups' understandings. During this lesson, some students have said that this text reveals how music connects us to our families and our cultures (as we saw with the narration and the scene at the radio station). Others have said that this also reveals how we are more than one thing or that our identities are varied, noticing how family, Mexico, and music are all a part of who Miguel is as an artist, a person, a son, and a brother. Most students who engage with this text, though, have noticed how language is a part of the identity of bilingual beings and sometimes we have been shamed for the way we speak in schools, at home, or with friends.

Step 5: Considering Our Own Stances

Our purpose with the first four steps with the text was to think not only about *how* the authors of texts develop ideas (using the protocol to help us as readers in our analysis), but also how these specific understandings revealed by the texts impact our own ideas about bilingual language practices and identity. Now it's time to open up a discussion about language practices, as a whole class, in small groups, or with partners. Sometimes simply posing a question about the text and language is all a class will need at this point; something like *Did you notice the moment when Miguel spoke and sang with his family in Spanish at the radio station?* may be enough to start a vibrant discussion that leads to comments on identity and bilingual language practices. Or we can pose questions that point more directly at identity and bilingual language practices:

- *What role do language practices play in Miguel's life?*

- *How does the way Miguel and his family use their language practices connect them to each other? To their cultures?*

- *What have we discussed today that relates to how you view your own bilingualism?*

- *Why do you think this about being bilingual?*

Whichever path you choose, the goal is the same: to help students synthesize the insights they've developed from their close reading of the text with their own stances and beliefs.

Step 6: Applying What We've Learned

At this point, we want students to reflect on the ways their classroom and/or school environment support or do not support bilingual language practices, followed by any recommendations. You can have students respond in a T-chart (see Figure 2.5) or in a paragraph in response to a question. You can post the following questions as options for reflections, sharing your response to one of them with the class, and asking students to respond in writing. Translanguaging should also be welcomed in students' responses.

- *How does our classroom and school either support or not support bilingual language practices?*

- *How do different groups of students or teachers feel about the ways the classroom and/or school address (or do not address) language practices?*

- *How do we experience language practices outside of school? How do those spaces outside of school support or not support our bilingual identities?*

- *What recommendations do you have for the classroom (lessons, activities, texts), larger school environment (signs, staff, translations, meetings with families, assemblies), and other learning spaces (home, community centers, after-school spaces, etc.) that would support bilingual language practices?*

You can collect their written responses to help you get a sense of how students' understanding of the text helped them form their own ideas and recommendations. You can also use these responses in planning the lessons that follow. Even if your learning community already implements liberating language practices, hearing the students' own interpretations of schooling is constructive to our growth as educators. It could be that bilingual students do not feel as welcomed in after-school programs, extracurricular activities, or spaces with families and friends as they do in the classroom. Hearing these perspectives is the first step in helping students navigate this dilemma and considering how you can create a welcoming space. Students' frankness might catch some of us off guard, but it may also inform our teaching.

Finally, give some time for students to hear from you about how this text has impacted your own understandings. Figure 2.5 presents some starting points to consider from the text and from our own teaching practice as we reflect on our "aha" moments from this engagement with the text. You can choose to start with a topic from the column labeled "Understandings from the Text," such as music, place, family, or language, asking students to share how their own understandings of this topic have changed, grown, or been affirmed as they engaged with this text. For more support, you can show one row from Figure 2.5 as an example and have students complete others in small groups. Our own responses in Figure 2.5 consider our understandings of the text and our life, in this case, our classroom/teaching practices. We can also invite students to help us to consider further actions we can take. How we respond to the texts and to our students reveals our pedagogical stance. This is an opportunity to show students that we are working toward "a translanguaging stance [that] always sees the bilingual child's complex language repertoire as a resource, never as a deficit" (García, Ibarra Johnson, and Seltzer 2017, 27).

Figure 2.5 Sample Life Applications Based on Viewing Miguel's Text

Understandings from the Text	Actions I Can Take Based on This New Understanding
Miguel and his family used music to connect with his history, family, and present gathering with family. (Music)	• I can ask students if this is the case with them. I can ask, "Is there any music that helps you connect with your family?" I can ask students to help me use this in my teaching. • I can ask students if there are other things that help them connect with their family. Food? Language? Hobbies?
Miguel's first visit to see a place connected to his history, family, and identity was an emotional experience. (Place)	• I can get to know where my students are from and what kind of meaning these places have for my students. • I can provide space (lessons, units) for students to write about these places and teach us about them.
It was important for Miguel to experience this trip with family. (Family)	• I can consider ways to connect the classroom experience with families. How am I integrating them into the school day, units of study, lessons, presentations?
Miguel tried his best to communicate with family, and when he could not find the words in Spanish to express himself, he used English and his father helped with translating. (Language)	• I can think about how I react to students who need translations. What do I feel? What do I say? • I can plan to have translation tools in the classroom. • I can engage in translanguaging practices myself and welcome students' translanguaging practices as well. • I can ask for support from colleagues, students, families, and other experts in bilingual language practices. • I can set up students to work in heterogeneous partnerships or triads so that together they can translate in discussion and for writing tasks.
Miguel comments on how his fans see him "solely as Black" and this trip gave him the opportunity to connect with his Mexican roots. (Identity)	• I can ask students to name the ways they self-identify, the reasons for their choices, and why they matter. • I can learn more about Afro-Latinx identity and Afro-Latinidad. • I can seek information on the history of anti-Blackness, its connections to colonialism, and how the Latinx community resists or responds.

Examining Our Own Stances on Language Practices

This lesson helps us to understand the tension between bilingual language practices, identity, and societal pressures to conform. It is an exploration of the relationship between language and power.

Preparing to Teach: Considering the Texts

> *I remember being caught speaking Spanish at recess—that was good for three licks on the knuckles with a sharp ruler. I remember being sent to the corner of the classroom for "talking back" to the Anglo teacher when all I was trying to do was tell her how to pronounce my name. "If you want to be American, speak 'American.' If you don't like it, go back to Mexico where you belong."* (Anzaldúa 1987, 75)

In her memoir, *Borderlands/La frontera: The New Mestiza*, Gloria Anzaldúa (1987) shares her experiences with the forces that try to control her being and her language practices and details the ways in which she resists. "How to Tame a Wild Tongue," a chapter from this memoir, offers us insights about language, power, and forging your own identity in the midst of oppressive circumstances.

In this lesson, we'll use excerpts from *Borderlands*. This text reveals the many ways people in authority and institutions oppressed Anzaldúa's language practices and her identity. These experiences are shared using features of English and Spanish. Selecting such a text that represents the experience and language practices of some language-minoritized communities both validates the practice and provides much-needed representation. Also, the fact that the author does not provide translation for each word in Spanish speaks to writing as a way of resistance and calling forth the existence of these other ways of being and communicating that are often marginalized.

Although the lesson is modeled using excerpts from Anzaldúa's Borderlands, *this lesson can also be used with the alternate texts listed. Middle-grade teachers can use the text in this lesson, or may choose alternate texts from the lists below. Grades 3–5 teachers can use texts suggested in the following lists.*

Text Options for Grades 3–5 and 6–8

- *Prietita and the Ghost Woman/Prietita y La Llorona* (1997) by Gloria Anzaldúa

- *Friends from the Other Side/Amigos del otro lado* (1997) by Gloria Anzaldúa

Key Text for Analysis (Memoir)

- Excerpt from "How Do You Tame a Wild Tongue?" in *Borderlands/La frontera: The New Mestiza* (1987) by Gloria Anzaldúa (for grades 6–8)

Alternate Texts for Grades 6–8

- *The Poet X* (2018) (National Book Award for Young People's Literature) by Elizabeth Acevedo

- *Growing Up Latino: Memoirs and Stories—Reflections on Life in the United States* (1993), an edited anthology by Harold Augenbraum and Ilan Stavans

- *They Call Me Güero: A Border Kid's Poems* (2018) (Pura Belpré Author Honor Book Award, 2019) by David Bowles

- *Marcus Vega Doesn't Speak Spanish* (2018) (ALSC Notable Children's Books, 2019) by Pablo Cartaya

- *Us, in Progress: Short Stories About Young Latinos* (2017) by Lulu Delacre

- *Aire encantado: Dos culturas, dos alas: una memoria* (2017) and *Enchanted Air: Two Cultures, Two Wings: A Memoir* (2015) (Pura Belpré Author Award, 2016) by Margarita Engle

- *Cajas de cartón: relatos de la vida peregrina de un niño campesino* (2002) and *The Circuit: Stories from the Life of a Migrant Child* (2002) by Francisco Jiménez

Alternate Texts for Grades 3–5

- *¡Bravo! Poemas sobre hispanos extraordinarios* (2017) and *Bravo! Poems About Amazing Hispanics* (2017) by Margarita Engle

- *América Is Her Name* (1998) by Luis J. Rodríguez

- *Separados no somos iguales: Sylvia Mendez y la lucha de su familia por la integración* (2017) and *Separate Is Never Equal: Sylvia Mendez and Her Family's Fight for Desegregation* (2014) by Duncan Tonatiuh

- *Soñadores* (2018) and *Dreamers* (2018) by Yuyi Morales

Step 1: Initial Reading

Some teachers choose to begin this lesson with an introduction to the author, Gloria Anzaldúa. This can be done through a quick biography, a short video clip of an interview with Anzaldúa, a picture slideshow talking through the moments in her life, or references to books of hers students may have already read (like *Prietita and the Ghost Woman/ Prietita y La Llorona* or *Friends from the Other Side/Amigos del otro lado*).

Other teachers have preferred to make this an interactive introduction, showing images related to school as liberating spaces or school as oppressive spaces (with historical and/or current events examples) and then having students discuss their observations. One of our favorite ways of introducing this text, especially given our focus on issues of language and power, has been to begin with students sharing experiences when they have felt that they were not allowed to be their truest or full selves in schools. We join these conversations, giving them examples from our own experiences (dealing with language, with ways of expressing our gender, with our undocumented status, etc.), and then have students discuss in groups.

Once the lesson has been introduced, we recommend you read the beginning of "How to Tame a Wild Tongue," up to the line that reads "language is a male discourse." We've found that reading carefully is helpful, as this text—like the alternative texts mentioned earlier—includes many comments on the issues of language, power, and identities.

Step 2: Use a Close Reading Lens

In preparation for the second reading of the text excerpt, move students into groups for their word choice analysis. Begin by asking the groups, *What words or phrases evoke strong emotion? What words or phrases touch on the relationship between language and power?* Reread and, just as we did for lesson 1, support one of the groups with an example before you move forward in having them discuss their observations. For example, at a school in the South Bronx, New York City, teachers read Anzaldúa's memoir excerpts and followed these steps themselves before they implemented this kind of reading with their students. They noticed how "caught speaking Spanish," "three licks on the knuckles," and "speak American" were phrases that evoked strong emotions for them. As one monolingual sixth-grade teacher in the South Bronx told us, "My students would definitely understand her perspective! They pointed these issues out when they were reading Francisco Jiménez's *The Circuit: Stories from the Life of a Migrant Child* and *Cajas de cartón: relatos de la vida peregrina de un niño campesino*." Her class had used excerpts from Jiménez's memoir to not only analyze character and theme development in a text, but also discuss how they experienced hardships growing up, one of them being restrictive language practices. Another teacher identified the lines "If you want to be American, speak 'American.' If you don't like it, go back to Mexico where you belong" and "Attacks on one's form of expression with the intent to censor are a violation of the First Amendment" as ones that name ideas that students would be able to trace across other texts.

Step 3: Identify Patterns

Once students have some observations written down, highlighted, or circled according to their focus, revisit the list of words to notice what they have in common. Some teachers ask students to write down the words or phrases on separate index cards and later sort them into different folders. Others have students write on sticky notes and post these on different columns across a sheet of paper. Then they walk around, asking students to explain the way they are sorting the words or phrases.

At a middle school classroom in upstate New York, students who read this text noticed a pattern across their observations that mirrored the work that teachers did in the South Bronx. After I showed them that I noticed a lot of words having to do with control or resistance, students discussed the patterns that they saw. They shared the following as the categories or patterns: culture, change, questioning, and authority. Some students color-coded their notes to show patterns, and others, in addition to the lens of word choice, took the lens of power (after having studied issues of power in literature) to notice who had power (classroom teacher, mother, university) and who was denied power (Gloria Anzaldúa). See Figure 2.6 for the patterns these students noticed.

This work is as powerful with adults as it is with children and adolescents. During professional development sessions, teachers have engaged in reading this text and following this protocol. They read further into that chapter, specifically the first paragraph under the "Overcoming the Tradition of Silence" section. They noticed patterns related to censorship and patriarchy as Anzaldúa says at one point that "language is a male discourse." See Figure 2.7 for the patterns one group of teachers in the South Bronx identified.

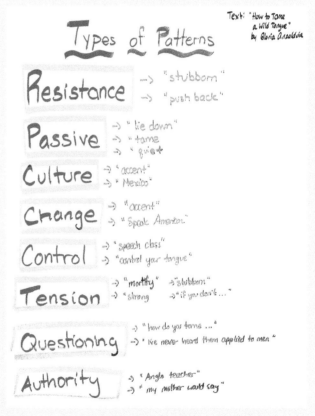

Figure 2.6 Sample Patterns Found by Middle-Grade Students

Figure 2.7 Sample Patterns Found by Middle-Grade Teachers

Restrictions	Patriarchy
"caught speaking Spanish"	"mal criada"
"sent to the corner of the classroom"	"nosotras"
"I want you to speak English"	"hocicona"
"required to take two speech classes"	"repelona"
"violation of the First Amendment"	"gossip"
	"talking back"
	"well-bred girls"
	"robbed of our female being"

Step 4: Develop Statements

Now, we challenge ourselves and our students to take the patterns or labels (i.e., *control*, *resistance*, *language*, or *restriction*) and turn them into sentences that make a statement on a topic or phrase from the text. It helps to have some sentence starters such as:

- In society . . .

- If . . . then . . .

- When schools . . . with students' languages, then . . .

See Figure 2.8 for some of the understandings developed by students in Upstate New York.

Teachers from the South Bronx came up with two critical takeaways from rereading the text and participating in this activity as they planned to follow this with implementation in their classrooms. A social studies teacher who works closely with the English department said

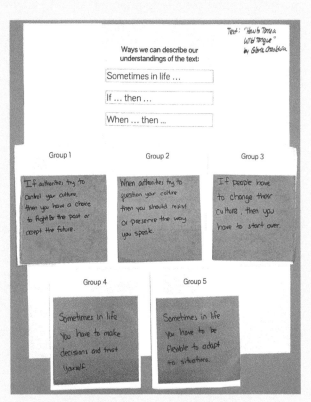

Figure 2.8 Sample Understandings Developed by Middle-Grade Students

that one central idea in the text or an understanding she gathered was that "not encouraging linguistic expression is a form of violence." Another teacher noticed that "dictating cultures and values robs oppressed cultures by extinguishing their language, gender, and influence in general." See Figure 2.9 for more examples of how teachers named understandings/statements connecting the patterns, and compare with your own understandings and the students' understandings.

One literacy coach from a school in Chattanooga, Tennessee, asked if the new understandings or idea statements created could include all of the categories or labels they came up with as a group. As a whole group, those teachers in Chattanooga had

Figure 2.9 Sample Understandings Developed by Middle-Grade Teachers

norms, points of view, minority, robbed, and *perspective* as the labels for the patterns they noticed. After a few minutes of discussing the text, issues, and patterns, one partnership came up with: "Even with established norms, there are different points of view in society and those in the minority could be robbed of their perspective."

Step 5: Considering Our Own Stances

This is the perfect moment for a deep breath and checking in on ourselves. We have just engaged with a powerful text that, for some, may trigger some painful memories of experiences similar to Anzaldúa's. For others, it may serve as a call to reconsider teaching practices. Alternatively, we may feel a combination of both as we remember moments from our own schooling and recent lessons we have taught or conversations we have had with students. The seemingly simple process of going through this text, with thought partners and with students, can help us to unlearn to make room for more humanizing teaching practices.

We can give students the opportunity to consider their own stances through discussion. In Inwood, New York City, at a middle school where the majority of the population consists of students from the Dominican Republic, one eighth grader said, "It's as if she's [Anzaldúa] showing us that language can be used in one way to control others, but in another way to resist." The student continued, "It's like people in her life have always tried to control the way she speaks. Her mom saying something about her accent and her college making her take speech classes. But she's also writing in Spanish in some parts and doesn't translate." The rest of the class enthusiastically went to the text to find those places, and they explained to each other what they understood from certain passages. Then, they discussed how they felt the reading voiced a lot of their own concerns and experiences with how their own speech had been silenced in the school.

You can support your students by giving them some guiding questions to launch the discussion. Just as we did in step 5 in the previous lesson, we can ask the following questions that help students discuss issues related to language practices, power, and identity:

- *What role do language practices play in Anzaldúa's life?*

- *What do others think about Anzaldúa's language practices?*

- *What have we discussed today that relates to how you view your own bilingualism?*

- *Why do you think this about your own bilingualism?*

Step 6: Applying What We've Learned

Here is where we revisit our ideas about language practices and translate these into linguistically sustaining classroom moves. Ask students to consider what recommendations for classroom and school life they might add to the list they started together in the first lesson (see Figure 2.5). Give students options for sharing their ideas: for example, they might continue the T-chart from lesson 1 (Figure 2.5) or they might write in a different genre or form, working on their own version of "How to Tame a Wild Tongue": an autobiographical bilingual story describing a moment or two from their lives, as Anzaldúa did in this introduction. Another extension of this work is to have students use this text as a starting point to create a skit where students perform a scene that helps the audience process the issues of language and power. This final way to wrap up the lesson can be left as a way for students to respond to the topic, text, and translanguaging practice in a way that gives them more options besides the "exit slip" kind of response with narrative writing, skit, song, poem, or sketch. This way, students are given time to engage with the topic and text, time to process across the texts, and time to share their responses in a creative way.

The lesson can end by sharing with students some of your own ideas about language practices, just as you did at the end of lesson 1, the questions that remain, and some goals you are setting up for yourself to learn more or continue this journey of "unlearning." See Figure 2.10 for some ways we can connect our understandings from the text with life applications.

Figure 2.10 Sample Life Applications Based on a Reading of Anzaldúa's Text

Understandings from the Text	Actions I Can Take Based on This New Understanding
Gloria Anzaldúa's experiences in schools revealed that her identity was not welcomed. For example, she was not allowed to speak in Spanish during recess, she got in trouble for telling the teacher how to pronounce her name, and she was required to take a speech class to get rid of her accent.	• I can make sure I learn how to pronounce students' names. • I can get to know the meaning behind their names with readings of name stories and having students share their own. • I can get to know students' translanguaging practices in class and outside of class. • I can be thoughtful about my language and ideas about varieties of language practices. For example, do I think any less or any more of certain ways of speaking? Do I make any judgments on any accents? Why?
The Spanish language is a gendered language. For example, Gloria Anzaldúa said "language is a male discourse" and gave the example of using the masculine word *nosotros* even when women are in the group.	• If I do not speak Spanish, I can learn more about the Spanish language to understand why this matters so much to Gloria Anzaldúa and other speakers of Spanish. • I can make connections between this understanding and the debate between using *Latinos, Latino/a, Latin@,* and *Latinx* for a group of people.
Sometimes our own family might subscribe to assimilationist approaches given the discrimination they have faced in the past and continue to face. For example, Gloria Anzaldúa's mother was "mortified" to hear Gloria speak with an accent.	• I can get to know my students' experiences and see if this is an issue with their interactions with loved ones. What are their ideas on accents? What comments have they made or heard about this in family gatherings? How does this make them feel? • I can get to know the experiences of students' families and the root of their ideas on language practices. • I can bring in guest speakers (in person and via online platforms) who engage in a variety of language practices.

Maybe our work to change our classrooms begins with pronouncing students' names correctly and validating the way they speak, as this was missing in Anzaldúa's schooling. Maybe it considers the ideas we have of different accents, the value judgments placed on them, and what this says about the hierarchy of racialized language practices (Flores and Rosa 2015) that are embedded in schools. Perhaps it is a combination of all of these as we consider our literacy instruction from the ways our students communicate their ideas in class, through speaking and written pieces, to the kinds of texts and experiences we share.

Reflecting on the Lessons: Topic, Texts, Translanguaging

Former president of the National Council of Teachers of English, Dr. Ernest Morrell, said in his 2014 Presidential Address, "There is no reason why an English class can't be multilingual when we have multilingual students" (2015, 317). We hope these paired lessons help you and your students to reach new understandings of bilingual/multilingual experiences and consider ways in which we can make our schools and classrooms places that encourage the full expression of our humanity. The discussion on the languages we value, the words we use in our classroom regarding language discrimination, and the ways we help students navigate their multiple language identities are crucial. By approaching these issues with critical lenses, we can provide spaces for our classroom communities to be agents of change. This work begins with us listening to our students and engaging in reflective and transformative practices.

Telling
Our Stories

Momento de aprendizaje

"Ya calladita mi hijita, pronto vamos a ver a tu papá." Carla read this line quietly as she shared excerpts from a draft of her personal narrative at a school in a Chicago suburb. The rest of the moment described (mostly in English) how her mother tried to quiet and calm her down as she was excited to be reunited with her father after a year of being separated—them in Chile and her dad in New York City. Turning to students, Carla asked, "Out of the list you wrote of moments that taught you something important about life, what will you choose?" The students talked in their small groups. A hand went up, and Carla walked to the back of the room to a student who whispered curiously, "So we can use Spanish in our stories, just like you did?" Carla and the students talked about the different ways they use Spanish in their lives, and how their stories can and should reflect this reality.

Reflecting on That Moment

Why might bilingual and multilingual students feel as if they cannot write using all of the language practices that they engage in throughout their lives? If we take a look at our curriculum and instruction, we may notice that a certain kind of English dominates our narratives. If we think even further back than our lesson planning sessions, thinking about our own teacher preparation experiences and our K–12 schooling, we may uncover that for most of us who completed our K–12 schooling in the United States, monolingual English dominated our learning. Many of our undergraduate and graduate students in our teacher preparation programs reveal that it wasn't until their studies in a bilingual education program or education course that they were exposed to stories that included more dynamic language practices. For several of us, it was a Sandra Cisneros text that we read much later in college where we felt *seen*. We struggle to see how our stories were reflected in our K–12 schooling. Many of the adults we teach ask the same question that this student asked. Now, they question not just whether they are "allowed" to use their full language repertoire but also how it will be perceived by their peers.

There is much vulnerability required when participating in this work. For this work to be healing and restorative—especially to those whose existence and ways of being have been marginalized—we must build on the work from the previous chapter, creating the spaces to validate students' identities and experiences, especially language-minoritized groups, like bilingual Latinx students. Whether it is the newcomer student who refuses to write because they have been shamed and only "seen" with a red pen that slashes through their drafts or the student who doesn't feel like school is a safe place where they can process their trauma through writing, all children should be given the space, the tools, and the options of how to process their experiences, when to do so, and who to share these with, in and outside of the classroom.

Our aim here is to create a space where all students can express themselves safely and more fully through the use of all their linguistic resources. A space where students are able to dig deeply into their stories and focus on the story setting, how they might use dialogue, and the various elements that make stories powerful, as we see with the stories of our mentor authors. This kind of storytelling may only be possible if we are able to let go of monolingual or language-separatist views in the bilingual classroom. The lessons in this chapter highlight authors as mentors who exemplify what it means to be a powerful storyteller, whose stories are enriched by the very dynamic language practices that many emergent bilingual students also engage with in their daily lives. These practices in writing can be a powerful tool to amplify stories so that they remain authentic and validate the ways our students communicate.

Protecting Students' Safety

- **Invite students to share stories and experiences; don't insist that they do so.** Whenever you ask students to share stories and experiences, offer students the option to share a story that they've researched rather than one they've lived. Don't wait for a student to show discomfort or to ask for another option.

- **Be clear about what you are not asking students to share.** Whenever you ask students to share their own or their families' experiences, remind them that they only need to share what they and their families are comfortable sharing. Do not try to coax more personal information out of students than what they volunteer—what students disclose in class may have repercussions beyond class.

Introducing the Sequence of Lessons

Figure 3.1 Sequence of Lessons

The lessons in this chapter encourage students to learn from authors and storytellers in their community to develop their own storytelling. We begin with exposing students to mentor/model texts by Latinx authors through a community reading, we follow that with a study of author's craft in those same texts, and we end with preparation for engaging our family and friends on this topic of stories from their lives (see Figure 3.1). We begin with our mentor authors, Yuyi (pronounced Zhoo-Zhee) Morales, Juana Martinez-Neal, and Meg Medina, focusing on our (im)migration journeys, name stories, and family and language practices. The first read of these stories introduces students to elements of storytelling. Then, we revisit these stories to study how these authors develop their own narratives. In the third lesson, we carefully plan for interviews with our family and friends to learn their stories and to notice how they tell these stories.

Although the lessons in this chapter are modeled using specific texts for grades 3–5, the lessons can also be used with the alternate texts listed. Middle-grade teachers can use the texts in this chapter or may choose alternate texts from the following lists.

Alternate Texts for Grades 3–5 (Realistic Fiction, Memoir, Biographies) and Grades 6–8

- *Marisol McDonald Doesn't Match/Marisol McDonald no combina* (2011) by Monica Brown, illustrated by Sara Palacios

- *Marisol McDonald and the Clash Bash/Marisol McDonald y la fiesta sin igual* (2013) by Monica Brown, illustrated by Sara Palacios

- *Los deseos de Carmela* (2018) and *Carmela Full of Wishes* (2018) by Matt de la Peña, illustrated by Christian Robinson

- *Última parada de la calle Market* (2016) and *Last Stop on Market Street* (2015) by Matt de la Peña, illustrated by Christian Robinson

- *Drawn Together* (2018) by Minh Lê, illustrated by Dan Santat

- *One of a Kind, Like Me/Único como yo* (2016) by Laurin Mayeno, illustrated by Robert Liu-Trujillo

- *Juana & Lucas* (2016) by Juana Medina

- *¿De dónde eres?* (2019) and *Where Are You From?* (2019) by Yamile Saied Méndez, illustrated by Jaime Kim

- *Mi papi tiene una moto* (2019) and *My Papi Has a Motorcycle* (2019) by Isabel Quintero, illustrated by Zeke Peña

- *Pasando páginas: La historia de mi vida* (2018) and *Turning Pages: My Life Story* (2018) by Sonia Sotomayor, illustrated by Lulu Delacre

- *Querido primo: Una carta a mi primo* (2010) and *Dear Primo: A Letter to My Cousin* (2010) by Duncan Tonatiuh

- *Pancho Rabbit and the Coyote* (2013) by Duncan Tonatiuh

- *Undocumented: A Worker's Fight* (2018) by Duncan Tonatiuh

- *El día en que descubres quién eres* (2018) and *The Day You Begin* (2018) by Jacqueline Woodson, illustrated by Rafael López

Digital Text Options to Complement Texts for Grades 3–5 and Grades 6–8

- "Soy yo" (2015) by Bomba Estéreo (song and music video in Spanish)

- "Un besito más" (feat. Juan Luis Guerra) (2015) by Jesse & Joy (song and music video in Spanish)

- Miguel's rendition of "Remember Me (Dúo)" (feat. Natalia Lafourcade) (2017) by Kristen Anderson-Lopez and Robert Lopez (song and music video in English and Spanish)

- *Spider-Man: Into the Spider-Verse* film scene with Miles Morales and family speaking in Spanish and in English (see the movie trailer) (Persichetti, Ramsey, and Rothman 2018)

- Interview with author and illustrator Juana Martinez-Neal (Candlewick Press 2018) (in Spanish and in English)

- Interview with author and illustrator Yuyi Morales (Holiday House 2018)

- Interview with author Meg Medina (Reading Rockets n.d.)

Alternate Texts for Grades 6–8 (Contemporary Fiction, Book Clubs, Author Studies)

- *They Call Me Güero: A Border Kid's Poems* (2018) by David Bowles

- *Ana María Reyes Does Not Live in a Castle* (2018) by Hilda Eunice Burgos

- *The Epic Fail of Arturo Zamora* (2017), *Marcus Vega Doesn't Speak Spanish* (2018), and *Each Tiny Spark* (2019) by Pablo Cartaya

- *Us, in Progress: Short Stories About Young Latinos* (2017) by Lulu Delacre

- *Stella Diaz tiene algo que decir* (2018) and *Stella Diaz Has Something to Say* (2018) by Angela Dominguez

- *Miss Quinces* (forthcoming) by Kat Fajardo

- *Tight* (2018) by Torrey Maldonado

- *The Revolution of Evelyn Serrano* (2012) by Sonia Manzano

- *Under the Mesquite* (2011) by Guadalupe García McCall

- *Merci Suárez Changes Gears* (2018) by Meg Medina

- *Silver Meadows Summer* (2019) by Emma Otheguy

- *Strange Birds: A Field Guide to Ruffling Feathers* (2019) and *The First Rule of Punk* (2017) by Celia C. Pérez

- *The Moon Within* (2019) by Aida Salazar

- *My Year in the Middle* (2018) by Lila Quintero Weaver

Alternate Texts for Grades 6–8 (Memoir)

- *Aire encantado: Dos culturas, dos alas: una memoria* (2017), *Enchanted Air: Two Cultures, Two Wings: A Memoir* (2015), and *Soaring Earth: A Companion Memoir to Enchanted Air* (2019) by Margarita Engle

- *The Distance Between Us* (Young Readers Edition) (2016) by Reyna Grande

- *El mundo adorado de Sonia Sotomayor* (adaptado para jovenes mayores) (2018) and *The Beloved World of Sonia Sotomayor* (Young Readers Edition) (2018) by Sonia Sotomayor

- *Darkroom: A Memoir in Black and White* (2012) by Lila Quintero Weaver

Supporting Translanguaging in the Sequence of Lessons

- Deliver the lesson in English, in Spanish, or using features of both.

- Have both English and Spanish versions of texts for all lessons available to encourage students to either hear one language and read the words in another or hear more than one language in one text.

- Have translation tools available, such as bilingual glossaries, dictionaries, or digital tools, to support students as they prepare for interviews during lesson 3.

- Engage in a translanguaging study of the ways authors use translanguaging in their texts and/or the ways family and friends use translanguaging during the interviews. This is one part of the author's craftwork for lesson 2 that can be done with the whole class or a small group.

- Encourage students to use their entire linguistic repertoire to:
  - *Discuss the texts (small groups and whole class).*
  - *Take notes on the texts.*
  - *Plan their interview questions (from role-playing with a partner to writing out the questions).*

- Accept and celebrate students' discussions and writing that include features of English, Spanish, and other languages.

Reading Stories from Latinx Mentor Authors

This lesson presents teachers with options to guide students in a community reading that encourages students to make connections between their own experiences and the text's characters, plot, setting, and themes. Although this lesson is modeled with three texts appropriate for grades 3–5, the texts can be used in grades 6–8 and the lessons can also be used with any of the alternate texts recommended.

The model texts in this lesson are as follows: Yuyi Morales (2018), in the 2019 Pura Belpré Illustrator award winner *Soñadores* and *Dreamers*, tells the story of her migration journey with her infant son and the role that libraries had in processing her transition from Mexico to San Francisco. In the 2019 Caldecott Honor book *Alma and How She Got Her Name* and *Alma y cómo obtuvo su nombre*, Juana Martinez-Neal (2018) tells the story of how a father explains the meaning behind each name given to his daughter, Alma Sofía Esperanza José Pura Candela, a name Alma believes is too long. In the 2016 Pura Belpré Author and Illustrator Award Honor book *Mango, abuela y yo* and *Mango, Abuela, and Me* by Meg Medina and illustrated by Angela Dominguez (2015), a grandmother and her granddaughter get to know one another a little better and figure out how to do this when abuela speaks Spanish and her granddaughter speaks English.

Each of these texts is available in Spanish and in English. Each book addresses a very real and important part of bilingual Latinx identities: our (im)migration journeys and names, how these reveal something about our families or family history, and communication with family when our language practices differ. Latinx identities are varied and complex and not all of us have the same (im)migration journeys, as we shared in Chapter 1 with our own experiences. Although these texts present particular experiences with relation to journeys, names, family history, and language practices, we hope you will also consider other texts as well, providing students with several examples.

Preparing to Teach: Reading the Texts in Community

Reading texts together is likely already a common practice in your learning community. Although reading with your students can support a wide range of literacy skills, the following sample plans offer models for reading with your classroom community for very specific purposes: to fully hear others' stories, to invite students to make connections to their own lives, and to lay the groundwork for students sharing their own stories in future classroom gatherings. Each sample plan focuses on both the content of the story (stories about movement or journeys, names, family, and language practices) and how we, as readers, can better understand the story by looking at characters, plot, or problems (and ways these are addressed), setting, and the lessons learned. You will find multiple opportunities for children to read out loud with a partner and with the class. Too often we find teacher-centered teaching in spaces with bilingual Latinx children, leaving very few moments for the students to practice and grow in their language practices. In Carla's Bilingual Literacy class with teacher candidates, her students create plans like these, implement them while recording themselves, and reflect on their teaching with a partner in their class. The most common feedback these preservice teachers give one another is to create more opportunities for the *students* in the class to speak, read, and engage with the book, just like Karina does in Figure 3.2.

We encourage you to try this cycle of read-aloud and reflection! Take notes on the duration of the moments you read out loud, the moments you share your thinking process out loud, and the moments students engage with the reading out loud. How many minutes are students getting to speak, to develop their language practices, to engage with the word and the world (Freire 1970), discussing life applications of these

Figure 3.2 Bilingual teacher Karina Espertin reads with her fourth-grade Bilingual Dual Language students.

stories in community? Notice how much time and space are given for your thought processes and language practices to be shared compared with students' opportunities in partnerships, triads, or small groups.

Therefore, instead of calling these "read-aloud" plans, we call them "reading in community" plans. (See sample plans in Figures 3.3, 3.4, and 3.6.) These center the reading practices of the entire classroom community, with opportunities for the teacher to read and demonstrate reading practices, for partnerships to read out loud together and discuss their ideas, and for the entire class to read together. Although each of these are options, you will see that all of them fit nicely as a text set on our journeys, our families, and our language practices. This means you can choose one of these depending on your student population, grade, and focus, or you can do two or all of the readings in community! There are several beautiful ways to share these powerful texts with your students, and the following plans are only one of many ways you can do so, while constantly considering topics, texts, and translanguaging. Following the three plans, you will find a guide (Figure 3.7) to help you plan your own reading in community, especially as you consider building on this work with the recommended texts.

In each reading in community plan, we recommend making a chart that will help set students up for the topic of the reading and to return to this topic throughout the reading or at the end during a whole-class discussion. We prefer having a written record as opposed to keeping it entirely discussion-based given that we are thinking about bilingual Latinx students who may not be used to seeing their language practices validated and used as more than a scaffold. In other words, having a class chart that reflects their language practices across conversations and the texts authenticates their existence. These small moves have a powerful impact.

Figure 3.3 Sample Plan for Reading *Soñadores* and/or *Dreamers* by Yuyi Morales in Community

Step 1: Setting Up for Our Reading in Community (5 minutes)

Choose an option to begin, being mindful of what students will want (or not want) to share:

1. Ask partnerships to talk about the journeys that people (themselves, their families, friends, people they've studied) have taken when coming to the (mainland) United States.

2. Ask students (in partnerships) to share the challenges that come up when people leave their home, su tierra, and come to the United States.

3. Have a whole-class discussion on ways they or others help people (their family and their friends) when someone has just arrived in the United States. Have students make a class chart to record and affirm their contributions. You can return to this chart throughout the reading or at the end with a whole-class discussion.

Step 2: Book Introduction (2 minutes)

Show the cover of the book and read the title and names of the author and illustrator. Connect this with the discussions students have just had, explaining that in this book we get to know Yuyi Morales' journey with her son from Mexico to the United States. Throughout this book we will get to know how the characters face the challenges of their journey.

Present vocabulary in context with supporting visuals (at least two for each): *inmigrantes, migrantes, ancestros, tenacidad*. Have students say the words with you and make connections with the images that you share. As you come across the words in the text, stop to consider the meaning of key words in the context of the story.

Step 3: Reading in Community (20 minutes)

Teacher Reading and Sharing Ideas #1 (pages 1–6)	Students Reading and Sharing Ideas #1 (pages 1–6)
Read the first four pages and share your thinking out loud, pausing after reading "Y cuando llegamos al otro lado . . . nos convertimos en inmigrantes." On the left side of a chart, write the challenges the characters face. For example: • "Adiós corazón" on page 4 makes me think that Yuyi feels like her heart is being left behind in her homeland. • "Sedientos, sobrecogidos" translates to "they were thirsty and scared." It wasn't an easy journey.	Ask students to pick their favorite page (or line) to reread out loud with them. Then, have students all reread it together (in Spanish or in English). Ask students to explain why they picked that line or page. What did they feel when they heard the words or when they read them out loud? What did they feel when they saw the illustrations? How do the words and illustrations help them understand the characters better?

Read "Migrantes, tú y yo . . . nuestros ancestros" together with students. If you went with options 1 or 2 when you started the reading experience, then you can add a column to the class chart (beside the challenges column) and discuss ways that they help others or what helped them when words were new to them or others. If you already have this chart started, then you can just discuss what you would add based on what you read so far in this book.

Teacher Reading and Sharing Ideas #2 (pages 11–20)	Students Reading and Sharing Ideas #2 (pages 21–24)
Read the next few pages when Yuyi and her son arrive at the library. Add to the "challenges" column of the class chart.	Ask the students: *How did the library and books help Yuyi and her son? How have books helped you in your life?* Let partnerships read pages 21–24 together. Listen to students' conversations and write phrases on a second class chart, "Ways books help me in my life."

Read the end of the book together with students at the same time, out loud.

Step 4: Class Discussion (5 minutes)

Ask students what *they'd* like to talk about, giving them some options:

1. **Focus on characters:** Discuss characters' journey, summarizing the challenges faced and applying that to our lives. Students can take this further by creating a list of books they would like to use to help new students or family members with their Spanish, English, or both.

2. **Focus on setting:** Discuss our interpretations of the meaning behind special places in our lives, gathering the words that Yuyi used to describe the library in Spanish and in English. Students can create a bilingual list of words to describe a special place in their life (their school library, public library, abuelita's home, home, etc.).

3. **Focus on themes:** Consider what the characters learned and then discuss how those lessons might help us in our lives. If students lean toward broad answers ("library," or "being bilingual," for example), help them develop these into theme statements: What about the library or books did this story teach us? You can return to the chart you started earlier on the ways books helped our lives. If you discuss a theme statement on immigration—such as What about the immigration journey did this book teach us or highlight for us?—then you can create a shared chart where small groups add their contributions that they write on sticky notes and bring up to the class chart.

Figure 3.4 Sample Plan for Reading *Alma y cómo obtuvo su nombre* and/or *Alma and How She Got Her Name* by Juana Martinez-Neal in Community

Step 1: Setting Up for Our Reading in Community (5 minutes)

Choose an option to begin:

1. Ask partnerships to share their name stories. To prepare for this, inform students several days in advance that you'll be asking them to share these stories. Remind them the day before this reading in community. This way, families have time to share these name stories. For students without connections to families for this information, another option can be given to share a name story they know about someone in their life (friend or character in a book).

2. Ask students (in partnerships) to share any questions they have about their names or the names of their family members.

3. Have a whole-class discussion on what the students know about their names.

Step 2: Book Introduction (5 minutes)

Show the cover of the book and read the title and names of the author and illustrator. Explain that in this book we learn about Alma's name as her dad explains the meaning behind each of the names given to her. Throughout this book, we will get to know the story behind each name and see how Alma changes.

Vocabulary in context presented with supporting visuals (at least two for each): *ciudad natal, vida cotidiana, ancestros, causas justas*. Have students say the words with you and make connections with the images that you share. As you come across the words in the text, stop to consider the meaning of key words in the context of the story. See Figure 3.5 for an example of a teacher introducing vocabulary with this text.

Step 3: Reading in Community (20 minutes)

Teacher and Student Reading #1 (pages 1–4)	Teacher and Student Reading #2 (pages 5–8)
1. Reads pages 1–4.	1. Continue reading pages 5–8.
2. When the text gives Alma's full name (Alma Sofía Esperanza José Pura Candela), everyone rereads it together.	2. When you reach, "Yo Soy Sofía," ask everyone to reread that line with you.
3. Say your full name.	3. Ask students to share with their partner what Alma thinks now. Listen and share out a few observations with the class.
4. Students say their full names in their partnerships.	
5. Share the problem in the text: Alma thinks her name is too long. Explain that we will continue reading to see how her father helps her think differently.	

Teacher and Student Reading #3 (pages 9–12)

1. Read pages 9–12.

2. Everyone rereads together: "¡El mundo es tan grande! Yo quiero conocerlo contigo, Papi. ¡Tú y yo juntos!"

3. Add to your observations about the story. For example: "I see that Alma is realizing that she has things in common with people in her family."

Teacher and Student Reading #4 (pages 13–16)

1. Read pages 13–16.

2. Everyone rereads together: "Tu abuelo me enseñó a ver y amar a nuestra gente." "Yo soy José."

3. Ask students to discuss how Alma is changing. Listen and share out two or three observations with the class.

Teacher Reading #5 (pages 17–20)

1. Read pages 17–20.

2. Share your observations. For example: "I see another way that Alma is changing is that she feels closer to her antepasados. She says hello to Pura. I can see how the character is changing with what she says and how she says it."

Student Reading #6 (pages 21–24)

1. Partnerships read pages 21–24.

2. Ask partnerships to discuss what Alma is learning about her family.

3. Listen and share out two or three observations with the class.

Reading Together (pages 25–28)

Read the end of the book together with the students, out loud, repeating "¡Alma Sofía Esperanza José Pura Candela!"

Step 4: Class Discussion (5 minutes)

Ask students what *they'd* like to talk about, giving them some options:

1. **Focus on characters:** Discuss character change: How did the character of Alma change in this book? What role did her father play? What did Alma learn about her family?

2. **Focus on themes:** Discuss the lessons the characters learned in the book, and then discuss how those lessons help us in our lives. If students lean toward broad topics (family, names, stories, or pride, for example), help them develop these into theme statements: What does this book teach us about our names or family? Why should we learn about the history of our names?

Figure 3.5 Sample Plan for Reading *Mango, abuela y yo* and/or *Mango, Abuela, and Me* by Meg Medina in Community

Step 1: Setting Up for Our Reading in Community (5 minutes)

Choose an option to begin, being mindful of what students will want (or not want) to share:

1. Ask students (in partnerships) to talk about their grandparents or caregivers in their lives.

2. Ask students (in partnerships) to share any challenges that come up when they speak with family members. Do they all speak the same way? How is it similar or different?

3. Have a whole-class discussion on ways they have helped people in their family learn another language. Have students create a class chart with their ideas and read it together.

Step 2: Book Introduction (2 minutes)

Show the cover of the book and read the title and names of the author and illustrator. Connect this with the opening discussion, explaining that in this book we see how the main character and her abuela help one another communicate in Spanish and in English. In this book, we will get to know how the characters not only learn more words but also learn more about each other!

Vocabulary in context presented with supporting visuals (at least two for each): *zigzagueante, merienda, escaparate.* Have students say the words with you and make connections with the images that you share. As you come across the words in the text, stop to consider the meaning of key words in the context of the story.

Step 3: Reading in Community (25 minutes)

Teacher Reading and Sharing Ideas #1 (pages 1–4)	Student Reading and Sharing Ideas #1 (pages 5–6)
Read the introduction and the next scene when abuela sits beside Mia. Name what you notice. For example: "I notice that two problems that abuela has are that her home is too big for just her and she lives too far away."	Ask student partnerships to discuss: *What problem does Mia have as this book begins?* Partnerships read the next scene where abuela shows the pluma and fotografía to Mia. Work with students to begin a chart of the problems they identify for each character.

Teacher Reading and Sharing Ideas #2 (pages 7–10)	Student Reading and Sharing Ideas #2 (pages 11–12)
Read the next scene where Mia and abuela walk to the park and later walk back home.	Ask the students to identify any new challenges they notice in the text. Add them to the chart. Partnerships read the next scene together where Mia's mami tells her to be patient. Then ask: *How do the characters help one another with these challenges? What advice would you give Mia?* Listen to students' advice and write some ideas on a class chart of advice for Mia.

Reading Together (pages 13–16)

Read these next two key scenes together out loud with the students, pausing and emphasizing those words that Mia and abuela teach one another in Spanish and in English while they make empanadas de carne and Mia posts sticky notes with words around their home.

Teacher Reading and Sharing Ideas #3 (pages 17–20)	Student Reading and Sharing Ideas #3 (pages 21–26)
Read the following part of the story when Mia and mami purchase a parrot for abuela. Comment on what you notice. For example, when Mia says, "He can keep her company when I'm at school," it shows that Mia is thinking not only about abuela learning English but also about abuela's feelings and how she misses her other home. Start a list of words to describe Mia, for example, add the words *kind* and *thoughtful*.	Ask the students: *How would you describe Mia and abuela? What words would you use to describe them and why? Think about this as you read with your partner.* Partnerships read the next few pages where we see the parrot in the home, a surprised papi, and abuela talking to neighbors in English. Listen to students' reading and conversations to add words to the second chart.

Reading Together (pages 27–30)

Read the end of the book together with students at the same time, out loud.

continues

Step 4: Class Discussion (5 minutes)

Ask students what *they'd* like to talk about, giving them some options:

1. **Focus on problem/solution:** Discuss characters' problems and solutions, summarizing how the characters faced their challenges and considering how you and the students might connect the characters' challenges and solutions to your own lives.

2. **Focus on characters:** Discuss our interpretations of characters, gathering the words everyone came up with to describe the characters in the book.

3. **Focus on themes:** Discuss what we learn about life from this book. Start with what the characters learned and then how those lessons help us in our lives. If students lean toward broad examples as topics (family, being bilingual, kindness, or change, for example), help them develop these into theme statements: What about family or kindness did this book teach us? You might find it helpful to return to a class chart (if option 3 was selected from step 1) and have students develop theme statements based on their contributions to the chart.

Figure 3.6 Pia Persampieri introduces vocabulary with her Bilingual Dual Language fourth-grade class.

Figure 3.7 Guide to Reading in Community (Narrative Texts)

Step 1: Setting Up for Our Reading in Community (5 minutes)

1. **Consider the themes and lessons of the book:** Ask partnerships to discuss questions you've designed to help them make connections to the subject, theme, or characters in the text. Focus on what may seem familiar to them.

2. **Involve the larger community:** In a whole-class discussion, ask students to discuss how they and the community might address a similar challenge to that of the story.

Step 2: Book Introduction (5 minutes)

Show the cover of the book and read the title and names of the author and illustrator. Connect the book with a previous activity.

Consider some of the vocabulary in context, using at least two visuals for each word or phrase. Have students say the words with you and make connections with the images that you share. As you come across the words in the text, stop to consider the meaning of key words in the context of the story.

Step 3: Reading in Community (20–25 minutes)

Teacher Reading and Sharing Ideas #1 (pages __–__)	Student Reading and Sharing Ideas #1 (pages __–__)
Prepare selection to read out loud followed by your observations, which are ideally connected to the purpose for reading this text in community (for example, problems and ways characters confront challenges).	Choose a meaningful line or page—or ask students to pick a favorite line or page—to reread out loud with students.
Keep track of your thinking in front of the students, using chart paper, notes in a notebook with document camera, a device projecting on a SMART Board, or whatever materials and technology you have available.	Asks students to explain what they felt when they heard the words or when they read them out loud. What did they feel when they saw the illustrations (if any)? How do the words and illustrations help them understand the characters better? If they chose the words that they read aloud, why did they choose them?

Reading Together (pages __–__)

Teacher and students read key lines from the story, and keep adding to the class chart.

continues

Teacher Reading and Sharing Ideas #2 (pages __–__)	Student Reading and Sharing Ideas #2 (pages __–__)
Repeat the practices used in the first idea sharing with the next part of the story. Keep adding to notes.	Ask students to reread a selection with a partner, triad, or small group. Then, prompt them to discuss a question or idea about the text that is related to the focus of this reading in community session.

Teacher Reading and Sharing Ideas #3 (pages __–__)	Student Reading and Sharing Ideas #3 (pages __–__)
Repeat the practices used in the first idea sharing with the next part of the story. Keep adding to notes.	Ask students to reread a selection with a partner, triad, or small group. Then, prompt them to discuss a question or idea about the text that is related to the focus of this reading in community session.

Reading Together (pages __–__)

Read key lines from the story. Continue adding to the class chart.

Step 4: Class Discussion (5 minutes)

Teacher asks students what *they'd* like to talk about, giving them some options (if options are needed):

1. **Focus on characters:** Discuss characters' journey, summarizing the challenges faced and focusing on how we can make personal connections and/or apply the character's experiences and choices to our lives.

2. **Focus on setting:** Discuss students' interpretations of why the author chose the setting. Why is it important? What connections can students make between their own experiences and the story's setting?

3. **Focus on themes:** Discuss what we learn about life from this book. Start with what the characters learned and then move on to how those lessons help us in our lives.

To download a reproducible version of this table, please visit http://hein.pub/comunidad and click on "Companion Resources."

Writing Our Own Stories

In this lesson, students write their own stories, enriching them with craft moves learned from the texts in lesson 1.

Preparing to Teach

Neither reading like a writer nor writing one's own story are simple tasks. In this lesson, students will identify elements of authors' craft in the stories they've read and use those moves to enrich their own stories. We recommend starting the writing work in this lesson but giving students time across several days to develop their writing. The purpose of this lesson is to return to stories that will inspire our own writing and not to push students to go through the whole writing process in one sitting. We heed the words of educator Dulce-Marie Flecha, considering trauma-informed teaching practices and the experiences of transient students: give them time to think of stories that they'd like to share instead of asking them to respond to prompts in the moment (Flecha 2018).

Step 1: Considering Your Own Stories

In the previous lesson, we read stories that covered different experiences from im(migration) journeys to name stories and the ways we communicate and grow with family members. In this lesson, we begin by creating the space for students to make a list of meaningful moments from their own lives and to start writing what they remember from one of those moments. You can set this up by having students make a list of connections they had with the books and how those connections can inspire them to write about their own lives. For example, if you connect with the name story from *Alma y cómo obtuvo su nombre* and/or *Alma and How She Got Her Name*, then you might make a list of the moments you remember that connect with your name. Another way to set this up or to give students a second option is to ask students to list moments from their lives that they'd like to write about (and eventually to share with the class) because it's important to them. Of course, heeding Flecha's words, we will remind students that they will not be asked to share this list or first story idea before they're ready to do so. Instead, you can encourage students to spend the first fifteen minutes processing moments that they care deeply about and that they may want to write because it helps them feel closer to this topic and/or closer to this community of learners.

Step 2: Revisiting the Texts

We all have those moments in our teacher life where so much is happening across our school day, school week, or even year that it becomes really difficult to keep track of what we have taught and what is coming up. Students also feel this way! To help students quickly reacquaint themselves with the craft of the texts, let them organize themselves in small groups (see Figure 3.8) and choose a focus for their discussion:

- **Setting:** Where and when does each story take place? How is the setting important to each story?

- **Character:** How does each character feel in the beginning, middle, and end of the story? How does each character change?

- **Problem:** What are the problems in the stories? How do the problems change or grow? Are there solutions to the problems?

- **Theme:** What is one lesson that each main character learns about life when they face a tough moment? What do students learn about life from these stories?

If students want to work on multiple story elements, you might also have each group focus on a different text and consider all of the story elements within that book. As students discuss their responses to the guiding questions, focus on "reading the room," taking notes on what they hear and how they respond to the questions. Are they referring back to the text? Are they translanguaging? Are they building on one another's responses? If not, gently remind them to do so in the remaining steps of the lesson.

Step 3: Discussing Ways Authors Tell Stories

Begin by modeling for students how you notice the author engaging in craft moves across the story. Reread an excerpt from one of the texts, pausing after the excerpt to name what you notice the author doing. Figure 3.9 gives a few examples of how you might discuss particular moves. Engaging in shared (re)reading practices, asking students to repeat some key lines with you, will also help bilingual students develop their language practices.

Figure 3.8 Karina Espertin revisits a reading with her fourth-grade Bilingual Dual Language students in a small group.

Figure 3.9 Ways Authors Tell Stories

	Alma y cómo obtuvo su nombre and *Alma and How She Got Her Name* by Juana Martinez-Neal	Ways the Author Tells This Story
En el principio . . . **In the beginning . . .**	Read the beginning three pages where we learn of Alma's name and what she thought about it at this point in the story.	• **Character:** The author is letting us know how Alma feels about her name. • **Problem:** The author shows Alma complaining about her name, so we can figure out that this is a problem for Alma.
A la mitad . . . **In the middle . . .**	Read pages 9–11 where Alma learns about her great-grandmother's name, Esperanza.	• **Dialogue:** The author shows us how Alma's papi speaks. I can tell from the way the author has written the dialogue that he knows each of Alma's ancestors well and he loves them all, too. • **Character:** The author shows Alma acting differently after hearing about each ancestor—like where she is excited to love to travel like her great-grandmother, Esperanza. The author shows us how Alma is changing.
Al final . . . **At the end . . .**	Read the last three pages where Alma shows that she loves the story of her name.	• **Character:** The author shows how Alma's feelings about her name have changed: at first she didn't like her name being so long, and now she loves it!

After students see how you are noticing storytelling craft, it is their turn to return to the text. Ask them to choose a brief excerpt and work in partnerships to discuss what the author did to show and develop the setting, characters, problem, and theme. Explain that they may notice that the author works with one story element or multiple story elements in their excerpt. Then, once they've worked through that excerpt, let them do the same with another excerpt of their choosing.

Step 4: Revisiting Our Narratives Inspired by Mentor Authors

Now is the time for students to use these examples as inspiration for their own writing. Ask students to return to their writing from the beginning of this lesson. All students will have made a list or two of moments inspired by the texts and selected one to develop. All students will have also started writing a scene from a meaningful moment in their life. Tell students that this is the time to return to that first scene that they wrote and elaborate on it using what they learned from mentor authors. Another option is for them to develop a second scene from that moment using a mentor author's craft. Before students resume their writing, ask them to jot down their writing goal or the part of the mentor author's writing they want to try out on their own. They can leave this goal written on the top of their notebook page or on a sticky note that's placed on their desk. You can then move around to note their mentors and leave them to write. Although this is a brief time to return to the moment they selected, plan to give them multiple writing periods to work on their pieces, making sure that the mentor texts are available to them while they write. Your one-on-one conferences can grow into small groups as you gather data on what the students are doing in their writing.

Step 5: Revisiting Our Purpose

Once students have written a scene or two that is inspired by their own experiences and the texts they revisited, come back together as a class to share the writing. Ask, *What is it about Yuyi Morales', Juana Martinez-Neal's, and Meg Medina's writing that you are trying out in your own story?* Ask students to share a line or two from their writing that shows how they were inspired by the mentor authors. They can do this in small groups or in partnerships. If you are discussing as a class, you can have this prepared by calling on two or three students whom you asked during their writing time (step 4) if they could share with the class. Another way to consider students' comfort level with sharing moments from their lives is to be intentional with writing partnerships. You may have done this already prior to starting this narrative reading-writing work, but consider having students provide input as to which writing partners/groups would be helpful for their narrative storytelling/sharing times.

Next, ask students, *What's special about this story that you are developing?* and *How did you feel writing out that scene?* Here, we are listening to students describe their stories and their feelings as well as setting them up for the work of the next lesson. Again, students can share in partnerships or small groups or you can ask a few to share with the rest of the class. Students benefit from hearing one another and from seeing how their teachers name the expertise in their community. As always, asking students for permission before putting them on the spot in front of the class is crucial in sharing narratives from their lives.

Learning More About Our Own Stories from Family and Friends

Students explore how the themes in the mentor texts are part of their worlds as they prepare to listen to their family and friends share stories of meaningful moments from their lives.

Preparing to Teach: What Do We Learn from the Stories Shared by Family and Friends?

In the previous two lessons, students have felt the power of stories as they connected to others' stories and wrote and shared their own stories. In this lesson, they will prepare to interview their families and friends to hear and share their stories, honoring their funds of knowledge (Moll et al. 1992). This abuelita knowledge—intergenerational storytelling—fuels healing and resistance to oppressive conditions (Nava 2017).

Before the lesson, consider what you would like to share with students to help them to see the power of abuelita knowledge. Will you share a meaningful story from your own life? Will you play a video or audio clip of someone in your own family relating a story? Or will you bring in the voice of one of the authors the students have studied?

Step 1: Why Do Stories Matter?

Begin by asking students why they tell stories or why they listen to stories. Then, share the personal story or the author interview that you've chosen to begin this lesson.

Author Interviews That Work Well with This Lesson

1. Interviews with Yuyi Morales
   a. "Yuyi's Story" (PBS 2012)
   b. "Dreamers" (Morales 2017)
   c. "Yuyi Morales" (*The Children's Book Podcast* 2018)

2. Interviews with Meg Medina
   a. "A Family of Storytellers" (Colorín Colorado 2016a)
   b. "Growing Up in Queens" (Colorín Colorado 2016b)
   c. "Learning to Read in Spanish" (Colorín Colorado 2016c)

For example, you might show "A Family of Storytellers," a three-minute-and-fifty-second excerpt from an interview with Meg Medina on the Colorín Colorado YouTube channel or website. After watching Meg Medina talk about the stories her abuelita shared and why they're important to her, you can revisit these words or have students share with one another—in writing partnerships or small groups—what the stories, their families, and their friends mean to them.

Step 2: Exploring Themes in Our Reading and in Our Lives

Tell students that in this lesson, they will prepare to interview family members or friends to learn about their stories. You can also begin by turning to the mentor texts you've read and studied with the students. Making sure that the students have access to the texts (see Figure 3.10), so that they can refer to them as necessary, ask them: *What themes or topics did you notice in the texts?* or *What themes or topics did you connect with in the texts?* Offer an example of a theme or topic that you noticed or connected with to get the conversation started. Record the themes or topics that students identify on a chart. Of course, these texts reveal several themes. We have included Figure 3.11 both to offer some starting points for discussion and to remind us all that the mentor texts are multifaceted and multilayered.

> *Meg Medina on stories and family:*
>
> "There are beautiful things from the places that we come from. Even if we left behind in difficult circumstances, there were things to love about there. There were things that left an imprint on our parents and on us. When I think about my grandmother, as the cuentista, and the stories that she told me, I'm just so grateful that she gave me that time." (Colorín Colorado 2016a)

Figure 3.10 A bilingual student reads a picture book.

Figure 3.11 Some Themes from Mentor Texts

	What Did We Learn from Our Mentor Texts?
Reading Yuyi Morales' *Soñadores* and/or *Dreamers*	• **On immigration:** Sometimes (im)migration journeys are taken by families together to unknown places. • **On immigration:** (Im)migration journeys to the United States sometimes are frightening because of the unknown. • **On being new to a place:** It can be confusing when you don't understand a language and you're in a new place. • **On libraries:** Libraries can be a place of refuge. • **On books:** Books can help people learn and find their voice.
Reading Juana Martinez-Neal's *Alma y cómo obtuvo su nombre* and/or *Alma and How She Got Her Name*	• **On names:** Our names reveal what matters to our families. • **On family history:** Learning the history of our names helps us get to know the history of our family. • **On change and growth:** Sometimes we need help understanding things that are unknown to us.
Reading Meg Medina's *Mango, abuela y yo* and/or *Mango, Abuela, and Me*	• **On language practices:** Learning another language can bring people together. • **On family and language practices:** It is tough when you can't communicate with family. • **On developing language practices:** It helps to be creative and kind when teaching and learning another language. • **On family:** Families help us through tough times.

Some students might say that *Soñadores* or *Dreamers* taught them about books or family; others might return to Medina's *Mango, abuela y yo* or *Mango, Abuela, and Me* and say that the book taught them about family, bilingualism, or change. Rather than relying on one-word answers that don't clearly explain what students have learned, help students to name their ideas with more specificity. Figure 3.12 shows some examples of how to support students in elaborating on their theme statements. You can help students develop those topics into theme statements by encouraging them to revisit the texts to see how the characters felt about those topics (*How did Yuyi feel about books? How did abuela feel when her granddaughter taught her words in English?*). Students might discuss how characters went from feeling scared to feeling hopeful or from feeling confused to feeling confident. Another way to help students go from topic to theme statements is to ask them to revisit the texts to notice how characters helped one another—for example,

Yuyi and her son, Alma and her father, abuela and her granddaughter. Then you can encourage students to think about what they were teaching one another. To create their theme statements (or explain an example from the chart) students can then remove the characters' names from their explanations, going from "Yuyi and her son were happy in the library" to "Libraries can be places that help people who are new to a place," or from "Alma's dad helped Alma learn about her family history and love her name" to "Learning the history of our names helps us learn more about our family history."

Figure 3.12 Developing Ideas on Themes

I can start thinking about a topic that the book revealed to me as I read it.	I can return to the text to see characters' feelings or characters' relationships.	I can think of how to say that without using the characters' names. How would I summarize that lesson learned to someone who hasn't read the book? How can I phrase this in a way that is universal? (That means that we see this in other books, movies, songs, and all over our lives!)
Immigration	In *Soñadores* or *Dreamers*, Yuyi and her son were scared when they arrived in the United States. They didn't know English.	Immigration journeys can be scary.
Names	In *Alma y cómo obtuvo su nombre* or *Alma and How She Got Her Name*, Alma didn't like her long name in the beginning. Her father taught her the meaning of each name. At the end she loved her full name!	Names can tell a family's history.
Family	In *Mango, abuela y yo* or *Mango, Abuela, and Me*, abuela and her granddaughter help each other learn English and Spanish.	Families can help us.

Step 3: Developing Interview Questions and an Interview Plan

Ask students to look at the list of themes you've identified together, and consider which themes are the most meaningful to them and to their family members. Then, ask them to consider which family member (or members) they might interview about one or more of these themes. Some family structures and constraints outside of the child's control will inform their decisions. For example, some students' immediate family might not live with them and they'll have extended family. For undocumented and/or transient students, the trauma associated with their family separation might lead them to consider revisiting some digital texts or books to conduct the "interviews" with those sources.

At this point, let students know when you expect them to have the interview completed: for some, their families might not be accessible if they are to complete this activity in a day. Use what you know about your students' home lives to inform the deadlines or duration for the interviews. You can also decide this together, especially if you do not have this information and need to listen to students to learn more about their families. Or you might have this information from beginning-of-the-year surveys and "meet-the-teacher" events with families.

Next, have students work in partnerships to create a plan for who they will ask, how they will ask, what questions they will ask, and how they will take notes. You may want to give students parameters for the assignment, including a recommended length of time for the interview (perhaps about ten minutes), that consider the grade or age range and deadlines for other assignments.

To help students develop questions based on the theme(s) that are of interest to them, offer some examples. We've included Figure 3.13 to spark some ideas for you as you consider how to model writing interview questions. Encourage students to come up with questions that are connected to their interviewee's experiences, keeping in mind that they can pull inspiration from the different texts.

Figure 3.13 Interview Questions Informed by Mentor Texts

	What Did We Learn from Our Mentor Texts?	What Can We Ask When We Interview Our Family and Friends?
Reading Yuyi Morales' *Soñadores* **and/or** *Dreamers*	• **On immigration:** Sometimes (im)migration journeys are taken by families together to unknown places. • **On immigration:** (Im)migration journeys to the United States sometimes are frightening because of the unknown. • **On being new to a place:** It can be confusing when you don't understand a language and you're in a new place. • **On libraries:** Libraries can be a place of refuge. • **On books:** Books can help people learn and find their voice.	1. Where were you born? 2. If you were born somewhere outside of the (mainland) United States, what did you leave behind? Tell me about the time you moved from ___ to ____. 3. What places are special to you? Why? 4. Have you ever found learning a language challenging? Tell me about that experience. 5. In the book *Soñadores* or *Dreamers*, we read about Yuyi Morales and how she and her son learned from books in the library. Are there any books that are special to you? Can you pick one and tell me why that book is special to you?
Reading Juana Martinez-Neal's *Alma y cómo obtuvo su nombre* **and/or** *Alma and How She Got Her Name*	• **On names:** Our names reveal what matters to our families. • **On family history:** Learning the history of our names helps us get to know the history of our family. • **On change and growth:** Sometimes we need help understanding things that are unknown to us.	1. What is your full name? 2. Can you share with me the story of your name? Where does your name come from? What does it mean? 3. Does your name remind you of anyone in your family? Tell me about a moment with someone in your family that is special to you (a gathering, birthday, trip, holiday, family moment). 4. In the book *Alma y cómo obtuvo su nombre* or *Alma and How She Got Her Name*, we learned that Alma didn't like her name because it was too long but her father taught her about the meaning behind her name and she loved it! Did you ever change your mind about something thanks to a family member or a friend who helped you think differently? Tell me about that lesson learned.

Reading Meg Medina's *Mango, abuela y yo* **and/ or** *Mango, Abuela, and Me*

- **On language practices:** Learning another language can bring people together.
- **On family and language practices:** It is tough when you can't communicate with family.
- **On developing language practices:** It helps to be creative and kind when teaching and learning another language.
- **On family:** Families help us through tough times.

1. Have you ever had challenges when communicating with family? Tell me about that time.

2. How have you or someone in the family learned another language? What worked? What didn't work? What advice do you have for us kids learning Spanish and English?

3. Was there ever a time when a family member visited from another place? How did you help them with the change? Tell me about that time.

4. In the book *Mango, abuela y yo* or *Mango, Abuela, and Me* by Meg Medina, we read about an abuela and her granddaughter who help each other with their Spanish and English. They use sticky notes to write words and even their parrot helps them with words! What helps you the most when you have to learn something new?

Step 4: Practicing the Interviewing Process

If this is the first time students are conducting interviews, consider dedicating some class time to helping students prepare for the interviewing process.

Try a role-play! Have students partner up with each other and try out some sample questions from Figure 3.13 or other questions that you develop as a class.

1. Partner A will write down two or three questions to try out in their note-book, leaving space between each to jot down the response.

2. Encourage students to be active listeners by acknowledging responses and being ready with a pen or pencil to write down answers. Of course, remind them to thank their interviewees for sharing a bit of their story.

3. Switch! Make sure everyone has a chance to play the role of Partner A.

4. Share out! Once everyone has had a chance to play the role of the inter-viewer, ask them to take a few moments to think about what they learned from their interviewees.

5. Then have them share their reflections in their groups, and perhaps a few of them can share with the entire class.

Your aim is to make sure that students understand that they should plan their questions before the interview, be active listeners and take notes during the interview, and thank their interviewees after the interview. They also may need to be reminded to take a few moments right after the interview to write in their journals some of their reflections, thoughts, or things that they learned from the interview while it's still fresh in their minds. They can use these notes as they share in class some of the stories learned and other important takeaways from interviewing their loved ones.

Once students have conducted their own interviews with their family members, ask them to bring their notes to class. Create space for students to share responses from their family interviews. This is a transformative way of validating students' and their families' lives, experiences, and journeys: the voices students have collected now become a part of the curriculum. Students become colleagues with their teachers as they bring to the "curriculum" table what is often missing: their voices, language practices, and stories. This means dedicating at least another three sessions where students can share their interview responses in peer conversations (partner or small groups) and create a representation of these responses (perhaps a "published" piece of writing with images, a song, artwork, etc.). This documented piece then can form part of the classroom and/or school library. Some teachers have created anthologies of these stories or displayed individual student pieces in gathering spaces so school staff, families, and other students across the school building can read and enjoy.

Reflecting on the Lessons: Topic, Texts, Translanguaging

In this sequence of lessons, we center the varied experiences and language practices of bilingual Latinx children and their communities, being intentional in disrupting the perpetuation of dominant language ideologies and the use of texts that do not reflect our students' stories. Of course, the fullness of Latinx identities or Latinidad cannot be expressed in three lessons or in these three texts. We encourage you to delve into children's literature and students' lives to find the complexity in experiences. Our mentor authors—Mexican, Peruvian American, and Cuban American—wrote stories that help us highlight important themes around journeys, names, family, and language practices, yet we want to caution that there is so much more to Latinx identities. We hope you will read the texts and your examples with an intersectional lens, noticing how your own students' multifaceted lives are experienced at the intersection of race, ethnicity, gender, language, documented status, ability, sexuality, religion, and other ways of identifying. Then, look to see how your text selection for read-alouds reflects these and broadens your students' understandings. Middle-grade teacher in Harlem, New York City, Jacqueline Perez does this work with her students (see Figure 3.14). We hope to do the same across several of our lesson sequences in this book! As teacher-educators, we revisit this process each semester as we prepare to teach our preservice teachers. We choose to really see our bilingual students' realities; and by truly highlighting these stories, we are creating a powerful counter-narrative, normalizing our students' varied experiences, and decentering whiteness. This is tough work. This is life work.

These lessons culminate by giving students opportunities to use their multiple literacies as they plan to listen to stories told by friends and family. We believe in the strength, wisdom, and healing across community knowledge, abuelita knowledge, and other funds of knowledge that are often dismissed in schools. Acknowledging these ways of knowing and bringing them into our curriculum validates what students have learned from their families and creates spaces for students' bilingualism and their Latinx identities.

May these lessons show students that we *do* love them, we *do* see their full humanity, and we *will* continue creating alternative learning opportunities to counter dominant oppressive practices that have excluded and minimized so many bilingual Latinx students.

Figure 3.14 Jacqueline Perez discusses *Merci Suárez Changes Gears* by Meg Medina with her Bilingual Dual Language sixth-grade students in a small group.

Knowing Our Histories to Understand the Present Moment

◇◇◇◇◇

Momento de aprendizaje

Years before ancestry kits were a trend and people began to claim Indigenous ancestry without tribal membership, Carla's sixth graders engaged in a partnership with the National Geographic Genographic Project, artist and humanitarian Yo-Yo Ma, and the Silk Road Ensemble. Thanks to funding from the Silk Road Connect Project, sixth graders (with permission from their family/caregivers) and their teachers received results from their kits that included information on their ancestors' patterns of migration along a world map. When Carla explained the information, showing her own results, a student we'll call Marcos enthusiastically got up from his seat yelling, "Profe, we're the same!" Students looked at him, then at Carla, then back at him, skeptical that they were in any way the "same" as Marcos described. Carla, a light-skinned Latina from Chile. Marcos, an Afro-Latinx from the Dominican Republic. You could hear several saying, "What do you mean? You make no sense!" Marcos described how his ancestors' patterns of migration and genetic group were the same as Carla's results. Marcos asked if the class could see the world map from his results. The class saw his ancestors' patterns of migrations and, sure enough, Marcos and Carla had the same starting point in an area on the continent of Africa with the end point at different places: for Carla, on the continent of South America, and for Marcos, in the Dominican Republic. Another student said she wanted to compare these with her results. When she saw the patterns of her ancestors' migrations projected on the screen, she said, "Miss, that's wrong. I ain't from Africa." The class erupted in chaos. "¡Tú no sabe tu historia!" "That's racist!" "You don't know the history of the Dominican Republic?"

Reflecting on That Moment

Why might some Latinx students reject connections to Africa? Why might some Latinx students respond to those rejections by calling that racism and questioning their peers' understanding of history? There is a long history of anti-Blackness, lack of understanding of the impact of colonization, and pervasiveness of internalized racism. This reality is as much present within schools as it is outside of schools. Most importantly, we must question how institutions, such as schools, are a part of perpetuating dehumanizing notions of self, of community, of history, and of our roles in the present moment. For example, how often have our students been a part of history lessons where marginalized experiences are centered? How often do the stories of marginalized people get taught? How often do these same stories get more than a paragraph in a history textbook? What about in our own schooling?

For Carla, studying the impact of colonization, resistance movements, and the complexity of Latinidad didn't come into play until graduate school. Thankfully, mentors, resources from Rethinking Schools and Teaching Tolerance, and courses like Multicultural Education helped Carla craft a yearlong, community-based response to the comments in her sixth-grade classroom. This included conversations with students on the documentary series *Black in Latin America*, specifically the episode "Haiti and the Dominican Republic: An Island Divided," which they watched with their families (Gates 2011), and research on concepts of beauty, especially considering how those concepts relate to whiteness and what is considered the "norm." What started with reading *Hairs/Pelitos* (1994) by Sandra Cisneros developed when looking at advertisements in magazines and in the community. These were tough conversations, but they were necessary to have when the beautiful Black and Brown children who made up the classroom community often felt like they were not beautiful or accepted.

For Luz, these understandings similarly developed later on during college, primarily through Chicanx and Latin American Studies courses. Often these types of experiences have been nonexistent in K–12 schooling, and it is little wonder that many students of color often choose to double or triple major in ethnic studies. Perhaps the most important revelation for Luz was learning about globalization, a continuation of colonization, and the way it deeply impacted Latin America (and continues to do so) and created predictable migration patterns, including that of her own family into the United States.

We shouldn't have to wait until undergraduate or graduate studies to learn about our histories and present movements and to build solidarity across groups. Unfortunately, this is the reality when whiteness is centered in institutional settings like schools. We see this through curriculum that dismisses the experiences of people of color, Indigenous people, and LGBTQIA+ individuals, among other minoritized groups. Sometimes these experiences are relegated to holidays or monthly celebrations (Black History Month, Hispanic Heritage Month, Asian American and Pacific Islander Heritage Month) and yet even those kinds of discussions are superficial because it's impossible to cover the diversity and complexity of these groups in a one-month or a one-day celebration. Latinx children should see their humanity throughout their schooling across the school year, just as white children see theirs, since it is presented as the norm in curriculum and texts.

Introducing the Sequence of Lessons

Figure 4.1 Sequence of Lessons

The lessons in this chapter highlight ways that teachers can create spaces for conversations, helping Latinx students learn more about their histories to have a better understanding of themselves and the present moment. There are histories that often go untold. Of course, it is impossible for one chapter to cover lessons that address the complexity of colonization and Latinx identities and the histories that need to be uncovered. Our selection of topics is intentional: it considers the populations of teachers and students we continue to grow with, and contemporary Latinx literature. The sequence of lessons follows an order that helps create an overview, keeping in mind that Chapter 5 will go more deeply into one of the topics from this chapter (see Figure 4.1).

We begin with a lesson on the importance of learning about ancient histories, specifically mythologies and folklore from different communities that have existed in the United States (in this example, a territory that was formerly Mexico) or brought to the mainland United States through (im)migration. In the first lesson, we focus on the ancient myths and ask, "How does learning about our past impact how we see ourselves and others?" In the second lesson, we focus on the importance of naming, looking at the terminology for injustice and resistance. In the third lesson, we raise students' awareness of present social movements that center those silenced and marginalized histories. The fourth and final lesson in the chapter launches students on creating and sharing their own counter-narratives.

Although the lessons are modeled here using specific texts for grades 6–8, the lessons can also be used in earlier grades.

Supporting Translanguaging in the Sequence of Lessons

- Teach the lesson in English, in Spanish, or using features of both.
- Have translation tools available, such as bilingual glossaries, dictionaries, or digital tools to support students as they engage with the texts in English.
- Engage in a study of the ways authors use translanguaging in their texts.
- Encourage students to use their entire linguistic repertoire to:
  - *Discuss the texts (small groups and whole class).*
  - *Take notes on the texts.*
  - *Plan their presentations.*
- Accept and celebrate students' discussions and writing that include features of English, Spanish, and other languages.

Exploring History to Better Understand Ourselves and Our Community

In this lesson, students will get to know a poem that addresses an aspect of Latinx history or culture through shared readings, choose a topic related to the poems to research, share their findings, and reflect on their new understandings.

To begin, decide on a pair of short texts to launch the class's work. Figure 4.2 includes a few of our favorite sources.

Figure 4.2 Paired Texts

Alternate Texts for Lesson 1 on Ancient Histories and Folklore from Latin America for Grades 3–5 and Grades 6–8		
	Grades 3–5	**Grades 6–8**
Chile	1. *Rayengey ti dungun: Pichikeche ñi Mapuche kumwirin/La palabra es la flor: Poesía mapuche para niños* (2011) by Jaime Luís Huenún Villa (bilingual edition Mapuzugun–Español) 2. *El soñador* (2010) or *The Dreamer* (2010) by Pam Muñoz Ryan, illustrated by Peter Sis	1. *Mapuche nütram: Historias y voces de educadores tradicionales* (2018) edited by Margarita Calderón, Diego Fuenzalida, and Elizabeth Simonsen (an online guide with profiles of Mapuche educators with poems and videos is available on the Universidad de Chile website [Universidad de Chile n.d.])

	Grades 3–5	Grades 6–8
Cuba	1. *Drum Dream Girl: How One Girl's Courage Changed Music* (2015) by Margarita Engle 2. *La selva* (2019) or *Forest World* (2017) by Margarita Engle 3. *Isla de leones: El guerrero cubano de las palabras* (2019) or *Lion Island: Cuba's Warrior of Words* (2016) by Margarita Engle 4. *Marti's Song for Freedom/Martí y sus versos por la libertad* (2017) by Emma Otheguy	
Dominican Republic and Haiti	1. *Las huellas secretas* (2002) or *The Secret Footprints* (2000) by Julia Alvarez 2. *Mama's Nightingale: A Story of Immigration and Separation* (2015) by Edwidge Danticat, illustrated by Leslie Shaun 3. *El color de mis palabras* (2004) or *The Color of My Words* (2001) by Lynn Joseph	1. *A Cafecito Story/El cuento del cafecito* (2001) by Julia Alvarez and Bill Eichner, illustrated by Belkis Ramirez, and translated by Daisy Cocco de Filippis 2. *Hurricane Child* (2018) by Kheryn Callender
El Salvador	1. *Talking with Mother Earth/Hablando con Madre Tierra* (2006) by Jorge Argueta, illustrated by Lucia Angela Perez 2. *A Movie in My Pillow/Una película en mi almohada* (2001) by Jorge Argueta, illustrated by Elizabeth Gomez 3. *Somos como las nubes/We Are Like the Clouds* (2016) by Jorge Argueta, illustrated by Alfonso Ruano	
Guatemala	1. *El tapiz de abuela* (1994) or *Abuela's Weave* (1993) by Omar S. Castañeda, illustrated by Enrique O. Sanchez, and translated by Aida E. Marcuse 2. *The Honey Jar* (2006) by Rigoberta Menchú with Dante Liano, illustrated by Domi	1. *The Only Road* (2016) by Alexandra Diaz

continues

	Grades 3–5	Grades 6–8
Mexico	1. *La Llorona/The Crying Woman* by Rudolfo Anaya, illustrated by Amy Córdova (2011) 2. *Prietita and the Ghost Woman/Prietita y La Llorona* (1997) by Gloria Anzaldúa, illustrated by Maya Christina Gonzalez	1. *Feathered Serpent, Dark Heart of Sky: Myths of Mexico* (2018) by David Bowles 2. *Flower, Song, Dance: Aztec and Mayan Poetry* (2013) by David Bowles 3. *The Storm Runner* (2018) and *The Fire Keeper* (2019) by J. C. Cervantes 4. *The Moon Within* (2019) by Aida Salazar

Collections of Folktales

1. *Tales Our Abuelitas Told: A Hispanic Folktale Collection* (2006) by F. Isabel Campoy and Alma Flor Ada, illustrated by Felipe Dávalos, Viví Escrivá, Susan Guevara, and Leyla Torres

2. *La matadragones: Cuentos de Latinoamérica* (2018) or *The Dragon Slayer: Folktales from Latin American* (2018) by Jaime Hernandez, illustrated by F. Isabel Campoy

3. *Once Upon a Time: Traditional Latin American Tales/Había una vez: Cuentos tradicionales latinoamericanos* (2010) by Rueben Martinez, illustrated by Raul Colón

4. *Tres Cuentos* bilingual podcast: www.trescuentos.com

As you make your decision on the texts and excerpts, we implore you not to reject texts that have topics that may make you feel uncomfortable. For example, some may have reservations about using *The Moon Within* because menstruation and/or gender fluid identity are topics that they have not previously discussed with their students. They may also not be familiar with how to discuss these topics with middle-grade children. However, these aspects of life are part of the lived experiences of many children and a part of humanity that cannot be ignored. We do great damage when only certain stories and experiences are highlighted while others are ignored as if they do not exist.

Whether you are an elementary teacher wondering whether you should use a Jorge Argueta poem (from *Somos como las nubes/We Are Like the Clouds*) that talks about the journeys of Central American minors or a middle-grade teacher wondering if you should select poems from *The Moon Within*, remember that we all have a responsibility to amplify the voices that have been silenced, marginalized, or relegated to spaces outside of our schools.

To model this lesson, we use the following texts:

- *Feathered Serpent, Dark Heart of Sky: Myths of Mexico* (2018) by David Bowles

- *The Moon Within* (2019) by Aida Salazar

David Bowles' *Feathered Serpent, Dark Heart of Sky: Myths of Mexico* is a rich text for middle-grade students on myths from Mexico. Besides the myths, the text includes a guide to pronunciation, acknowledging Indigenous Mexican languages like Nahuatl and Mayan, and a glossary. In this lesson, pairing *Feathered Serpent, Dark Heart of Sky: Myths of Mexico* with *The Moon Within* allows us to address the connections between traditions and what has been lost or unknown. In the coming-of-age novel *The Moon Within*, Aida Salazar weaves Indigenous Mexican mythologies and beliefs about moon ceremonies and gender expansiveness to detail a young girl's reactions to her changing body and her best friend's gender fluidity.

Although the texts that we are using as models in this chapter's lessons are for middle grades, the following approaches to these conversations—all of which focus on topic, texts, and translanguaging—can be adapted for younger children using a different text pairing from the list in Figure 4.2. After reading the paired texts in preparation for your teaching, you can return to the texts, noticing the themes that reflect connections with one's past, connections with the earth, and connections with one another.

Begin with Shared Reading: Poetry Bringing Us Together

In Figure 4.3 you will find a guide for beginning the shared reading work across the week to help you with a replicable structure. Shared reading, often used in K–2, supports students with fluency and meaning-making work, addressing high-frequency words and vocabulary and helping them with letter-sound correspondence. We find shared reading just as beneficial to students through grade 8 because of the community it builds, the questions that can arise when delving into a text across time, and the support it provides bilingual and multilingual students in using their linguistic resources as they grow their language practices.

> "But it wasn't until I took a world literature class in college that I read a single Aztec or Maya myth. Amazing. I had attended schools just miles from the Mexican border, but not one of my teachers had spoken of Quetzalcoatl or Itzamna, of Cihuacoatl or Ixchel. My family also knew nothing of these Mesoamerican gods."
>
> —David Bowles
> in *Feathered Serpent, Dark Heart of Sky: Myths of Mexico* (2018, 10)

Figure 4.3 Shared Reading Across the Week

	Shared Reading Session 1	**Shared Reading Session 2**	**Shared Reading Session 3**
Setting the stage/ regrouping (5 minutes)	Introduce the text and context. • Poem and poet • Scene from a picture book or novel and author • Song and artist	Partnerships discuss the text and content. They revisit their ideas about the meaning of the text to create questions (on words, overall meaning, life application) about the text. Listen in on one or two partnership conversations and document observations.	Ask a small group to share (after checking in with them at the end of their conversation during the previous session) what they learned or practiced together. Possibilities include the following: • New understandings of meanings of the text • Vocabulary or new understandings of words • Questions • Translations
	Read the text while students follow with a copy of their own or enlarged copy (chart paper, projected on screen).	Everyone reads the text out loud with students participating in the reading with the part they selected during a previous reading.	
Partnerships (4 minutes)	Students select a part of the text they'd like to read out loud. They practice this in partnerships. Listen in on one or two partnership conversations and document observations.	Students select an additional part of the text they'd like to read out loud. They practice this in partnerships or small groups. Listen in to one or two partnership conversations and document observations.	Partnerships or small groups reverse roles and read something that someone else has chosen to read in previous sessions. Maybe change characters (if dialogue or perspectives differ in text) or roles.
Reading in community (1 minute)	Everyone reads the text out loud with students participating in the reading with the part they selected.	Everyone reads the text out loud with students participating in the reading with the part they selected.	Everyone reads the entire text together.

	Partnership discussion on the meaning of their selection and reasoning behind selecting that part to read out loud. Listen in to one or two partnership conversations and document observations.	Small-group discussion (two partnerships together) where students share their questions. Listen in on one or two discussions and document observations.	Whole-class conversation on meaning, new understandings, questions that remain, vocabulary practiced.
Discussion (5 minutes)			

Use short texts for shared reading at the start of the lesson to set the context for the work. Students may have already read the text in book clubs or as a whole-class read-aloud, but even if students are not familiar with the text as a whole, excerpts connected to the journeys of two characters are accessible with your brief introduction on the text (reading from the book jacket, the author's website, or a teacher guide). This helps bilingual students not only engage with this very powerful text and topic but also to engage in translanguaging and expanding their language practices.

> Our ancient ancestors honored
> our flowering in this way.
> It is a ritual taken away from us
> during so many conquests.
>
> —"Moon Ceremony" poem in
> *The Moon Within* (Salazar 2019, 10)
>
>
> In our ancestral Mexica tradition, Ometeotl
> is our Creator spirit that is neither
> female nor male but both—divine duality.
> Marco has Ometeotl energy
> a person who inhabits two beings
> the female and the male at once.
>
> —"Not Magda" poem in
> *The Moon Within* (Salazar 2019, 126)

Let the texts and experiences speak for themselves, and give students that platform to launch discussions in your classroom. For example, when Carla has used "Moon Ceremony," which is at the beginning of Salazar's book, or "Not Magda," which is toward the second half of the book, she begins by reminding students of what they may already know about Aida Salazar's text (from previous lessons in this book) and how "Moon Ceremony" sets the scene for readers to learn about the different perspectives that the main character, Celi, and her Mima have on Celi getting her period. For Mima, Celi's "moon will soon come," but for Celi, it's "a period." If you begin this work with the poem "Not Magda," then you might introduce it with a reminder of discussions on gender-expansiveness or conversations you've already had about identity. You can recall work from the previous lessons that address identity with a focus on race/ethnicity, language, or documented status, and explain that you are growing that understanding to address how people identify with their gender.

Carla began the conversation with her students on these topics by discussing her own experiences of how she associated shame with her body (getting her period when she had to sing at church, staining her outfit, singing in jeans while the rest of the group was in their uniform). "Students were familiar with this moment because Carla had mentioned it in her writer's notebook during a personal narrative writing unit. Carla also shared how a family member who identifies as gender nonbinary shared how they were uncomfortable shopping with their mom for clothes when clothes were labeled for "women" and "men" in clothing stores. After this experience, Carla searched for several texts to learn more about gender expansiveness and gender diverse cultures and how gendered expectations are entrenched in society, including school culture.

Partner and Group Research

For this next part of each day's session, you can choose to group students based on the questions you heard during the shared reading time or based on topics they select (such as moon ceremonies, traditions that have changed over time, mythologies, gender diverse cultures, etc.). Make sure that there are resources for students to engage in this research. This might mean bins of books, devices with internet access to websites that you have preselected, or copies of the texts you have been studying as a class. If you are using *The Moon Within* (2019), you may want to refer to the teacher's guide (2019) that Carla created for the book—it's available on Aida Salazar's website. As you visit different partnerships, note the kinds of observations and questions that come up, coaching students to consider key questions on how this knowledge helps them with an understanding of themselves and their communities and ways that they can share this information with others. See Figure 4.4 for support with your feedback for research groups.

Figure 4.4 Feedback for Research Groups

If the students ask . . .	You can have them consider . . .
• What does _____ mean? • How is _____ viewed by different people? • What are the traditions around _____? • How does colonization/imperialism impact traditions? • What are examples of how people resist colonization with their traditions?	• Looking at books, articles, and videos you have curated on this topic • Asking family members for context or about their own related experiences • Connecting examples of colonization from history with present-day examples

The suggestions you make and the resources you choose will depend on the text you are studying with students. For example, if you are using *The Moon Within* as your anchor text, you might consider sharing resources on the menstrual cycle—the Oscar-winning documentary "Period. End of Sentence" (Zehtabchi 2019) is a wonderful resource—or asking students to connect examples of colonization from history with present-day examples, just as Salazar connects contemporary discomfort with discussing menstruation to a history of colonization. If you are using *Feathered Serpent* as your anchor text, you may ask students to track the changes within belief systems/traditions with a timeline of key events to create comparison charts with different deities and creation myths, to research other cultures or traditions that have nonbinary deities, or to view the film *A Place in the Middle* (Hamer and Wilson 2014), which explores the Hawaiian concept of mahu, comparing it with other gender diverse cultures. You can also access a discussion guide on the film *A Place in the Middle*, available on the film's website (Rogow, Hamer, and Chang n.d.).

Sharing Our Notes: Gallery Walk

Invite students to post their notes/findings from their research so that others can walk from one poster/page to another during a gallery walk session. Set up students with sticky notes to use to respond to others' work with comments and questions. You can guide students to leave comments that make connections or provide recommended readings. You can also guide students to ask questions, recalling the work that they have probably already done in social studies and science classes, asking the questions that historians ask or scientists ask when studying a topic. These notes from their peers will help students prepare their presentations in lesson 4. This work also helps the transition to the next lesson, where you and the students will learn about histories and perspectives on histories that are often overlooked in school settings, focusing on the stories of marginalized populations, particularly those that reflect the experiences and cultures of bilingual and multilingual Latinx students.

Personal Reflections

To close the lesson, give students a brief moment to write down their personal reactions to the activity and readings. They can respond to any of the following questions or you can leave the writing open-ended:

- *How did reading these texts make you feel? Why?*

- *What new information did you learn?*

- *Has anything that you've learned changed a perspective you held previously? If so, what has changed?*

- *What connections did you make across your research?*

- *What more do you want to learn?*

- *What new questions do you have?*

Tracing Colonization in Texts, Terminology, and Our Own Lives

In this lesson, we use text excerpts and vocabulary charts to share new terminology with students, knowing that although students may have experienced these realities in their lives, they may need to process the different ways that we name injustice and resistance.

Preparing to Teach

Before the lesson, preview the key terms you'll be discussing with students: *dominant narrative, counter-narrative, colonize, colonization, imperialism, expansion, hierarchy, missions,* and *resistance*. Figure 4.5 features some important terms for this sequence of lessons with a brief explanation. We encourage you to expand and give specific examples whenever possible based on your focus of study.

Figure 4.5 Colonization Terms Everyone Should Know

Dominant narrative	An account, story, or history that is widely accepted as being factual. It often centers the experiences of the dominant society and gives an account from the perspective of those in power.
Counter-narrative	A story, account, or history from the perspective of those who have been negatively impacted by the actions of the dominant society.
Colonization/ colonized	The cultural/political/social imposition often by force for the purposes of exploiting a group of people and/or land.
Imperialism	A practice in which larger and/or stronger countries (militarily) gain political and economic control/power over smaller and/or less militarized nations.
Expansion	Refers to the growing of power by controlling a larger space or territory for political and economic gain, often through war or policies to forcefully remove people already living and having a claim to a land.

continues

Slave trade	Forced movement of enslaved people for profit across geographic and political boundaries, but also within nation-states.
Hierarchy	A societal order of power and privilege often established by those in power to sustain their privileged position.
Missions	Religious establishments by a variety of Christian denominations with the intent to forcefully convert people (often Indigenous or African) to Christianity.
Resistance	A movement or organization of people who come together to stand in opposition to a policy, a government, or an injustice.
Thanksgiving	A national holiday in the United States celebrating what has been described as a gathering between the Wampanoag and the Pilgrims at Plymouth, Massachusetts. Some have resisted this celebration, noting that this was a part of a genocidal project.
Columbus Day	A national holiday in October that celebrates the arrival of Christopher Columbus in the Americas. Some states like Florida and some major cities such as Los Angeles have banned Columbus Day and instead celebrate Indigenous Peoples' Day to honor Indigenous people and culture.

Recalling What We Already Know

For a quick check-in with students to listen to or read what they already know about colonization, you can begin this lesson by asking students to discuss or write down what they have learned about a few of the following events:

1. Latin American colonization

2. European imperialism

3. Thanksgiving

4. Columbus Day

5. Slave trade

As you listen in or read students' responses, consider: What do they already know about colonization in history? Which of the terms related to colonization are they already using? Which terms or concepts may need to be taught?

Bilingual/Multilingual Vocabulary Charts

Based on what you see in the students' thinking, identify a term from the list in Figure 4.5 to introduce. Create a chart with your class using the four elements in the Bilingual/Multilingual Concept Guide in Figure 4.6 to introduce one of the terms to students.

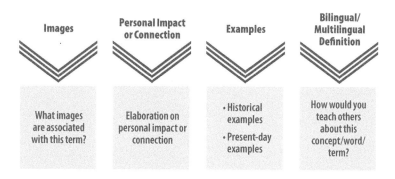

Figure 4.6 Template for Bilingual/Multilingual Concept Guide

Think aloud as you provide images, connections, examples, and a definition, explaining to students how you are identifying each. If you need to rely on other resources—perhaps to find an image or a helpful definition—let them see you do that.

After your demonstration, support students as they work in groups to create their own bilingual/multilingual vocabulary chart for another term from the list. This allows students to share their own understandings of the terms with images, definitions, and examples. Be sure that students have access to the same resources you had access to (perhaps the internet and the definition of the word, provided in Figure 4.5) when you created your model chart.

Challenge students to identify numerous examples and personal impacts for each term. Ask them to consider: *Where do I see this in my life/my world/in my current reality?* When each group has completed its work, give students the opportunity to teach their classmates about the term they have researched.

You can find several examples of multilingual vocabulary charts with images, definitions, and examples in Part 3, "Language Development," of *Translanguaging: A CUNY–NYSIEB Guide for Educators* (Celic and Seltzer 2013), available on the CUNY–NYSIEB website.

Dominant Narrative vs. Counter-Narrative: Historical and Present-Day Examples

Now, return to one of the events students had a lot to say about earlier in the lesson (a holiday or specific event related to U.S. or Latin American history) to introduce the concept of dominant narratives (what is traditionally taught about this event from the perspective of those in power) and counter-narratives (perspectives on the same event from those in marginalized groups), as well as present-day ways that people share this counter-narrative. See Figures 4.7 and 4.8 for examples of what the completed charts might look like.

Figure 4.7 Dominant Narrative vs. Counter-Narrative Chart Sample #1

Event: Fourth of July		
Dominant Narrative of the Event	**Counter-Narratives of the Event from History**	**Counter-Narratives of the Event Shared Present Day**
Pictures that glorify symbols related to the Fourth of July, such as: • U.S. flag • Fireworks • Family celebrating • Statue of Liberty • U.S. government building • Parades Historical documents shared: • Thomas Jefferson's words in the Declaration of Independence "Life, Liberty, and the Pursuit of Happiness"	Excerpts from "What to the Slave Is the Fourth of July?" speech on July 5, 1852, by Frederick Douglass Congressional Resolution on "Juneteenth Independence Day" (2018)	Meme with a scene from the film *Avengers: Infinity War* (Russo 2018) with the character Black Panther (played by Chadwick Boseman) shaking his head and waving no. Above the picture it reads: "4th of July." Below the picture it reads: "We don't do that here." Picture books depicting Juneteenth celebrations: • *Juneteenth for Mazie* (2015) by Floyd Cooper • *Juneteenth Jamboree* (1995) by Carole Boston Weatherford

Figure 4.8 Dominant Narrative vs. Counter-Narrative Chart Sample #2

Event in History	Dominant Narrative	Counter-Narratives
1492—Christopher Columbus arrives in Bahamian islands and Hispaniola (present-day Haiti and Dominican Republic)	Examples: • Christopher Columbus as hero • Christopher Columbus as "discovering" America or the New World • Examples of the dominant narrative of Columbus: *A Picture Book of Christopher Columbus* (1991) by David Adler and *Christopher Columbus* (1991) by Stephen Krensky • Welcomed by Native peoples, no resistance to arrival/conquest	Examples: • Columbus was responsible for the death of millions of Taínos on the island of Hispaniola, as explored in "The People vs. Columbus, et al." teaching activity by Bill Bigelow, available in *Rethinking Columbus: The Next 500 Years* (Bigelow and Peterson 2003) and on the Zinn Education Project (n.d.) website. • Indigenous resistance and impact on populations existing on land when Columbus arrived and with later conquest on lands can be seen in *El pueblo seguirá* (2017) and *The People Shall Continue* (2017) by Simon J. Ortiz. • *A Coyote Columbus Story* by Thomas King, illustrated by William Kent Monkman (1992), tells of the intentions Columbus had and the way Native Americans were treated through a trickster tale format. • Correcting the myth "Columbus discovered America" or "Columbus discovered the New World" because for something to be discovered, it needs to be something new with no ownership. See Debbie Reese's critical literacy lesson to search for the "discovered" narratives in picture books in her blog post " My Response to 'Can You Recommend a Book About Columbus?'" (Reese 2018).

Once you've demonstrated how to complete a chart of this kind, students can remain in their previous groups to work on their own chart, following either example, for any event or holiday, listing three elements: (1) dominant narrative example; (2) counter-narrative from history; and (3) counter-narrative from the present day. Encourage students to try using the new terms they have learned in their charts.

Reflections: Returning to Our Lives

At the end of the lesson, have groups pause their work to discuss how they see colonization working in their lives. For example, how do children celebrate or reflect upon the events surrounding the Fourth of July, Thanksgiving, or Columbus Day? What new perspectives did they learn? What are the counter-narratives that they found and that made them feel a certain way? For example, for those studying Columbus Day and creating their own dominant narrative and counter-narrative chart in their groups, what did they find out about Indigenous Peoples' Day celebrations as counter-narratives? Student reflections are helpful not only for them to process their feelings surrounding these events, but also for you to get a sense of students' discussions and the charts they created because these reveal their understandings of the concepts.

Identifying Dominant Narratives and Counter-Narratives

Students investigate the narratives that marginalize as well as those that center the experiences of a variety of Latinx populations. In this lesson, we use timelines to engage students in conversations and develop their own understandings of their story. Students might refer to the following sources in this work:

- *Latino USA: A Cartoon History (2000) by Ilan Stavans, illustrated by Lalo Alcaraz*

- *PBS "Latino Americans: Timeline of Important Dates" (2013)*

Note-Taking with a Purpose

Tell students that for this lesson, they will be presented with a selective timeline of events having to do with colonialism, imperialism, immigration, and political developments across the United States and Latin America and that they will be given the option to decide what focus they would like to take when they look at the timeline. They can focus on a topic such as land ownership, or they can track events connected to a specific place such as Mexico or Puerto Rico. (See more options in Figure 4.9.) This helps students "zoom in" on patterns, create questions, and add to the understandings that they have been developing in the previous lessons.

Why set up students this way? First, providing student choice is crucial in increasing engagement. Second, seeing the names of these countries and territories as options to *focus* on is really pushing the boundaries of what has been the norm in learning history. By highlighting these places and their connections to land, religion, language, and issues of immigration, it means that we are validating and centering the experiences of those on the margins. We are questioning the dominant narratives and amplifying the voices of the counter-narratives.

Figure 4.9 Note-Taking Options/Lens

Tracking Observations Across a Timeline by Following One Focus	Tracking Events Between Specific Countries and Territories and Mainland United States
1. **Land ownership**, "expansion," and conquest—from the point of view of conquerors and impact on Indigenous peoples and their resistance, past and present (example: Puerto Rico)	1. **Mexico**
	2. **Caribbean** (Cuba, Haiti, Dominican Republic, and other islands)
2. **Role of religion**—from the point of view of religious leaders from Europe and point of view of Indigenous peoples who had other spiritual practices	3. **Central America** (Costa Rica, El Salvador, Guatemala, Honduras, Nicaragua, Panama)
	4. **South America** (Argentina, Bolivia, Brazil, Chile, Colombia, Ecuador, *French Guiana, Guyana, Paraguay, Peru, Suriname, Uruguay, Venezuela)
3. **Language**—laws, bilingual education	5. **Puerto Rico**
4. **Immigration**—laws from the perspective of the U.S. government and experiences of those leaving their countries for the United States	* French Guiana is an overseas territory (department) of France.
5. **Resistance**—examples of resistance from marginalized groups against the dominant group in power	

Interactive History Journey

Have you ever been captivated by a biopic, a biographical movie, so much so that you are left searching for your breath and wondering how this film came together? Carla will never forget the first time she showed scenes from Spike Lee's *Malcolm X* (1992) film to her students during a unit on civil rights and social change. Students were captivated by the imagery, the storyline, and examples of resistance to injustice. There is so much to unlearn and relearn about history, and in teaching Latinx bilingual students—really *all* students—it is imperative that we provide a space to unpack historical narratives.

Figure 4.10 offers a timeline of selected events in the history of Latinx people in the United States. Begin by providing students with the timeline and asking them to share in groups which terms, people, and places they are familiar with compared with those that are new to them. Students can color-code the boxes with a different highlighter that notes their familiarity with the events. Share with students that you'll be facilitating an interactive history journey focusing on three to five events from the timeline. Research the events in preparation to teach students about them. In addition to discussing the dominant narrative of the event, also be prepared to explain the counter-narrative to provide context that the dominant narrative lacks and to share images and/or video relating to the event. Resources provided by Stanford University Education Group's *Reading Like a Historian*, the History Channel, PBS, Rethinking Schools, and the Zinn Education Project are helpful resources in this work. Figure 4.11 offers additional resources that may be of help to you at this stage in the lesson or to your students later in the lesson.

Figure 4.10 Select Events of Latinx History in the United States

Before 1900	1900s	2000s
1565—Saint Augustine introduces Catholicism and Spanish language to Florida. Knights from Spain build churches in St. Augustine, Florida. First European settlement.	1917—Puerto Ricans are granted U.S. citizenship; Congress passes Immigration Act of 1917 with literacy requirement on all immigrants.	2010—Ban on Mexican American studies program takes place in Tucson, Arizona, schools.
1607—Jamestown, Virginia, colony is founded.	1921—Limits are placed on immigration to the United States for the first time in history.	2012—Deferred Action for Childhood Arrivals (DACA) is created (United States).
1680—Pueblo Indians revolt (Spanish territory at the time of the revolt; currently New Mexico).	1925—Border Patrol is created by U.S. Congress.	March 2014—National Council of La Raza president Janet Murguía calls President Obama the "deporter-in-chief."
1718—San Antonio Mission is founded.	1930s—Between 300,000 and 500,000 Mexican Americans are deported from the United States.	November 2014—President Obama uses executive action to expand DACA.
1803—Louisiana Purchase is made.	1946—*Mendez v. Westminster* trial on California School Segregation occurs.	June 16, 2015—President Trump declares candidacy and makes disparaging remarks about people coming to the U.S. from Mexico.

continues

Before 1900	1900s	2000s
1819—Florida is taken from Spain.	1947—Puerto Rico becomes a commonwealth.	2015—More than 10,500 unaccompanied minors arrive in the United States, mostly from El Salvador, Guatemala, and Honduras.
1836—Battle of the Alamo occurs.	1954–1958—Operation Wetback by U.S. government deports 3,800,000 people of Mexican descent.	2016—Proposition 58 removes the ban on bilingual education in California.
1845—Texas becomes a part of the United States. 1848—Mexican American War and the Treaty of Guadalupe Hidalgo occur.	1964—Civil Rights Act and the Bracero Program are implemented in the U.S.	September 2017—Hurricane Maria, a category 5 hurricane, hits Puerto Rico.
1859—Cubans arrive in Florida, Louisiana, and New York.	1965–1970—Delano Grape Pickers Strike by the United Farm Workers and the Agricultural Workers Organizing Committee occurs (California).	December 2017—Ban on Mexican American studies program in Tucson, Arizona, is ruled unconstitutional by U.S. federal judge A. Wallace Tashima.
1895—Jose Martí leads resistance in Cuba.	1968—East LA high school walkouts occur—about 10,000 students protest peacefully.	May 2018—U.S. Department of Health and Human Services admits to losing track of 1,500 undocumented immigrant children separated from their families and placed in homes with sponsors.
1898—United States declares war on Spain and claims Puerto Rico as its territory.		

Figure 4.11 Alternate Texts for Lesson 2 on Dominant Narratives and Counter-Narratives

Texts Based on Historical Time Periods	Informational Texts on Latinx History
1. *¡Bravo! Poemas sobre hispanos extraordinarios* (2017) and *Bravo! Poems About Amazing Hispanics* (2017) by Margarita Engle, illustrated by Rafael López (various time periods)	1. Book: *An African American and Latinx History of the United States* (2018) by Paul Ortiz
2. *Jazz Owls* (2018) by Margarita Engle, illustrated by Rudy Gutierrez (Zoot Suit Riots of 1943, Los Angeles, California)	2. Book: *Latino USA: A Cartoon History* (2000) by Ilan Stavans, illustrated by Lalo Alcaraz
3. *The Revolution of Evelyn Serrano* (2012) by Sonia Manzano (1960s, New York City)	3. Book: *Harvest of Empire: A History of Latinos in America* (2011) by Juan Gonzalez (also a documentary)
4. *Shame the Stars* (2016) by Guadalupe García McCall (1915, U.S.-Mexico borderlands)	4. Book: *Occupied America: A History of Chicanos* (2014) by Rodolfo F. Acuña
5. *All the Stars Denied* (2018) by Guadalupe García McCall (the Great Depression/1931, Texas border town)	5. Book: *Our America: A Hispanic History of the United States* (2014) by Felipe Fernandez-Armesto
6. *Echo* (2015), *Esperanza Rising* (2000) and *Esperanza renace* (2002) by Pam Muñoz Ryan (rise of Nazi Germany, the Great Depression, World War II)	6. Book: *Latino in America* (2009) by Soledad O'Brien
7. *Dactyl Hill Squad* (2018) by Daniel José Older (Civil War era, New York City)	7. Documentary series: *Latino in America* (CNN 2009)
8. *Out of Darkness* (2019) by Ashley Hope Pérez (1937, New London, Texas)	8. Documentary series: *Black in Latin America* by Henry Louis Gates, Jr. (PBS 2011)
9. *The Wind Called My Name* (2018) by Mary Louise Sanchez (1930s, Wyoming)	9. Article: "The Brutal History of Anti-Latino Discrimination in America" by Erin Blakemore (2018)
10. *My Year in the Middle* (2018) by Lila Quintero Weaver (1970s, Alabama)	10. Timeline and video clips: "Latino Americans: Timeline of Important Dates" (PBS 2013)
	11. Article: "Key Facts About Young Latinos, One of the Nation's Fastest-Growing Populations" by Mark Hugo Lopez, Jens Manuel Kronstad, and Antonio Flores (2018)
	12. Article: "Afro-Latino: A Deeply Rooted Identity Among U.S. Hispanics" by Gustavo López and Ana Gonzalez-Barrera (2016)
	13. Resources: "Latino History" (National Museum of American History n.d.)

After you discuss the first event, give students a few minutes to check their notes with others, in partnerships or groups. If they have any questions, ask them to first ask their classmates and to compare their notes. Address any questions that students cannot answer using their notes and check for any misunderstandings. Repeat this process with the remaining topics you've researched. We summarized these steps and the students' own small-group research into dominant narratives and counter-narratives in Figure 4.12.

Figure 4.12 Guide to an Interactive History Journey Focusing on Dominant Narratives and Counter-Narratives

	Teacher	Students
Part 1	Research student expertise.	Discuss what they know about a preselected list of events. Events can be focused on a time period or theme, or paired with texts being read in other courses/subject areas.
Part 2	1. Share dominant narratives and counter-narratives on event #1 (including teacher notes and observations from students). 2. Research students' understandings. 3. Transition to connections with event #2.	1. Listen. 2. Discuss questions, take notes, and process information in small groups. 3. Listen for connections with event #2.
Part 3	Repeat steps 1–3 above for event #2.	Repeat steps 1–3 above for event #2.
Part 4	Repeat steps 1–3 above for event #3.	Repeat steps 1–3 above for event #3.
Part 5	Support students in small groups by doing one or more of the following: 1. Helping students select 3–5 events based on time frame, topic, or country/territory. 2. Helping students with the research process (questions → sources → comparing dominant narrative and counter-narratives → putting their notes in their own words). 3. Showing examples of interactive historical timelines.	1. Pick a focus to return to these events and others on the preselected handout: time, topic, country/territory. 2. Research information on the events with a small group. 3. Create an interactive historical timeline for this set of events that teaches people about the dominant narratives and counter-narratives.

Students Delve into Their Own Studies of
Dominant Narratives and Counter-Narratives

Ask students to look over the table in Figure 4.10 and to determine the time frame, topic, or country/territory that they will focus on. Explain that they will be working in groups to create an interactive historical timeline with images, video clips, and dominant narratives with counter-narratives. If your class has access to a class set of devices, each student can use a device to research a specific event to find the images, context, dominant narrative, and counter-narrative. If there is limited access to devices in your classroom, students can share one device in a group or rotate the use of a classroom device as they work with other resources to gather information.

Depending on the time you have in your own curriculum pacing and planning with colleagues, you may want to extend Figure 4.10 across different sessions. This also depends on how much of this information has already been covered and processed in social studies and/or humanities courses. For some teachers, this work is more of a review. For others, this is a much-needed introduction, and therefore, more time is needed to fully understand the dominant narrative and counter-narratives across these events in history. Most importantly, students may have already been introduced to some of these events but only through the lens of the conqueror (dominant narrative). In other words, they haven't studied counter-narratives or processed what these reveal. It is critical to consider what you know about students to make sure you are intentional with the selection of dominant narratives and counter-narratives that you will cover. For instance, we were intentional about using Christopher Columbus as hero vs. Christopher Columbus as part of a genocidal project, as our example in the previous lesson, because this is a widely known example. Additionally, counter-narratives may be present in the events dominating the current news cycle or in students' own experiences—particularly those that impact the most vulnerable in society—even if the initiating event is far in the past. We encourage you to include related current events in your own sharing in this last part of the lesson.

Lesson Closure

For the final few minutes of class, encourage students to make a list of their questions, concerns, or information they'd like to share with others in a future lesson. Maybe they are thrilled with the images, context, dominant narratives, and counter-narratives that they found for an event and can't wait to share their interactive timelines with other groups! Maybe they are not ready to share. Let them know that in the next lesson, they'll look at more examples of counter-narratives and have time to create their own.

Creating Counter-Narratives That Honor Our Community

Students share their learnings by creating counter-stories and grow in solidarity with Black, Brown, Indigenous, and gender nonconforming communities.

> *[C]ounter-storytelling stems from critical race theory . . . and offers students exposure to stories of the lived experiences of minoritized people rather than the pervasive master narrative . . . [A]t all grade levels, counter-storytelling allows students to see themselves, their histories, their ancestry, and their identity as an integral part of the historical narrative.* (Fernández 2019, 34)

Immersing Students in Methods for Counter-Storytelling

There are several ways for students to consider how to develop their own counter-stories. In your preparation, consider the methods you've already engaged in as a class, such as counter-narratives in books (such as Aida Salazar's *The Moon Within*) and in families' experiences through storytelling (see the sequence of lessons in Chapter 3).

To begin this lesson with students, immerse them in a range of counter-narratives. The following resources offer starting points in a range of media. Once you begin looking for counter-storytelling and have developed a keen sense of listening to the voices of resistance to the dominant narrative, you'll be surprised by how often you witness counter-narratives at work in the world.

Counter-Narratives in Social Media
- #1000BlackGirlBooks
- #BlackLivesMatter
- #MeToo
- #NoDAPL
- #SayHerName
- #WhatLatinosLookLike
- #NoKidsinCages

Counter-Narratives in Media

- Video clips of interviews with one or more of the following are appropriate for all grade levels:

  - Marley Dias, a New Jersey teen who started the #1000BlackGirlBooks campaign. She is also a published author. You can show images from her book, *Marley Dias Gets It Done: And So Can You!* (2018).

  - Emma González, a gun control activist and survivor of the Marjory Stoneman Douglas High School shooting.

  - Xiuhtezcatl Martinez, an Indigenous environmental activist. You can show excerpts from his book, *We Rise: The Earth Guardians Guide to Building a Movement That Restores the Planet* (2017).

- Options for older students:

  - A clip from the sitcom *One Day at a Time* can be used to connect with the #MeToo movement: Season 3, Episode 2, "Outside" (Fryman 2019), shows the family having a conversation about consent and harassment. In this episode, the teen daughter shares why she feels unsafe, the teen son shares his confusion around a picture he shared on his social media, and female characters retell episodes of harassment.

  - The first five minutes of Kimberlé Crenshaw's (2016) TED Talk, "The Urgency of Intersectionality," where she discusses the problem we face in society when Black women are not seen. It also includes video clips of police violence against Black women. In the final three minutes of the TED Talk, Dr. Crenshaw says the hashtag #SayHerName and the names of Black female victims of police shootings are read aloud.

Latinx Counter-Narratives in Art

- Melanie Cervantes and Jesus Barraza—Several posters, prints, buttons, and stickers on their Dignidad Rebelde website (We recommend starting with *Viva la Mujer* [Barraza and Cervantes 2018], *Tumbling Down the Steps of the Temple* [with quote about bilingualism] [Cervantes 2012], and *Solidarity with Standing Rock* [Barraza and Cervantes 2016].)

- Maya Christina Gonzalez—Several books and book covers (We recommend *They She He Me: Free to Be!* [Gonzales and SG 2017] and *The Gender Wheel* [2018]; also, pages from *Coloring the Revolution* [2017].)

- Nathalie Gonzalez—Illustrations on her website and the *Women's History Month* series she did for MAKERS, also available on her website (2018)

- Ricardo Levins Morales—See the artwork on the Liberation Calendar as well as *Peace Is a Product of Justice* (2010) and *My Hands/Mis Manos* (2014)

- Robert Liu-Trujillo—Illustrations on his blog on the Rob Don't Stop website, https://work.robdontstop.com

- Ruben Guadalupe Marquez—*Jakelin Ameí Rosemary Caal Maquin* and *Yalitza Aparicio*, some of several you can find on his Instagram and Etsy

- Yocelyn Riojas—*My Dreams Are Not Illegal* (2018)

- Favianna Rodriguez—*No Human Being Is Illegal* (2013), *You Are Welcome Here* (2017), and several other works on immigration and women's rights
- Julio Salgado—*Undocumented, Unafraid and Unapologetic* (2015) and *No LGBTQ Exclusion!* (2016)

Text Sets About Counter-Storytellers

- **Sylvia Acevedo**
  - Biography: *Path to the Stars: My Journey from Girl Scout to Rocket Scientist* (2018) by Sylvia Acevedo
  - Podcast episode: "From Girl Scout to Rocket Scientist—Sylvia Acevedo's Story," on Houghton Mifflin Harcourt website (Hanault 2018)
  - Podcast interview: "Portrait of: Sylvia Acevedo," on NPR *Latino USA* (NPR 2019)
  - Video: "Sylvia Acevedo: 2018 National Book Festival," talk on the Library of Congress (Library of Congress 2018)
  - Video: "Meet Sylvia Acevedo," on the Girl Scouts of the USA YouTube Channel (2016)
  - Article: "Conoce a Sylvia Acevedo, la científica espacial de origen latino a cargo de las 'Girl Scouts,'" by Parija Kavilanz (2017)

- **Pura Belpré**
  - Picture book: *Sembrando historias: Pura Belpré: bibliotecaria y narradora de cuentos* (2019) and *Planting Stories: The Life of Librarian and Storyteller Pura Belpré* (2019) by Anika Aldamuy Denise, illustrated by Paola Escobar
  - Picture book: *The Storyteller's Candle/La velita de los cuentos* (2008) by Lucia González, illustrated by Lulu Delacre
  - Poem: "Dos idiomas en la biblioteca" and "Two Languages at the Library" by Margarita Engle in *¡Bravo! Poemas sobre hispanos extraordinarios* and *Bravo! Poems About Amazing Hispanics* by Margarita Engle, illustrated by Rafael López (2017)
  - Audio clip: "How NYC's First Puerto Rican Librarian Brought Spanish to the Shelves," on NPR's *Boundbreakers: People Who Make a Difference* (Ulaby 2016)
  - Documentary trailer: "Pura Belpré, a Storyteller (Trailer)," available from the Center for Puerto Rican Studies–Centro (2012) YouTube Channel
  - Documentary: "Pura Belpré, Storyteller," available from the Center for Puerto Rican Studies (2012)
  - Teaching Guide for Documentary by the Center for Puerto Rican Studies: "Centro Teaching Guide," compiled by Victoria Nuñez for the Center for Puerto Rican Studies (2012)

- **Sandra Cisneros**
  - Video: "Sandra Cisneros, Pioneering Latina Writer" (MAKERS n.d.)
  - Video: "Sandra Cisneros Reads at the Librotraficante Caravan Banned Book Bash in San Antonio" by Bryan Parras (2012) on YouTube

- Audio: "'House on Mango Street' Celebrates 25 Years," on NPR *Morning Edition* April 9, 2009 (NPR 2009)

- Audio: "Sandra Cisneros" on the Penguin Random House Audio website where you can hear an excerpt from *The House on Mango Street* (Penguin Random House n.d.)

- Article: "The Many Homes of Sandra Cisneros," interview with Sandra Cisneros, August 24, 2016 (Ramos 2016)

- Letter: "Dear Sixth-Grade Students of Ms. Jill Faison, Hogan Middle School, Vallejo, California," a letter from Sandra Cisneros (2015)

Dolores Huerta

- Picture book: *Side by Side: The Story of Dolores Huerta and Cesar Chavez/ Lado a Lado: La historia de Dolores Huerta y César Chávez* (2009) by Monica Brown, illustrated by Joe Cepeda

- Video: "Dolores Huerta, Co-Founder, United Farm Workers," on MAKERS website (MAKERS n.d.)

- Podcast interview: "Yes She Did: Dolores Huerta," on NPR *Latino USA* (Hinojosa 2017)

- Podcast interview: "Dolores Huerta and Her Daughter Talk Gender and Power," on NPR *Latino USA* (Paliza-Carre 2018)

- Documentary: "Dolores," documentary on the life of Dolores Huerta, released on January 20, 2017; directed by Peter Bratt (2017) (Available on YouTube, Amazon Prime Video, and other places where films can be purchased or rented.)

José Martí

- Picture book poetry biography: *Martí's Song for Freedom/Martí y sus versos por la libertad* (2017) by Emma Otheguy, illustrated by Beatriz Vidal

- Picture book biography: *Cuando los grandes eran pequeños: José Martí* (2007) by Georgina Lázaro-Leon, illustrated by María Sánchez

- Poem: "La magia de las palabras" and "The Magic of Words" by Margarita Engle in *¡Bravo! Poemas sobre hispanos extraordinarios* (2017) and *Bravo! Poems About Amazing Hispanics* (2017) by Margarita Engle, illustrated by Rafael López

Sylvia Mendez

- Picture book: *Separate Is Never Equal: Sylvia Mendez and Her Family's Fight for Desegregation* (2014) by Duncan Tonatiuh

- Article: "Sylvia Mendez and California's School Desegregation Story" by Lesli A. Maxwell (2014)

- Podcast clip: "'No Mexicans Allowed': School Segregation in the Southwest," conversation with Sylvia Mendez on NPR *Latino USA* (Echevarri and Bishop 2017)

- Documentary: "*Mendez v. Westminster*: Desegregating California's Schools," by PBS Learning Media (PBS n.d.)

- **Óscar Arnulfo Romero**
  - Picture book biography: *Telegramas al cielo: La infancia de monseñor Óscar Arnulfo Romero/Telegrams to Heaven: The Childhood of Archbishop Óscar Arnulfo Romero* (2017) by René Colato Laínez, illustrated by Pixote Hunt
  - Podcast: "The Canonization of Archbishop Oscar Romero," interview with Associate Professor of Theology and Latin American Studies at Fordham University Michael E. Lee about Salvadoran archbishop Oscar Romero by Latino Media Collective Latino Rebels Radio (Latino Rebels 2018)
  - Documentary: "Monseñor: The Last Journey of Oscar Romero" by Ana Carrigan and Juliet Weber (2012)

- **Arturo Schomburg**
  - Picture book poetry biography: *Schomburg: El hombre que creó una biblioteca* (2019) and *Schomburg: The Man Who Built a Library* (2017) by Carole Boston Weatherford, illustrated by Eric Velasquez
  - Podcast: "Vanessa Valdés Discusses Biography of Arturo Schomburg" (Kazi 88.7FM 2017)
  - Website: Schomburg Center for Research in Black Culture
  - Livestream archive: "Arturo Schomburg Lecture" from the Schomburg Center 2016 Celebration. (Dean Schomburg, Arturo Schomburg's grandson, gives an introduction on Arturo Schomburg's life at 11:40 minutes—20 minutes into the celebration.) (Schomburg Center n.d.)
  - Livestream archive: "Diverse Voices in Latinx Children's Literature LIVE STREAM! A Celebration of Bilingual Books and Latinx Communities at Bank Street College," conversation with Eric Velasquez (both in 2018 and 2019!), illustrator of *Schomburg: The Man Who Built a Library* on Kidlit.tv (KidLit n.d.)
  - Video clip: "The 2015 Puerto Rican Day Parade Honors Arturo Schomburg" (Schomburg Center 2015)

- **Sonia Sotomayor**
  - Picture book: *Pasando páginas: La historia de mi vida* (2018) and *Turning Pages: My Life Story* (2018) by Sonia Sotomayor, illustrated by Lulu Delacre
  - Picture book: *Sonia Sotomayor: A Judge Grows in the Bronx/La juez que creció en el Bronx* (2009) by Jonah Winter, illustrated by Edel Rodriguez
  - Chapter book/young reader intermediate edition: *El mundo adorado de Sonia Sotomayor* (2018) and *The Beloved World of Sonia Sotomayor* (2018) by Sonia Sotomayor

The Classics: Latinx Authors of Counter-Narratives in Fiction and Nonfiction

- Alma Flor Ada, Cuban. *Bajo las palmas reales: una infancia cubana* (2009) and *Under the Royal Palms: A Childhood in Cuba* (1998)
- Isabel Allende, Chilean. *Mi país inventado: un paseo nostálgico por Chile* (2004) and *My Invented Country: A Nostalgic Journey Through Chile* (2003)*

* YA or older content

- Julia Alvarez, Dominican. *En el tiempo de las mariposas* (2005) and *In the Time of the Butterflies* (1994), *De cómo las muchachas García perdieron el acento* (2007) and *How the García Girls Lost Their Accents* (1991), *Antes de ser libres* (2002) and *Before We Were Free* (2002)

- Rudolfo Anaya, Chicano. *Bless Me, Ultima* (1994)

- Jorge Argueta, Salvadoran. *Somos como las nubes/We Are Like the Clouds* (2016)

- Monica Brown, Peruvian. *My Name Is Celia: The Life of Celia Cruz/Mi nombre es Celia: La vida de Celia Cruz* (2004), *My Name Is Gabriela: The Life of Gabriela Mistral/Mi nombre es Gabriela: La vida de Gabriela Mistral* (2005), *Pablo Neruda: Poet of the People* (2011), Lola Levine series, Marisol McDonald series

- Melissa Cardoza, Honduran/Garífuna/Lenca. *13 Colors of the Honduran Resistance/13 colores de la resistencia hondureña* (2016)*

- Raquel Cepeda, Dominican. *Birds of Paradise: How I Became Latina* (2013)*

- Sandra Cisneros, Mexican American. *La casa en Mango Street* (1994) and *The House on Mango Street* (1991), *Woman Hollering Creek and Other Stories* (1991)

- Angie Cruz, Dominican. *Soledad* (2001)*, *Dominicana* (2019)*

- Margarita Engle, Cuban. *Aire encantado: Dos culturas, dos alas: una memoria* (2017) and *Enchanted Air: Two Cultures, Two Wings: A Memoir* (2015), *The Poet Slave of Cuba: A Biography of Juan Francisco Manzano* (2006)

- Martín Espada, Puerto Rican. *Alabanza: New and Selected Poems 1982–2002* (2002)

- Cristina García, Cuban. *Dreaming in Cuban* (1992)*

- Juan Felipe Herrera, Mexican American. *Cinnamon Girl: Letters Found Inside a Cereal Box* (2016)*

- Francisco Jiménez, Mexican American. *Cajas de cartón: relatos de la vida peregrina de un niño campesino* (2002) and *The Circuit: Stories from the Life of a Migrant Child* (2002), *La Mariposa* (1998)

- Sonia Manzano, Puerto Rican. *The Revolution of Evelyn Serrano* (2012)

- Nicholasa Mohr, Puerto Rican. *El Bronx Remembered* (1993), *Nilda* (1996)

- Pam Muñoz Ryan, Mexican descent. *Echo* (2015), *El soñador* (2010) and *The Dreamer* (2010), *Esperanza renace* (2002) and *Esperanza Rising* (2000)

- Luis J. Rodríguez, Chicano. *Always Running: La Vida Loca: Gang Days in L.A.* (1993), *América Is Her Name* (1998)

- Esmeralda Santiago, Puerto Rican. *Cuando era Puertorriqueña* (1994) and *When I Was Puerto Rican* (1993)*

- Carmen Tafolla, Chicana. *That's Not Fair! Emma Tenayuca's Struggle for Justice/¡No es justo! La lucha de Emma Tenayuca por la justicia* (2008)

- Piri Thomas, Puerto Rican-Cuban. *Down These Mean Streets* (1967)*

* YA or older content

Exposing students to these artists and movements not only fulfills the purpose of representation but also creates a space where bilingual and multilingual Latinx students see that they too are a part of historical and present movements for social justice. As you review the counter-narratives, highlight how they have the following in common: they *de*center whiteness, validate the experiences of those who have been on the underside of history, and center the stories of oppressed peoples (people of color, Indigenous, LGBTQ+, undocumented, etc.). Also, note the creativity of the counter-narratives of the past and of today, using song, the arts, and even subverted elements of the dominant narrative.

Social Movements as Counter-Storytelling

Now that students are familiar with some examples of present-day activists and their methods of sharing counter-narratives, you can move toward situating this work in historical social movements at the center of Latinx liberation. There are several to choose from, but in Figure 4.13 we highlight two movements to help you tell their stories. For example, using images and narratives from the *Palante* bilingual newspaper of the Young Lords Party, students can learn about this group's efforts to provide health care, education, food, clothing, and clean streets for residents in El Barrio, New York City. You can also read an excerpt from Sonia Manzano's middle-grade historical fiction novel *The Revolution of Evelyn Serrano* (2012), as the main character comes to learn about why the Young Lords Party took over a church to provide services for the community. After each example, you can ask students to identify the injustices, followed by the interventions by these groups, and finally, reflect on what they'd do if that were happening to people now. We are most interested in how students connect with these movements as we highlight work that has been done by leaders in the Latinx community across the United States (the Young Lords Party in Chicago and New York City, the United Farm Workers Union in California). In having students reflect on their own feelings on the movements and how they would contribute to correcting the wrongs if this were happening now, we are creating spaces for students to envision themselves as agents of change. In having this activity follow the previous introduction with social media and artists, students see that they too can effect change and have a responsibility to be in solidarity with those who are most oppressed in society. After going through this process together on one social movement, students can work in small groups to do the same with artifacts from another social movement, such as the *Mendez v. Westminster* (1947) case that challenged the segregation of Latinx students in California schools, or the East Los Angeles Walkouts where students protested injustices in the schools in the late 1960s.

Figure 4.13 Social Movements Starter Sheet

Social Movement/ Group for Advocacy	The Young Lords Party	The United Farm Workers Union
Time	1960s–1970s	1960s–Present
Place	Chicago and New York City	California
People	José (Cha-Cha) Jiménez, Iris Morales	Cesar Chavez, Dolores Huerta
Message	13 Point Program	Rights for agricultural workers
Symbols/ signs/artifacts	*Palante* bilingual newspaper	United Farm Workers flag with the Aztec eagle
Texts	• Book: *The Revolution of Evelyn Serrano* (2012) by Sonia Manzano • Book: *Palante: Voices and Photographs of the Young Lords, 1969–1971* (Abramson and the Young Lords Party 2011) • Book: *Through the Eyes of Rebel Women: The Young Lords 1969–1976* (2016) by Iris Morales • Documentary: "¡Palante, Siempre Palante! The Young Lords" (Morales 1996)	• Book: *Side by Side: The Story of Dolores Huerta and Cesar Chavez/Lado a Lado: La historia de Dolores Huerta y César Chávez* (2009) by Monica Brown, illustrated by Joe Cepeda • Video: "Dolores Huerta, Co-Founder, United Farm Workers" (MAKERS n.d.) • Podcast interview: "Yes She Did: Dolores Huerta" on NPR *Latino USA* (Hinojosa 2017)

Creating Our Counter-Stories

What are the historical events or social issues that students have felt most connected to at this point in the sequence of lessons, considering their lives, the classroom community, local community, country, and the world? In the previous lesson on Latinx history, students learned that they could develop some of the counter-narratives that they began to research. They were also given options with more examples in the introduction to this fourth lesson. Now it is time for students to select the counter-story they'd like to share. You can decide with the students who the audience will be: classroom, grade, school community, families and friends, or an online community. Maybe they'd like to teach their classmates or focus on sharing the information with the rest of their peers in their grade. Or maybe this is an opportunity for engaging the outside community so that counter-stories can shape new understandings of historical events and social issues.

During this time you will want to have available all of the resources from these lessons so that students can revisit and have mentors for both content and representation. Some students might choose the route of illustrations and captions to represent historical events (such as *Latino USA: A Cartoon History* by Ilan Stavans and Lalo Alcaraz [2000]). Others might be moved by the artwork of Favianna Rodriguez, Melanie Cervantes, and Nathalie Gonzalez, and use them as a guide. The poetry in *The Moon Within* can also inspire students to write their own poetry to tell stories of experiences, identities, changes, and coming-of-age moments that challenge the norm.

Once students have created their counter-stories, create spaces in your learning community for them to share their work. Whether you are in an urban area or rural area, a school with mostly bilingual Latinx students or a school with just a handful of bilingual Latinx newcomers, the pressing issues of our time behoove all educators to consider social justice issues, movements, and their impact on the most vulnerable of children. And that reality—the ways that society has inflicted harm on the most marginalized and how from the margins resistance rises and teaches us how to love more of humanity—is for all teachers to teach and all children to learn.

Reflecting on the Lessons: Topic, Texts, Translanguaging

Our aim is for students to not only learn more of the stories from the underside of history, but also learn of the resistance and critical hope of movements that inspire us to create and share counter-stories. As researcher and social justice educator Anita Fernández explains, "the end goal" of counter-storytelling exercises is to "[develop] a critical consciousness with which to view the world and move ourselves and our communities towards liberation" (2019, 35). This matters not only for the bilingual and multilingual Latinx students in your classroom, but also for the non-bilingual, non-Latinx students in your learning community who have been deprived from learning these histories, and these ways of knowing and surviving/resisting. We are not providing a "voice for the voiceless" or "speaking for the marginalized." We must correct that harmful narrative. Instead, the spaces we are creating for students with the lessons in this chapter allow for the stories of the marginal*ized* and minorit*ized* to be amplified and have a larger audience. In undoing harmful narratives we also want to consider our own language use and what we mean by language-minoritized populations, or as Nelson Flores calls these student populations, "racialized bilingual[s]" (2019). We want these counter-stories to be shared and revisited by the learning community. These lessons help:

- teachers address a lack of understanding of historical movements—"reframing and rewriting history to authentically represent our students" (Fernández 2019, 37)

- bilingual/multilingual Latinx students see themselves in history in a variety of ways (not always as oppressed but also as resisters, as luchando por la justicia).

In the next chapter, we take one of the issues mentioned in this sequence of lessons, immigration, and develop it across a series of lessons, providing spaces for children to process through narrative and informational multimodal texts and argumentative writing. We hope the lessons in this chapter help pave the way, not only in your knowledge of historical movements to integrate in your classroom, but also in your own journey as you continue to process your identities and role within education. As the authors of "What Is Ethnic Studies Pedagogy?" note, "To embody a sense of purpose and a culturally and community-responsive pedagogy, [teachers] must be reflective and be able to critically interrogate their own identities and experiences" (Tintiangco-Cubales et al. 2019, 24). We see this sequence of lessons as a "starter set," a set that can launch your teaching and your own personal reflections to consider what we've known, what we don't know, what we assume, what is missing, and how to reveal the varied histories of bilingual/multilingual Latinx students.

Taking an Informed Stance Against Injustice

◇◇◇◇◇

Momento de aprendizaje

Yo no soy inmigrante. Yo tengo papeles.

—Mateo

At this moment, Mateo was considered a recent arrival in Luz's classroom. He had arrived to the United States from the Dominican Republic just a couple of years earlier. They were reading a news article about the testimony of two young siblings who had been traveling for weeks from Central America and had been detained at the U.S.-Mexico border (Morales Almada 2014). In the context of the article, the class discussed what it meant to be an immigrant, and how in this class, many were immigrants (all students in this class were immigrants or U.S.-born children of immigrants). That is when Mateo made his statement.

Reflecting on That Moment

What was it about the word *inmigrante* that offended Mateo when Luz referred to him as such? For Mateo, calling him inmigrante had another connotation, "undocumented." When Luz clarified what each of these words meant, he was less reluctant to identify himself as an immigrant, and, we hope, in the future if anyone thinks he might be undocumented, he won't consider himself as less than anyone else. For Luz, the question that immediately came up was, "How has the rhetoric around immigration impacted how youth like Mateo might see themselves and others who identify as immigrants or undocumented immigrants?"

This moment with Mateo laid bare the shame that he had associated with immigrants, growing up in a society where the dominant narrative dehumanizes immigrants from minoritized communities. That moment is also an affirmation that this work and this learning are both important and necessary.

The lessons in this chapter aim to give students the power to change the narratives that dehumanize them. In this chapter, we will use the topic of immigration as an example, but you may decide to focus on another dehumanizing force.

Introducing the Sequence of Lessons

Figure 5.1 Sequence of Lessons

This chapter lays out an approach for engaging students in social justice issues to challenge dominant narratives that is reflected in Figure 5.1. Although this chapter uses the issue of immigration as its example, the lessons work with any social justice issue. The first step is to make personal connections to the issue. Next, students will use primary sources to learn about the issues directly from those impacted by them. You'll then work with them to look at the secondary sources, specifically how the media portrays the issue, and survey the similarities and differences between these primary and secondary accounts, keeping in mind how dominant narratives and counter-narratives impact perceptions of events affecting minoritized groups. The next step is to learn about the policies that support or undermine the social justice issue that you're studying. What are the different positions and arguments surrounding each policy?

Finally, students can use what they have learned to engage with their community in an authentic way with a culminating project meant for an authentic audience. Students can bring awareness, devise advocacy approaches, and/or offer informed stances and solutions.

Identifying a Focus

To begin, consider where you and your students will focus your energy. What issues have had a dehumanizing effect on your students or on their community? You are probably familiar with the issues that are keeping your students questioning, wondering, and curious to understand more of the world, but you might also survey students to ask them about what issues are important or concerning to them. Most importantly, the objective of this work is to humanize those whom society has dehumanized, keeping Mateo's opening comment from this chapter in mind. Figure 5.2 provides you with some sample social justice issues across grades 3–8 on matters of education, environment, gender and sexuality, health, immigration, Latin America, race, and safety. The suggestions are based on our work in classrooms with Latinx students across grades 3–8 as well as in teacher preparation programs with elementary- and middle-grade teachers. You can also revisit the resources shared in Chapter 4's lesson 4 (related to teen activists) to launch discussions with grades 3–5.

Figure 5.2 Sample Social Justice Issues to Study for Grades 3–8

Topic	Social Justice Issues
Education	• Bilingual education • Diverse books (see #DisruptTexts, #WeNeedDiverseBooks) • Ethnic studies • School dress codes • Standardized testing

Environment	• Animal rights • Climate change • Clean water (Dakota pipeline, Flint) • Emergency preparedness/response to hurricanes (New Orleans, Puerto Rico) • Indigenous rights
Gender and sexuality	• Family diversity • Gender expression • Pronouns • Toxic masculinity • Transgender children
Health	• Mental health (availability of counselors in schools) • Physical education/recess • School lunch • Universal health care • Vaccines
Immigration	• DREAMers • Family separation • Children in cages • Immigration reform • Welcoming new students
Latin America	• Revitalization of Indigenous languages • Welcoming immigrants • Political movements
Race	• Anti-Blackness • Black Lives Matter • Flint clean water crisis
Safety	• Gun reform • School policing

Protecting Students' Safety

As teachers, we are responsible for our students' safety. Although the lessons in this chapter aim for critical consciousness and affirmation in the learning community, they address topics that can heighten feelings of vulnerability. The lessons ask students not only to consider an issue of social justice—issues that, by their nature, can be triggering—but also to connect their own identities and personal experiences to that issue. It is up to you, their teacher, to ensure their safety in this work by recalling our recommendations from Chapter 3, which included inviting students to share stories and experiences, not insisting that they do so, and being clear about what you are not asking students to share. In addition, we recommend that you:

- **Plan for how students will interact with the dominant narrative.** Addressing a dehumanizing dominant narrative involves understanding that narrative. When it is time to consider dominant narratives, begin with the students' connections to these issues. Ask yourself: What do my students already understand about this dominant narrative? Have I dedicated time to getting to know my students' experiences with these topics instead of assuming what they do not know? For some of the topics, students may be the experts on these issues, considering their lived experiences. These may differ from your own. It is crucial to create that space for students. Next, decide whether you will provide resources for your students or whether you will let them do the research themselves. If you decide to provide resources for students, consider their appropriateness for classroom use or if they're genuinely helpful to your students. Ask yourself: What do my students need to know about this dominant narrative that they don't already know? What can I show to help them see this dominant narrative at work? What might be triggering given their experiences? How might unpacking a particular example help them to see the pernicious effects of this dominant narrative at work? How might seeing a particular example do more harm than good?

- **Be prepared for big emotions.** As Mateo reminds us in the opening of this chapter, how a student from a minoritized community has internalized a dominant narrative can shape how the student sees themselves. It is important for students to know that the classroom is a space where these feelings and experiences can be shared. What happens when these are harmful to the student and others? It is our responsibility as teachers to address these, explaining the power dynamics and why they are harmful. For example, when anti-Black comments came up in Carla's classroom (see opening anecdote in Chapter 4), it took several lessons, readings, classroom meetings, and family meetings for these issues to be explored. In a classroom where critical consciousness is at the center, it is imperative that this isn't confused with freedom to express hateful speech. If you believe students need more time to process their experiences, we recommend going through the lessons from the previous chapters leading up to this lesson sequence.

Throughout your work in this chapter, remember that your aim is to help students challenge dominant narratives that oppress minoritized groups. Let your students and the dominant narratives dominating the national conversations be your guide when determining a topic. Although some students or classes may be eager to share personal experiences, others may not. And although some may want to directly address some of the most hate-filled examples of dominant narratives at work, others may be traumatized by those examples. Success in this work is not measured by the stories students share or by the magnitude of the examples of counter-narratives. Instead, success in this work is when minoritized students feel affirmed in their own identities, confident in their understandings that counter-narratives can rise above, celebrating the truths of their lives.

Supporting Translanguaging in the Sequence of Lessons

- Encourage students to discuss and write texts using all their language repertoire.
    - *Annotate a text bilingually.*
    - *Collaborate with peers and share out using their entire language repertoire.*
    - *Brainstorm and/or prewrite using their entire language repertoire.*
- Provide students with bilingual texts and encourage them to use the texts flexibly.
- Provide students with multimodal texts (videos, images, etc.) in both languages to encourage students to use all their meaning-making potential.
- Share authentic texts, including personal narratives that are bilingual or in any language.
- Deliver the lesson in English, in Spanish, or using features of both.
- Have digital translation tools available or bilingual glossaries or dictionaries.
- Accept and celebrate students' writing that includes features of English and Spanish.

Hearing and Sharing Personal Narratives/Mi origen

This will be a two-day lesson: students will listen to your immigration story or a primary account, and then get ready to interview a family member to gather their own immigration stories or seek other primary accounts. Considering ways that we have personally experienced or can connect at some level to our topic of study is a great way to get students to become engaged in the learning. At the same time, be mindful of the points raised in the previous section, "Protecting Students' Safety," as well as modifications for students who are not able to interview family members.

This lesson aims for a personal connection with the topic at hand even if you, personally, may not have a firsthand connection. For example, if you and your students will be studying immigration, we are aware that not everyone is an immigrant. If you do not have any personal connections with immigration, if some of your students are not immigrants, or if stories of immigration are no longer within a family's living memory, share primary accounts from immigrant youth instead. Don't let a lack of personal experiences—your own or your students'—hold you back from studying immigration. Issues surrounding immigration are a reality for a significant number of Latinx children in the United States and a pressing concern considering the way the national conversation around immigrants and immigration is dehumanizing when it concerns children of color. The Pew Research Center (Radford and Noe-Bustamante 2019) reported that as of 2017, there were 44.4 million immigrants living in the United States and over half of those are Latinx.

Preparing to Teach

Make sure students have access to their notebooks or computers to plan out their questions, and make some time for them to practice these with their classmates. It is a good idea to plan ahead and send the family a notice about this project so that they are aware of the interview option, the purpose of this sequence of lessons, and their choice in how to participate. Depending on the families' experiences across their immigration journeys and support (or lack thereof) from institutions, they may or may not feel safe enough to share details of their immigration story with their child for a school assignment. Unfortunately, with incidents of racism and bigotry in schools across the United States on the rise, we must be understanding of issues of mistrust. From racist displays at schools with teachers dressed as the border wall for Halloween to Immigration and Customs Enforcement (ICE) vans parked outside of schools in Latinx neighborhoods, families have a right to seek safety for their children. With this reality in mind, we approach the sharing of stories in lesson 1. And again, we invite you to refer to the section on protecting students' safety.

Step 1: Sharing Our Stories and Introducing the Purpose of the Lesson

Share your story or a primary account first! We should share our own testimonies if we are giving our students the option to share theirs. Consider who your ancestors are. Some of us can track down our origins more easily than others, so this may also require some digging for educators as well. You can share a timeline of your family's immigration or a family tree. You can also speak on your family's linguistic, cultural, and national origins (everyone has this!), or you can use an artifact or a photo to anchor your story in that particular object or image. You can also consider sharing an important or lasting memory about your or your family's immigration experience—Chapter 1 contains some examples from our own journeys. With the exception of Indigenous people who are native to this land, and the Mexican people in the Southwest whose land was taken in the Mexican War (as it is known in the United States), or the American Intervention in Mexico (as it is known in Mexico), we all have some kind of (im)migration story. For some, it is a story that goes back to the forced removal of people from territories in Africa to fund the capitalist colonial economy of the slave trade. For others, it is a story that extends across generations and geographical regions that may have included asylum or refuge from political turmoil.

Tell students that you are sharing your own story with them because you will invite them to do the same. It could be that they, themselves, have vivid memories of their immigration experience, but their story might become more complete with the input of their family. If they are first- or second-generation immigrants, or beyond, then they will definitely have to consult with their family members or elders to try to make sense of their family's immigration story. If they are transient students who have been separated from their family, you will also provide options for them with texts that they can engage with for their research.

Step 2: Piecing Together Our Stories

In sharing your story with your students (or a primary account from those listed in lesson 2), you've created an entry point for students to begin to think about the questions they may have about their own stories (or the primary account you shared), and this is important since you will all collaboratively coconstruct the interview questions that they will then ask their family members and/or caregivers (or questions they'll use for research into other primary accounts). You may want to involve the whole class in creating some basic questions they might all use, but then encourage students to work with a partner or with a small group to consider what else they may want to ask depending on their particular experiences. Figure 5.3 contains some sample questions students can start with if they are studying immigration. It is imperative that students also note that they do not need to disclose any information they are not comfortable sharing, including immigration status, again, keeping in mind the guidelines for protecting students' safety outlined earlier in this chapter. Discuss these questions as a class to give your students an opportunity to personalize them, but make sure they also take time to come up with questions that are meaningful to their own experiences.

Figure 5.3 Questions to Begin Our Immigration Study

Question	Purpose
1. What country or territory does your family originate from? (Everyone should have an answer, including members of a First Nations/Indigenous community who have been the original inhabitants on colonized land.)	To establish origin
2. If you migrated to the (mainland) United States, when did you do so?	To establish a timeline
3. Whose decision was it to migrate?	To identify the key people involved in the decision
4. Why did you make the decision to migrate?	To identify the push/pull factors
5. What do you remember most about your (im)migration journey? Is there an object or a photo that brings up an important memory?	To identify meaningful memories
6. What do you miss the most from your place of origin?	To identify meaningful memories

Once students have adjusted the suggested starter questions to fit their own experiences, and they have had a chance to think of any other questions they'd like to add, have them practice asking these to one another in partnerships. Refer to Chapter 3 for suggestions on getting your students ready to conduct an interview. Remind students that it is okay to ask more questions while they are conducting the actual interview. Sometimes the most meaningful questions are those that come up during a conversation, and which we often cannot plan. The questions can be written in English or Spanish, or both. Ask students to conduct the interviews in any language they believe will encourage more in-depth responses from their loved ones. They can also conduct their interviews bilingually and document what they learn.

One way students can keep track of comments during the interview is to take notes of key words or phrases that they hear while audio recording the interview so that they can return to the recording at a later time to take down full responses to some questions. Many parents and caregivers may have smartphones with voice-recording capabilities that can be used as an audio recorder for their children's assignments. Another way students can take notes is to ask their interviewee to repeat their statements and students can write down the most important parts of their responses (one or two sentences for each response).

Step 3: Making Sense of Our Stories

After students interview their family member(s) or engage with texts on these themes (see list of resources in lesson 2), ask them to look over their notes from their interviews and give them a moment to process these stories. Give them some time to write in their journals some reflections from that experience. You can pose the following questions to guide students to add more to their writing:

- *Synthesize what you learned from the interview.*

- *Did you learn anything new? What was surprising?*

- *How did you feel while listening to this story?*

- *What else would you like to know?*

- *Do you feel like there might be anything missing?*

Let them share if they're comfortable. They can share in their small groups or with a partner using their entire linguistic repertoire. While students engage in sharing, circulate around the room and sit with some groups to listen in on some of these stories.

Step 4: Create a Visual Representation of Your Collective Stories

Create a class timeline by drawing a line across a few sheets of large chart paper or butcher paper. If students were able to gather some dates during their interviews, have them write down the date or year and the event on a sticky note. It is possible for students to have multiple years of migration to the United States reflected within a family, as it can sometimes take many years for families to be reunited, if at all. In both of our cases, our fathers migrated first, and then the rest of the family followed once certain things were set in place (i.e., they found work and a place to live and saved up money for the family to travel and for passports with tourist visas, etc.).

Once they have written the year and the event associated with that year, have the class organize their notes into chronological order to create a class immigration time-line—a visual representation of your students' and their families' immigration move-ments. Encourage students to contribute more than one entry whenever possible. It's important to have this visual because you might be able to connect some of these years to immigration policies that students will learn about later on in this sequence of lessons.

You can close this lesson by asking students to notice some patterns from the experiences of the class as a whole. What do they notice? Do they have any more questions for their parents/family members? If so, have them write these down in their notebooks so that they don't forget. Tell them that in the next lesson, they will be learning about the immigration stories of kids their own age, who migrated by themselves. They will also learn to look for any similarities and differences between their own stories and the stories of these youth.

Deepening Our Understanding with Primary and Secondary Sources

Preparing to Teach

Begin by introducing students to firsthand accounts of experiences related to the topic of migrant youth, particularly accounts by children their age. One rich resource, the Voice of Witness (voiceofwitness.org) oral history project, is dedicated to capturing the firsthand experiences of those impacted by injustice. You can access articles that contain some of these stories, blogs, and webinars, but you can also find links on this website to texts for more complete accounts. The list below includes resources for finding and accessing stories of immigrant youth in particular:

Online Articles and Websites

- "From Solito to Solidarity" by Steven Mayers and Jonathan Freedman (2018), Voice of Witness
- "Meet Young Immigrants," Immigration: Stories of Yesterday and Today (Scholastic n.d.)
- "My Immigration Story: The Story of U.S. Immigrants in Their Own Words" (My Immigration Story n.d.)
- "Border Children Tell Their Stories: Why We Came to the US" by Lisa Riordan Seville and Hannah Rappleye (2014), NBC News
- "What Happens When a Child Arrives at the U.S. Border?" by Patty Gorena Morales and Joshua Barajas (2018), *PBS NewsHour*

Books

- *Enchanted Air: Two Cultures, Two Wings: A Memoir* (2015) and *Aire encantado: Dos culturas, dos alas: una memoria* (2017) by Margarita Engle
- *The Distance Between Us* (Young Readers Edition) (2016) by Reyna Grande
- *My Family Divided: One Girl's Journey of Home, Loss, and Hope* (2018) by Diane Guerrero and Erica Moroz
- *Voces sin fronteras: Our Stories, Our Truth* (2018) by Latin American Youth Center
- *Solito, Solita: Crossing Borders with Youth Refugees from Central America* (2019) edited by Steven Mayers and Jonathan Freedman

There are a variety of options in organizing these stories to get them ready for your students to study. You can print a curated set of stories that represent a variety of experiences, or you can have students explore the various resources available and choose a story of a young person that calls to them.

To do further background reading for yourself as you prepare to teach this lesson, visit the American University's Center for Latin American and Latino Studies' Unaccompanied Migrant Children from Central America: Content, Causes and Advocacy Responses Project and the UCLA Reimagining Migration Project. Both are robust resources for gaining an in-depth understanding of this issue.

Step 1: Introducing Firsthand Accounts: Learning About Migrant Youth Experiences

To show students how we can make sense of these readings, do a shared reading of one testimony together as a class. Before you read the story, model how to read with a specific focus by showing the following guiding questions and any other questions that you feel may be important to keep in mind as you're reading. For example, if you're reading an account of someone who immigrated from a Central American country or Mexico and was detained at the southern border of the United States, you might ask:

1. *What are the reasons that led this young person to make the long journey north?*

2. *How long did it take?*

3. *What were some challenges they faced during their journey?*

4. *What happened when they tried to cross the border into the United States?*

5. *Where were they detained?*

6. *What were their experiences in the detention centers?*

As you come across some of these answers in your reading, show students how they might annotate the text, and underline or highlight so that they can easily locate these important points in the story.

After you have finished reading and annotating your shared reading text, tell students that now it will be their turn to try the same steps with the story that they've either been assigned or have chosen.

Step 2: Engaging with Firsthand Accounts

Once students have been assigned or have found a story they'd like to focus on, they're ready to read on their own, with a classmate, or in a small group. Again, remind them to annotate the texts using their entire linguistic repertoire, as well as highlight or underline important points that may answer some of the guiding questions posed above.

When students have had a chance to carefully read the testimonies of youth, you can ask them to share with a partner or in their small groups. Open up the discussion to the whole class and record students' responses so that the class has access to these notes (chart paper, board, or a device that projects text). Compare and contrast the different experiences in the different stories of youth your students chose to focus on. This way, students can also keep track of the patterns that are emerging from the various accounts. Pose the following questions to reinforce the fact that you're trying to look for patterns:

- *What are the reasons many of these youth are migrating?*

- *What are the similarities and differences?*

- *What are some connections you notice about their experiences throughout their journey?*

- *If they were detained, what were their experiences in detainment?*

Step 3: Identifying the Dominant Rhetoric

In this step, students will find out what secondary sources report about their issue. Continuing the immigration example, you might show students how they could conduct an online search for news reports and other takes on migrant youth. For instance, you might want to find news articles, YouTube videos from official media outlets, political cartoons, or tweets (search for specific hashtags on Twitter, such as #migrantkids, #migrantyouth, #unaccompaniedminors, #nokidsincages) that address this topic. Do a quick review of what comes up with a simple search. Make note of some things that you notice from these secondary sources: What is the overall messaging that is conveyed? How are groups positioned? How are cause and effect discussed, if at all?

If you are having students conduct their own research, there are some ways partners or groups can take on different sources. Perhaps one pair can focus on YouTube videos, another pair can look at news articles from a variety of news media outlets (from varying political leanings), another can focus on searching for political cartoons, and another can focus solely on looking for tweets using the specific hashtags described here to stay focused. You can decide what other secondary sources you may want to consult and assign those to remaining pairs.

Another approach is to use preapproved sources, for example, the two resources we recommended previously for your own research: American University's Center for Latin American and Latino Studies' Unaccompanied Migrant Children from Central America: Content, Causes and Advocacy Responses and UCLA's Reimagining Migration Project. For younger grades you might select sources from *Scholastic*, *Time for Kids*, *Newsela*, and others that may already be in your classroom assuming there are any existing school subscriptions.

Searching online using terms that exemplify ways people in power continue to dehumanize immigrants and other minoritized groups can result in triggering images and words. Rather than attempting to "protect" children from these images and words or to avoid painful topics, we can find age-appropriate ways to do this work with our students without inflicting trauma. After all, many children, especially minoritized children, are already exposed to and living in this reality. One way to proceed is by providing a preselected list of sources. Another is to prepare students for the upcoming content by letting them know what they will be seeing and reading, whether you are talking about racism in the United States and will prepare eighth graders for a visual timeline that includes images of Emmett Till and Trayvon Martin, or preparing fourth graders for a lesson on the violence enacted on Indigenous communities with images from boarding schools to water protectors resisting/protesting.

Once the students have a sense of the overall messaging that is coming across from their secondary sources, ask them to write some observations on sticky notes. They can work in groups to discuss and identify patterns, and once they're finished organizing these, ask them to share with the class. Your job will then be to facilitate the connections across the groups. You can also return to the guide we shared in Chapter 2 if you'd like a more structured protocol for close reading/analysis in finding patterns. Ask them to identify some major points or takeaways from analyzing secondary sources. Ask them to think about the firsthand accounts of the children that they read just before, and ask, *What are the differences? What are the similarities? How are children being depicted in these secondary sources? How does it differ from what they say about their own experiences?* You can record some of this discussion on a chart paper that you can title: "How are migrant youth being portrayed?" You can also add the sticky notes that students wrote onto this chart.

Step 4: Reflection and Planning

Ask students to write a reflection in response to the previous questions. If students would like help in focusing their ideas, you might ask them to consider what surprised them most in their reading, what resonated with them, or where they saw discrepancies. Again, encourage students to draw from their entire linguistic repertoire in their writing. They will use this writing later as they work toward their culminating project.

Students might also zoom in on a particular aspect of what they learned. For example, in a study of immigration, they might focus on a question such as *What happens during and after detainment?* In this case, the student might review the information gathered (the first-person accounts of the minors) to get a good idea of what detainment might be like from the detained child's perspective, and some of the things that happen after initial detainment. Sometimes, minors are released to an adult sponsor or family member as they await their court hearing. Those without sponsors may wait an undefined amount of time in the detention centers until they are able to make their case before a judge.

Researching Policies

Preparing to Teach

It is helpful, again, to do some background research on the policies that affect your issue before beginning this lesson. If you're preparing to teach this lesson in relation to immigration, here's an example of the general information you might find, using both secondary and primary sources: policies that address both authorized immigration pathways and guidelines on acceptable grounds for obtaining asylee or refugee status. Let's begin with the first. Authorized immigration pathways are limited. *Business Insider* published a helpful infographic that shows the possibilities and roadblocks for authorized migration based on information gathered from the U.S. Citizenship and Immigration Services. You can access this infographic on the *Business Insider* website with the title "A Trump Adviser Told DACA Recipients to 'Get in Line' to Immigrate to the US—Here's Why They Can't" (Mark 2017).

If you'd like to also consult the primary source of information, visit the United States Citizenship and Immigration Services government website, where you can also access information about the limited pathways available for authorized immigration. However, it is important to keep in mind that many of the unaccompanied minors are seeking asylum since they're generally fleeing life-threatening circumstances in their home countries. Still, this process is similarly complicated, and the rules for what counts as credible grounds for asylum keep changing.

Step 1: Words Matter: Understanding Terms and their Impact

Begin by ensuring that students are familiar with the terms and processes that relate to the policies you'll be discussing. Figure 5.4 shows some of the terms that might be relevant in our immigration example. We might also choose to share an overview of the complicated process of immigration to the United States using an infographic, such as the one available from *Business Insider*.

Figure 5.4 Immigration Terms Everyone Should Know

Term	Definition
Refugee	**Who is a refugee?** Refugees are people who cannot stay in their home countries because they are facing life-threatening conditions or persecution due to a variety of factors, including race/ethnicity, religion, nationality, political stance, and affiliation to certain social groups.
Asylum	**What is asylum?** Asylum is a status that can be granted to people who meet refugee conditions. Asylum grants people authorization to remain in the country under certain conditions.
Migrant/immigrant	**What is the difference between a migrant and an immigrant?** Migrants typically move within a nation-state/autonomous nation. Immigrants move across politically established international boundaries or borders. Sometimes these terms are used interchangeably.
Undocumented status	**Who is undocumented?** People who do not have legal authorization to reside in a country are called "undocumented immigrants." This status can change once they have been granted a visa or another form of authorization to remain in the country. People with this status are sometimes referred to as "illegal" immigrants, but this is a dehumanizing term and we firmly stand against its use.
DACA	**What is DACA? Who is eligible?** Deferred Action for Childhood Arrivals (DACA) is a temporary protected status for people who were brought to the United States as children and have resided in the country since 2007 without interruption. DACA recipients may be eligible to renew their status every two years and can also receive a work permit to work in the United States if they continue to meet certain guidelines. Protected status means that they can avoid being deported, but this is not always the case. DACA recipients are often referred to as "DREAMers."
Green card	**What is a green card?** A green card is a permanent resident card that allows people to permanently live and work in the United States. After several years, people with green cards can apply for U.S. citizenship. Only those with U.S. citizenship are eligible to vote.

For more information, visit www.uscis.gov.

When discussing these terms, put them into context by discussing how they relate to one another. For example, it may also be helpful to remind students that asylee or refugee status may be obtained on a case-by-case basis, and sometimes, it can take years for people to receive this status. Also, an important reminder is that people can be denied and are expected to return to their home countries or seek asylum elsewhere. What is more, it is crucial to remind students that labels for immigrants can often be dehumanizing, and the best way to avoid these is by learning the terms that are widely accepted and are not degrading in any way.

Step 2: Policy: A Form of Dominant Narrative

Consider which of the resources you relied on in your research would help students understand the policies at work in relation to their focal issue, or look for resources that will be more helpful for your students. For example, in an immigration-focused lesson with grades 3–5, you might use the resources from the United Nations High Commissioner for Refugees Teachers' Toolkit, which includes visuals to help teach terms, graphics of facts and figures about refugees, and other teaching materials. With middle grades, you might rely on the following online resources:

- "An Overview of U.S. Refugee Law and Policy," American Immigration Council (2019)

- "Refugee Act," Wikipedia (2019)

- "U.S. System for Refugee, Asylum Seekers Explained," NBC News (n.d.)

- "Fact Sheet: U.S. Asylum Process" by the National Immigration Forum (2019)

- "Refugees & Asylum," United States Citizenship and Immigration Services (2015)

Do a shared reading of these resources, beginning by asking a few anchoring questions, and then having students follow along with you and annotating, as they did before, by using their entire linguistic repertoire.

Introduce the following guiding question and subquestions before the shared reading:

- *What is the official report or position on seeking asylum or refugee status?*

  - *Who is eligible for asylum or refugee status?*

  - *Who is not eligible for asylum or refugee status?*

  - *What is the typical process like?*

Then, use the guiding questions to engage students in a discussion about some key facts and details about this policy. Students can discuss in small groups as you circle around and sit in with a few of them, or you can engage the whole class in a discussion. Students can also create posters in their groups that reflect the facts and details regarding these policies to present to the class.

The discussion and/or students' work should reflect the central policy points related to the topic. Continuing the example of immigration, this might include points such as the following:

- Asylum, as mentioned before, is a protected status that can be granted to people fleeing their homelands for fear of persecution based on a variety of factors like race/ethnicity, nationality, religion, political opinion, or affiliation to certain social groups.

- Asylum seekers (who meet the requirements mentioned before) would have to either have already entered the United States or be seeking entry into the United States at the international border to be able to have grounds to claim asylum.

- Claims are evaluated on a case-by-case basis, and sometimes the vetting process can be lengthy.

- Immigration policies are not static; they change depending on the political climate.

Step 3: The Counter-Narrative Account of Federal Policies

Now it's time to look at these policies from the perspective of advocates and human rights organizations. These perspectives often show how official policies can be interpreted differently from official reports based on the political climate of the time. Counter-narratives are often accompanied by case studies of real people being impacted by these decisions.

Find resources that show a counter-narrative to federal policies—you might begin your search by looking for organizations that work to counter those policies. Look for texts that are short, quick reads. A few exemplar texts relating to immigration:

- "U.N. Reaffirms Refugees' Right to Seek Asylum in U.S." by Stephanie Nebehay, Reuters (2018)

- "I Welcome: Protecting the Rights of Refugees and Asylum-Seekers," Amnesty International (n.d.)

- "USA: 'You Don't Have Any Rights Here,'" Amnesty International (n.d.)

- "Fact Check: What Is the National Emergency? Do We Need a Wall?," International Rescue Committee (2019)

Then, share the resources with students following a similar format as in step 2, beginning by giving students a few guiding questions to keep in mind as they read. For example:

- *What are human rights advocates reporting on asylum seekers or asylum-seeking policies?*

  - *Who is being deemed eligible for asylum?*

  - *Who is being denied asylum?*

  - *What are some conditions or experiences refugees and asylum seekers are reporting?*

Repeat the process outlined in step 2 to guide your students or groups in the reading. Then ask students to compare their annotations and their notes or posters from the previous informational text.

Step 4: Synthesizing Information

To close lesson 3, ask readers to notice any inconsistencies or patterns and to come up with their own interpretation of the information. For instance, students studying immigration might notice that although official policy states that people fleeing persecution have the legal right to seek asylum, they are being turned away at the border by U.S. Border Patrol, which is a violation of asylum policies. Record student responses in a class chart to make sure that everyone can have access to these statements for future use.

Countering a Harmful Dominant Narrative

Preparing to Teach

This lesson gives students an opportunity to speak back to the dominant narrative they've been studying in the previous three lessons. Because it includes working through the entire writing process, including publication to an authentic audience, it may take place over several days. Pace your class as needed.

Step 1: Gathering Ideas

Give students a few minutes to privately list the most important things they have learned in the previous three lessons. What surprised them? What feels most important to them? Then, ask them to share their lists and, as a class, identify one thing that needs to be changed—perhaps a policy, a school rule, or a community's awareness or understanding of an issue. Once they've established what changes they think need to be made, ask them, *Who can help to make that change?*

Explain that in the work of this lesson, they will be working to convince that audience to make that change.

Step 2: Planning

Work with students to identify a way in which they can get their message to the people who need to hear it and are in positions of power to do something about it. Here are a few examples:

- a letter-writing campaign to a local government representative to advocate on behalf of a social justice issue

- an infographic or other public service announcement to bring facts about this topic to the school/community

- a play to reenact a social justice issue as a way to bring awareness to the school/community

- a compilation of student personal narratives to show the impact of the issue on the school community

- a social media campaign run from a class account

- a report that you present to a local government agency (e.g., city council) to advocate for a particular action on a current issue.

Next, have students identify the features of the genre they've chosen. For example, if they'll be sharing stories, ask them to name what was powerful about the counter-narratives they read in earlier lessons—perhaps specific details or emotional recollections. Or, if they'll be writing letters to representatives, show them models of letters to representatives so that they can see how the letters include arguments and calls to action. If they'll be planning a social media campaign, ask them what makes posts popular on different social media platforms—how might they use hashtags, include images, or reach out to online influencers to "make some noise" online? For students working on social media campaigns, we highly recommend Marley Dias' (2018) book, *Marley Dias Gets It Done: And So Can You!* The text walks readers through Marley's journey in creating #1000BlackGirlBooks and gives recommendations for youth developing their own campaigns. When looking at mentor texts, students might also consider how the texts might be expressing a stance as well, individually or collectively: conversations happening online and in the news can often drive the national conversation on any given topic, resulting in creating enough public pressure to change how policies are enacted. For instance, this can occur when a lot of people are making "noise" on social media coupled with online-based campaigns, even the creation of hashtags, to drive support on an issue.

> Encouraging students to make use of all of their linguistic resources at every step of the writing process can often enable them to add more detail and depth to their writing since they are not being restricted to a single set of language features.

Ask students to map how they will use the features of the genre to convey their message. Let them organize their thoughts into an outline, an idea web, a flowchart, or whatever method works best for their genre.

Step 3: Drafting

Ask students to use their notes to write the first draft of their message. Remind them that they can refer back to the informational texts they read throughout the sequence of lessons to add facts and details to strengthen their message.

Students should be encouraged to draw from their entire linguistic repertoire as they are drafting their writing.

Step 4: Revising/Editing

Give students opportunities to work with peers to revise and edit their writing, keeping their audience in mind: the style they might use for one genre may not be helpful in another. If it seems helpful to the students' message for you to suggest grammatical, usage, or mechanical edits, do so, but let students decide whether and how to use your feedback.

Step 5: Publishing and Sharing/Celebrating

When the students' messages are ready, it's time to get them to their intended audience: mail the letters; launch the social media campaign; hang the infographics in the school hallways; invite families, community members, and administrators to hear students present their essays; or hold a public service announcement viewing at your school. Share widely! You have just engaged your students in meaningful work, and it should be celebrated. The celebrations might include inviting school administration, families, and community members to a panel presentation or a reading in the school. Some teachers have taken the campaigns outside of the classroom and asked if students can share in community spaces (coffee shops, libraries, community centers, universities). With students' and families' permission, some teachers have shared class products on social media, using a student-created hashtag as well as other hashtags that are popular in the educator community to amplify the students' voices—#NCTE, #EduColor, #EduChat, and #EdEquity, for example.

Reflecting on the Lessons: Topic, Texts, Translanguaging

The sequence of lessons described here sets students down the path of rejecting dehumanizing dominant narratives and finding ways to publicly counter those narratives. We are in an age where there is a massive flood of news from many different directions. These lessons teach our students to discern the dehumanizing nature of dominant narratives, to identify the resistance of counter-narratives, and to approach the experiences of minoritized groups with empathy and an open mind. Students have an opportunity to learn to interrogate the counter-narratives as presented through multimodal texts as well as to engage with several examples—given the time, space, and support. Students also have the opportunity to deeply engage with various texts by drawing from their entire linguistic repertoires through the opening of translanguaging spaces in these lessons. This work not only helps our students to reject the current narratives that hurt minoritized groups, but also prepares them to develop their advocacy in contributing to a more just society.

Sustaining the Community Across the Year with Poetry

◇◇◇◇◇

Momento de aprendizaje

In Carla's class of bilingual Latinx sixth graders, students had been working on their poetry anthologies (their culminating assignment for the sixth-grade poetry unit) and were enjoying a musical performance by an artist who was visiting the school as part of the Silk Road Connect partnership. Just as the final notes faded away, Aileen, one of the students, spontaneously asked if she could read her poem to the class. Aileen titled it "Bilingual Matters" and began to read:

Bilingual Matters

Some people are like
"What did he say?"
but I knew what he said.

Why don't you be
bilingual?
'Cause I know what
he said.

It gives you more
Ad-van-ta-ges
'Cause I know what
he said.

Listen guys this is what he said
"Vamo comer mucho platano
con salami ahorita."

(Translation to people who are monolingual)
We're going to eat some
sweet plantains with salami later.

Holla & Peace Out.

Reflecting on That Moment

The class erupted in applause. Carla gave them time to share feedback and other students shared their own bilingual poems. The class loved her poem and delivery so much that they asked to include it in our culminating performance at New York City's Central Park SummerStage with Yo-Yo Ma and the Silk Road Ensemble. Not only did the message of Aileen's "Bilingual Matters" make it to the New York City community, but Yo-Yo Ma and Damian Woetzel of the Aspen Arts Institute also shared it with students in a Chicago school, who then performed it. The performance made it on the local Chicago news, the link was emailed to us, and Aileen was able to see how her message made it beyond the page, beyond the bulletin board and the portfolio. There was something powerful and transformative for everyone involved: Aileen felt her own identity as a bilingual poet affirmed, Carla witnessed the power of making room for student voices (it wasn't in the lesson plan!), the performer understood the impact of their art on Aileen, and all of the students felt the community of sharing their bilingual experiences through bilingual poetry.

Why Poetry?

In the poem "Como tú" (translated as "Like You"), Salvadoran poet Roque Dalton reminds us that poetry is for everyone (2000). This is what we hope for: poetry is for everyone. Whether your classroom has just one bilingual Latinx student or it's a Bilingual Dual Language class where all the students are bilingual Latinxs, poetry continues to expand understandings and sustain communities.

Poetry as Resistance

Poetry helps us resist injustices in the world around writing expectations, language practices, identity formation, social issues, and so much more! It frames resistance to injustice with love at the center and a critical sense of hope. Poetry that centers Latinx experiences resists the ways bilingual Latinx students have been ignored or misunderstood.

Poetry as Healing

A lot of wrongs have been done to and continue to be done to bilingual Latinx students. Reading poetry that shares these wrongs and how poets react to injustices helps children process. We are not alone in our struggles. We get reenergized. We heal. Poetry plays a role in allowing children to find that community. For those who haven't experienced those wrongs, it helps them to investigate why and how society privileges certain people, experiences, and identities. As a classroom community, this kind of healing process is crucial in times when words are used in mostly harmful ways. So when a child and a teacher read David Bowles' "The Newcomer" in the novel in verse *They Call Me Güero: A Border Kid's Poems* (2018), they can consider how they too can welcome others. They can consider how immigrants are treated. They can create plans for the class and the school to welcome new students.

Poetry as Teaching

Poetry teaches us many things if we listen deeply to the experiences shared by the poets. Poetry instruction that centers students' voices and the experiences of minoritized children can have a lasting impact on the ways children love themselves, love one another, and love the land with which we all are responsible to be in reciprocal relationship throughout our lives. For first-year teachers in Carla's Multicultural

Education course, poetry taught them about Arturo Schomburg (thanks to Carole Boston Weatherford and Eric Velasquez's book), José Martí (thanks to Emma Otheguy and Beatriz Vidal's book), and the poets who were growing within them (thanks to inspiration from Jason Reynolds, Elizabeth Acevedo, and Jacqueline Woodson). Previously, poetry was something the teachers had avoided, but after one class session of reading and sharing poetry together, they learned that so much of their approach to poetry had to be unlearned, just like they were helping their grade 1–6 students unlearn the prescribed writing constraints that they brought with them to the classroom, along with assumptions about minoritized people.

Introducing the Sequence of Lessons

Figure 6.1 Sequence of Lessons

The examples in this chapter continue to center the experiences of bilingual Latinx students, this time using poetry as the medium that helps students be in community with themselves, with one another, and with the earth. Following from the lessons in Chapters 4 and 5, we seek to continue to spotlight bilingual Latinx children, especially as they grow up in a society that dims their light. In the tradition of poet Pedro Pietri in "Love Poem for My People" (2008), we want children to see the beauty, the magic, the gift that they are and that they hold within! Also, as poet Jason Reynolds recommends in the *PBS NewsHour* segment "How Poetry Can Help Kids Turn a Fear of Literature into Love" (2017), we use poetry to counteract common practices that expose students to imposing, dense texts that do not speak to them. In Reynolds' words, "They need not fear a thing created to love them and for them to love."

In the first lesson of this chapter, we show how poetry that centers bilingual Latinx experiences can be integrated throughout the week, one text per week, for only a few minutes a day, and focusing on one poet per month. In truth, this is more of an approach than a single lesson, as it could span several days and it is highly flexible. Considering what we've done in previous lessons (rethinking language ideologies, telling our stories, knowing our histories to understand the present moment, unmasking dominant narratives and counter-narratives, and processing social issues), this practice of poetry sustains the community of learners by continuing to amplify the voices of bilingual Latinx children. In the second lesson, we take a different approach by using poetry text sets and discussion protocols, building on the work we did in Chapter 2 with the topics of language, identity, and power. In the third lesson, we provide guidance on poetry performances, considering content and method in alignment with our focus on topics, texts, and translanguaging, as we have shown throughout the lessons in this book.

Supporting Translanguaging Through Poetry

- Read poems in English, in Spanish, or using features of both.

- Have readings/audio versions of poems available online (some books have the readings available digitally).

- Have translation tools available, such as bilingual glossaries, dictionaries, or digital tools to support students as they engage with the poems in English.

- Engage in a translanguaging study of the ways authors use translanguaging in their poems.

- Encourage students to use their entire linguistic repertoire to:

  - *Discuss the poems (small groups and whole class).*

  - *Take notes on the poems.*

  - *Rehearse their poems for performances.*

  - *Accept and celebrate students' discussions and poems that include features of English, Spanish, and other languages.*

Sharing Poetry Reading Across the Week

In planning with elementary school teachers at a school in El Barrio, Spanish Harlem, in New York City across the 2017–2018 school year, Carla noticed that poetry did not show up in any of their literacy plans.

The school was at a crossroads: it had recently undergone changes in administration and increased accountability measures with more preparation for high-stakes standardized testing. At the same time, the school was embracing a Bilingual Dual Language education program, rather than an assimilationist approach. The bilingual teachers felt that Spanish/English instruction would be most helpful for the children, yet they hadn't received any professional support for these changes: all of the curriculum was in English, faculty meetings and grade team planning meetings were in English, and the bilingual teachers still needed to find the time to translate materials and/or find materials in Spanish. Adding to the urgency of the situation, after the devastation from Hurricane Maria, new students were arriving from Puerto Rico, where they had experienced the lack of U.S. government aid and response to people on the island. In the face of these changes and challenges, the teachers at the school made a brave and daring choice: instead of retreating into simplified instruction or compliance, the teachers prioritized the students, creating the most welcoming space possible for newcomers—with poetry.

To Start: Read! Just Read!

Each day, as soon as students entered the classroom in the morning, we had the Poem of the Week posted up for everyone to see. Next, students were immersed in the poem: on the first day of the week, they heard the poem read by famous poets on platforms like You-Tube or by their teacher. Then, once they had "met" the poem, they joined in the reading with a line, with a stanza, or sometimes selecting to read the entire poem with the teacher. On the remaining days of the week, they began by reading the poem together. Because of each day's time crunch, we knew that if we wanted to be sure that poetry was not forgotten or squeezed out of the schedule, it needed to be the very first thing we did each day.

There's no extensive introduction to the topic, poet, text, or discussion. We read. Just read. Otherwise, it could have become a teacher-centered moment in which the adults talked about how much they knew about this poet, or how much they loved this poem, or how this topic had impacted them, while missing out on students' reading and engaging with poems. The unpacking, the review of vocabulary, the discussions, and short reminders of figurative language can come in time, after students have had the opportunity to engage in multiple readings of a particular text. But first, we focus on the love of poetry, the love of community, and how both can happen if we just let children read and listen to one another.

Figure 6.2 shows a sample list of Poems of the Week that we read over the course of one month in the elementary school. Figure 6.3 shows a sample list for Poems of the Week for middle grades. You'll notice that some of the poems are available in Spanish and English, while others are written mostly in English, using features of Spanish from the poet's life throughout their writing. These poems resist the monolingual, white narratives that dominate poetry in classrooms.

Figure 6.2 Sample Grades 3–5 Bilingual Spanish-English Poetry Shared Reading Plan on Celebrations Across a Month

Duration	Topics	Poem
Week 1	Bilingualism Bilingual identity	"Bilingual"/"Bilingüe" (2015) by Alma Flor Ada in *The Poetry Friday Anthology for Celebrations: Holiday Poems for the Whole Year in English and Spanish* (Listen to this poem—#6—on the Bilingual Poem Performances from the Poetry Friday Anthology for Celebrations SoundCloud website)
Week 2	Family Family time	"Family Day"/"Día familiar" (2015) by Francisco X. Alarcón in *The Poetry Friday Anthology for Celebrations: Holiday Poems for the Whole Year in English and Spanish* (Listen to this poem—#21—on the Bilingual Poem Performances from the Poetry Friday Anthology for Celebrations SoundCloud website)
Week 3	Books Libraries	"Two Languages at the Library"/"Dos idiomas en la biblioteca" (a poem about Pura Belpré) by Margarita Engle in *¡Bravo! Poemas sobre hispanos extraordinarios* by Margarita Engle, illustrated by Rafael López (2017) and *Bravo! Poems About Amazing Hispanics* (2017) by Margarita Engle, illustrated by Rafael López
Week 4	Challenges Hope	"Sharing Hope"/"Compartiendo esperanza" (a poem about Roberto Clemente) by Margarita Engle in *¡Bravo! Poemas sobre hispanos extraordinarios* by Margarita Engle, illustrated by Rafael López (2017), and *Bravo! Poems About Amazing Hispanics* by Margarita Engle, illustrated by Rafael López (2017)

Figure 6.3 Sample Grades 6–8 Bilingual Spanish-English Poetry Shared Reading Plan

Duration	Topics	Poem
Week 1	Bilingualism Bilingual identity	"Losing My Accent" (2015) by David Bowles and also in verse in the novel *They Call Me Güero: A Border Kid's Poems* (2018) by David Bowles
Week 2	Family	"In a Neighborhood in Los Angeles"/"En un barrio de Los Ángeles" by Francisco X. Alarcón in *From the Other Side of Night/Del otro lado de la noche: New and Selected Poems* (2002) by Francisco X. Alarcón (also available on Poets.org website)
Week 3	Books Libraries	*Schomburg: El hombre que creó una biblioteca* (2019) and *Schomburg: The Man Who Built a Library* (2017), a picture book in verse by Carole Boston Weatherford, illustrated by Eric Velasquez (select excerpts from the book in English)
Week 4	Challenges Hope	"The Newcomer" (in verse in the novel *They Call Me Güero: A Border Kid's Poems* [2018] by David Bowles)

Lingering with a Poem (5 minutes)

After reading the poem together (on Day One as a class, and on the other days of the week in small groups or partnerships), you'll want to give time for students to discuss their reactions. You might ask, *How did you feel when we read this poem? What does this poem mean to you? What did you picture while we read this poem?* The purpose of these conversations is to continue growing the community and using poetry as a way to have meaningful conversations. In Figure 6.4, we show different options for the class conversations as you revisit the same poem across the week. For one of the days, we recommend looking at a translated version of a poem. If translations are not available, ask children how they might say a certain line or how the translations might differ across the regional varieties of Spanish that the children may speak.

Figure 6.4 Shared Poetry Reading Across the Week

Day One	Day Two	Day Three	Day Four
1. Teacher reads the poem. 2. Teacher points to the words and the class reads together out loud. All students should have access to the poem (projected, on chart paper, or on individual copies). 3. Class discusses or names reactions to the poem.	1. Class reads the poem together. 2. Small groups or partners read together. 3. Partner or small-group discussions on the poem.	1. Class reads the poem together. 2. Small groups or partners read together. 3. Discussion on translation (includes similarities, differences, reactions).	Option #1—Children in partnerships or small groups add on to the poem; they create their own additional lines! Option #2—Children write their own poems inspired by the poem of the week. Option #3—Children rehearse the poem for performance in the next lesson.

Extending the Conversations Across the School Year

Figure 6.5 shows how you can identify poets and poems to extend the shared poetry reading work across the school year.

Figure 6.5 Poetry Across the School Year

Poet of the Month	Poem Week 1	Poem Week 2	Poem Week 3	Poem Week 4
Margarita Engle	Poems from *¡Bravo! Poemas sobre hispanos extraordinarios* (2017), *Bravo! Poems About Amazing Hispanics* (2017)			
Pat Mora: Poems from *My Own True Name: New and Selected Poems for Young Adults* (2000)	"Immigrants"/ "Los inmigrantes"	"Elena"	"Learning English: Chorus in Many Voices"	"To My Son"

continues

Poet of the Month	Poem Week 1	Poem Week 2	Poem Week 3	Poem Week 4
Langston Hughes	"Dreams" in *The Collected Poems of Langston Hughes* (1994)	"My People" in *Selected Poems of Langston Hughes* (1990)	"I, Too" in *Selected Poems of Langston Hughes* (1990)	"Mother to Son" in *Selected Poems of Langston Hughes* (1990)
Kwame Alexander	Poems from *El crossover* (2019), *The Crossover* (2014)			
David Bowles	Poems from *They Call Me Güero: A Border Kid's Poems* (2018)			
Emma Otheguy	Poems from *Martí's Song for Freedom/Martí y sus versos por la libertad* (2017)			
Various: Poets featured in *Hip Hop Speaks to Children*, edited by Nikki Giovanni (2008)	**Pedro Pietri** "Love Poem for My People"	**Eloise Greenfield** "Books"	**Lucille Clifton** "Why some people be mad at me sometimes"	**Tupac Shakur** "The Rose that Grew from Concrete"
Nikki Grimes: Poems from *One Last Word: Wisdom from the Harlem Renaissance* (2017)	"Lessons"	"Through the Eyes of an Artist"	"A Safe Place"	"No Hamsters Here"
Jacqueline Woodson	Poems from *Brown Girl Dreaming* (2014)			
Jason Reynolds	*For Every One* (2018)			

An easy place to begin is with holidays, as the start of the school year roughly aligns with celebrations of Hispanic Heritage Month. Margarita Engle's poetry book *Bravo!*, which comes with beautiful illustrations, can be a wonderful starting point. However, don't limit yourself to holidays or cultural celebrations to celebrate and highlight the voices of minoritized populations. The purpose of this work is to weave poetry into students' relationships with themselves, with one another, and with the earth across the entire year.

Exploring Language, Identity, and Power with Poetry

In an English as a New Language fifth-grade classroom—a class where English is typically the dominant language of instruction—Anel's students read E. J. Vega's "Translating My Grandfather's House" (1994) along with Francisco X. Alarcón's "In a Neighborhood in Los Angeles"/"En un barrio de Los Ángeles" in *From the Other Side of Night/Del otro lado de la noche: New and Selected Poems* (2002). What began as a way to share the memories people have with their grandparents and special places in their lives grew into uncovering how some parts of the students' lives felt "smaller" or "hidden" from what they were sharing in school. Some students said this reminded them of how they use less Spanish sometimes because they want to prove that they can learn English; others were upset about the ending to Vega's poem (the child in the poem draws a childhood home, but the teacher disapproves, and then the child proceeds to draw what everyone else draws to get the

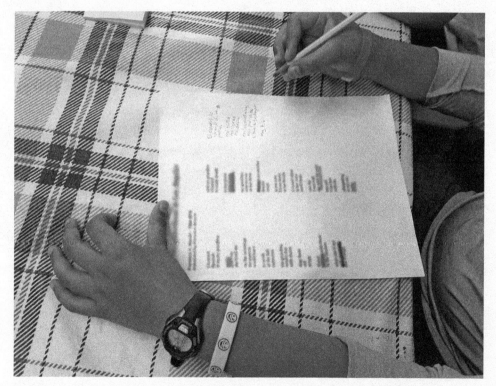

Figure 6.6 A middle-grade student works on their own poem after reading Francisco X. Alarcón's poem "In a Neighborhood in Los Angeles"/"En un barrio de Los Ángeles."

teacher's approval). Their anger triggered memories for them that revealed how they, too, were not really themselves because they felt that school made them change to be accepted.

In a bilingual middle-grade classroom in New York City, students read the words to Elizabeth Acevedo's "Hair" (2014) after watching her performance. They say that the poem makes them want to learn more about the history of advertisements and beauty supplies in the Dominican Republic. Several students connect with Acevedo's experience. We follow this up with the TED Talk spoken word performance "3 Ways to Speak English" (2014) by Dr. Jamila Lyiscott, and students who had been shamed for how they spoke English or Spanish express a deep connection to the poem. At the same time, they really want to learn more about language rules.

Just a few blocks from that school, watching and reading Lyiscott's poem causes a very different reaction from middle-grade students in an English as a New Language course; this time, the poem unites the students in thinking about how their language practices are beautiful, bringing students who speak Arabic, Bengali, and Spanish together.

All of these powerful responses come from a simple yet powerful approach to planning. First, teachers curate poetry text sets on topics that highlight their students' experiences and tackle aspects of bilingual identity formation. Then, students are immersed in the poems. Finally, the students are given an opportunity to discuss the poems.

Curating the Poems and Building the Text Sets

The best way to find poems is to read and listen to poetry widely, with an eye toward texts that are accessible to students and that will resonate with them, always looking for a variety of perspectives and experiences conveying diverse Latinx journeys. In sustaining community in monolingual, bilingual, and multilingual settings where we are highlighting the lives of minoritized populations, it is crucial not to think that a single poem by a Mexican poet about their experience on the borderlands encapsulates the journeys of all Latinx people. We are aiming for text sets that get the conversation started with voices from across the spectrum of Latinx histories, present movements, challenges, and hopes.

Figure 6.7 includes poets and poems that can help you to get started with your curation. Resources such as the Poetry Foundation website and specific poets' books will help you to get to know poets' work and backgrounds. We also noted which poems are more age-appropriate for middle grades, considering adult language and topics. Many of the poems included here are widely available online and directly on the poets' websites.

Figure 6.7 Poems on Language, Power, and Identity

Poet	Poems/Texts
Alma Flor Ada Born and raised in Cuba **F. Isabel Campoy** Born in Spain	*¡Sí! Somos Latinos* (2014) and *Yes! We Are Latinos: Poems and Prose About the Latino Experience* (2013)
Francisco X. Alarcón Born in California Grew up in Guadalajara, Mexico	• "Family Day"/"Día familiar" by Francisco X. Alarcón in *The Poetry Friday Anthology for Celebrations: Holiday Poems for the Whole Year in English and Spanish* (2015) • *Poems to Dream Together/Poemas para soñar juntos* (2005)
Julia Alvarez Born in New York City Grew up in the Dominican Republic	"Bilingual Sestina" in *The Other Side/El otro lado* (1995)
Gloria Anzaldúa Born and raised in Texas	"To Live in the Borderlands Means You"* in *Borderlands/La frontera: The New Mestiza* (1987)
Richard Blanco Born in Madrid Child of Cuban migrants Grew up in Miami	• "Translation for Mamá" in *Directions to the Beach of the Dead* (2005) • "América"** in *City of a Hundred Fires* (1998) • "One Today: A Poem for Barack Obama's Presidential Inauguration, January 21, 2013" (2013)*
David Bowles Mexican American Grew up in South Texas	• "Border Kid" (available on David Bowles' website and in *Here We Go: A Poetry Friday Power Book* by Sylvia Vardell and Janet Wong [2017]) • "Losing My Accent"* (available on David Bowles' website [2015]) • "The Newcomer"* in *They Call Me Güero: A Border Kid's Poems* (2018)

*Recommended for older audiences in middle grades.

**Recommended for older audiences; note adult language.

continues

Poet	Poems/Texts
Julia de Burgos Born and raised in Puerto Rico	"A Julia de Burgos"/"To Julia de Burgos"
Mayda del Valle Born in Chicago Child of Puerto Rican migrants	• "A Faith Like Yours" (2009)* • "Descendancy" (2010)*
Margarita Engle Born in California Cuban mother and North American father	• *Drum Dream Girl: How One Girl's Courage Changed Music* (2015) • *Enchanted Air: Two Cultures, Two Wings: A Memoir* (2015)* *and Aire encantado: Dos culturas, dos alas: una memoria* (2017)* • *Soaring Earth: A Companion Memoir to Enchanted Air* (2019)*
Martín Espada Born in Brooklyn	"Jorge the Church Janitor Finally Quits"/"Por fin renuncia Jorge el conserje de la iglesia" in *Poetry Like Bread: Poets of the Political Imagination from Curbstone Press* edited by Martín Espada (2000)
Juan Felipe Herrera Born in California Son of migrant farm workers	"Borderbus"* in *Notes on the Assemblage* (2015)
Yesenia Montilla Born and raised in New York City Afro-Latina Daughter of immigrants	• "A Perfect Game" • "Ode to Dominican Breakfast" • "The Day I Realized We Were Black"** All poems are available on Yesenia Montilla's website
Pat Mora Born and raised in Texas	*My Own True Name: New and Selected Poems for Young Adults* (2000)*

*Recommended for older audiences in middle grades.

**Recommended for older audiences; note adult language.

José Olivarez Born in Chicago Son of Mexican immigrants	• "I Walk into Every Room and Yell Where the Mexicans At"* • "(Citizen) (Illegal)" (2018)* • "This is a poem" All poems are available on José Olivarez's website
Willie Perdomo Born and raised in New York City Puerto Rican	Poems from *Where a Nickel Costs a Dime: Poems (1996)***
Pedro Pietri Born in Ponce, Puerto Rico, and raised in New York City	"Puerto Rican Obituary"** in *Pedro Pietri: Selected Poetry* (2015)
Anthologies	• *Red Hot Salsa: Bilingual Poems on Being Young and Latino in the United States* (2005) edited by Lori Marie Carlson • *Cool Salsa: Bilingual Poems on Growing Up Latino in the United States* (1994) edited by Lori Marie Carlson • *The Tree Is Older Than You Are: A Bilingual Gathering of Poems and Stories from Mexico with Paintings by Mexican Artists* (1995) edited by Naomi Shihab Nye

*Recommended for older audiences in middle grades.

**Recommended for older audiences; note adult language.

Once you have a rich collection of poems to choose from, organize the poems into initial sets. Set up copies of the texts in baskets, bins, or folders at students' tables (about one for every two to four students). Label each of the folders or baskets with a short thematic description. For example, a folder with the poems by Bruchac and Alarcón mentioned in Figure 6.8 might be labeled "Earth" or "Seasons." For those in younger grades, illustrated books of poetry—which provide support for students' conversations—may work as their own "sets."

Figure 6.8 Sample Poetry Text Sets

Sample Grades 3–5 Text Set	Sample Grades 3–8 Text Set	Sample Middle-Grades Text Set
Topic: Learning About Different Family Experiences	**Topic: Taking Care of the Earth**	**Topic: How Others See Me and How I See Myself**
1. Poems from *¡Si! Somos Latinos* (2014) and *Yes! We Are Latinos: Poems and Prose About the Latino Experience* (2013) both by Alma Flor Ada and F. Isabel Campoy 2. "In a Neighborhood in Los Angeles"/"En un barrio de Los Ángeles" by Francisco X. Alarcón in *From the Other Side of Night/Del otro lado de la noche: New and Selected Poems* (2002) by Francisco X. Alarcón (also available on Poets.org website)	1. *The Earth Under Sky Bear's Feet: Native American Poems of the Land* (1995) by Joseph Bruchac 2. Poems by Francisco X. Alarcón: • *Laughing Tomatoes: And Other Spring Poems/Jitomates risueños: y otros poemas de primavera* (1997) • *From the Bellybutton of the Moon and Other Summer Poems/Del ombligo de la luna: y otros poemas de verano* (1998) • *Angels Ride Bikes: And Other Fall Poems/ Los ángeles andan en bicicleta: y otros poemas de otoño* (1999) • *Iguana in the Snow: And Other Winter Poems/ Iguanas en la nieve: y otros poemas de invierno* (2001)	1. "Hair" (2014) by Elizabeth Acevedo 2. "Translating My Grandfather's House" (1994) by E. J. Vega 3. "The Right Way to Speak" in *Brown Girl Dreaming* (2014) by Jacqueline Woodson

Discussions on Language, Power, and Identity

Once students have read the poems in their set, give them an opportunity to discuss what they've read.

To continue centering these voices and to sustain the lives of those who have been relegated to the margins, we recommend using the following guiding questions to facilitate the group discussions:

- *What parts of the poem stand out for you? Why?*

- *How does the poem make you feel?*

- *How did the poet use language (English/Spanish, word choice) to develop their ideas or make you feel a certain way?*

- *How do the poet's experiences compare with your own life?*

- *What did you learn from this poem?*

- *What more do you want to learn about after reading this poem?*

Students can engage in discussions on both the content of the texts with its focus on matters relating to bilingual identities and what the illustrations make them feel, think, see, and consider.

Students Rename Text Sets

Once students have had an opportunity to discuss the poems in their set, ask them what might connect the poems. In other words, create the space for children to be in community through poetry and to use their creativity to rename the set of texts. For example, a set that was initially named "Earth" or "Seasons" may become "Taking Care of the Earth." Students can rename their folders/bins with texts after each "text club" or "book club" meeting if they are gathering in groups for this purpose.

Performing Poetry for Resistance, Healing, and Teaching

In this approach, we amplify the voices of students by supporting them in sharing their original poetry or poems written by other poets through performance.

Rehearsing Poetry Performances

You can introduce students to different ways of sharing their poetry through poetry centers/stations/groups.

Center 1: *Watching spoken word poetry*

Students watch video clips of different performances by children or youth their age with a partner or in a small group. This is helpful for students who have never seen a poetry performance. Viewing these videos and discussing them with each other helps students sustain a classroom community, while also addressing the content and approaches to sharing poetry with an audience.

Center 2: *Rehearsing favorite poems from text sets and/or shared reading*

Here, students return to poems that they already know from shared reading sessions during class or text sets from group discussions. Just as with center 1, this second center gives students more opportunities to engage with texts that they are familiar with, which helps those who may not want to or may not be ready to share their own writing with an audience. These same students would benefit from center 5 where they create digital media with readings of their favorite poems.

Center 3: *Rehearsing students' own poems*

Students use this space to rehearse their performances of their own poems if they feel they are nearly ready or willing to share. It might be helpful for them to have spent some time in center 1 so that students can see examples of what it "looks" like to perform a poem. They can take turns rehearsing their poems with each other in a small group and give each other constructive feedback based on any criteria you can develop together as a class. Or it can simply be a space for offering each other words of encouragement and finger snaps!

Center 4: *Creating digital media with students' readings of their own poems (audio, video, presentation with images and audio)*

Students use this space to create any kind of digital media using their own poetry performances. For instance, they might want to create a presentation of their poetry partnered with GIFs, memes, images, or other visual media that they'd like to add to create a new artistic representation of their poetry. They can also add or manipulate audio or video files of their performances, if available.

Center 5: *Creating digital media with students' readings of poems from class (audio, video, presentation with images and audio)*

Students in this center create digitally based artistic representations of their favorite poems or poetry performances. For instance, some students may want to take a poem or collection of poems they can perform and create a video combining their voice narration with a slideshow of curated images that visually conveys the poetry.

Performing in Community

Not all students will share as Aileen did in the opening anecdote in this chapter and read their poem in front of the class. For some, performing a favorite poem by a mentor poet might be something they'd like to prepare for and share. For others, performing in a small group is a more accessible option. Discuss these different approaches as students prepare to share with their authentic audience (classmates, grade, school, families/community members). For those with the privilege of being in the presence of a fellow poet/classmate as they share a poem, listening deeply and being present in that moment is crucial. As supportive audience members, students can be coached to notice any of the following:

- how the poem makes them feel

- how the poet made them think about language, power, identity

- how the poet was purposeful about their word choice

- how the poet created rhythm.

We highly recommend limiting the guidance to three to five focal areas and not making this about students having to identify a list of poetic devices. If a child sees a list of literary terms such as *alliteration, onomatopoeia, repetition,* and *imagery,* it can shift the focus to a discussion on poetry checklist items and take the joy out of the poetry experience when reading, creating, and sharing. If poetry indeed is to be used as resistance to injustice, then we cannot devise poetry instruction in ways that take part in that injustice. Our goal in this work is to help children process these topics, learn more about poets, and share their love (or newfound love, we hope) of poetry. The community will grow as a result.

Reflecting on the Approaches to Using Poetry: Topic, Texts, Translanguaging

Like the earlier chapters in this book, this chapter highlights the importance of getting to know a variety of bilingual Latinx experiences. In this chapter, however, we've switched gears from building community and developing counter-stories to sustaining community and understandings. Also, in embedding more student-centered work—such as shared reading, the creation of text sets, and rehearsals for performance—poetry becomes, like the poet Roque Dalton says, for everyone (2000). When Carla made her transition from divinity studies at Princeton Theological Seminary to bilingual education studies at Hunter College, City University of New York, there was something powerful about reading about and living through learning experiences that centered love. Whether it was being introduced to critical pedagogy through classes that lifted the voices of the students (enacting what was being read in Paulo Freire, Ira Shor, and bell hooks' writing) or truly listening to the plethora of Latinx journeys, it was evident that this practice requires love to be sustained. Poetry is at the heart of this work, and we hope that these activities breathe more life and community in your classrooms across the school year.

Being a Reader, Writer, Researcher, and Advocate with and for Bilingual Latinx Students

◇◇◇◇◇

Momento de aprendizaje

"Of course you can attend! Just make sure to prepare to share with your colleagues when you get back." These were the words we heard often over the course of our teaching career. Our administration was consistently supportive of professional learning that would develop the teaching and experience of the many newcomers and Emergent Bilingual Learners in our respective school community.

Reflecting on That Moment

In all of these moments, whether outside of the school community or within the classroom, we were encouraged to think critically about teaching, curriculum, and relationship building in our classroom. Our students were celebrated and encouraged to think deeply about their learning experiences. This meant that the learning was happening for students and for teachers, across schools and community organizations, and all felt that their voices and experiences mattered. Connecting with others—at conferences, workshops, museums, and local organizations—reaffirmed this calling, this sense of advocacy that is grounded in seeking an equitable, inclusive, and a more just educational experience for language-minoritized students. Because white supremacy is entrenched in society and seeps into educational institutions through curricula, disciplinary practices, tracking systems, standardized testing, and other systematic forms of discrimination, it was crucial to grow and be sustained in this work alongside a community of educator-activists.

This book has presented a series of lessons around a variety of topics and texts, all of which enact a pedagogical approach that is culturally and linguistically sustaining. However, for this pedagogical practice to truly liberate students from oppressive teaching practices and curricula, we, as educators, must do more than teach these lessons. We must also develop a clear and actionable plan for supporting and advocating with and for bilingual students, grow a coalition of edu-activists, and build a community of practice.

Support and Advocate with and for Students

Supporting and advocating with and for students will be an ongoing effort. An action plan will help you to keep your goals clear and within sight. You might consider keeping a teaching journal and jotting down some of your responses to the following guiding questions:

1. **Decide on a focus.** What are your students asking of their classroom experience? What is your dream/goal in creating a supportive, engaging, and thriving experience for your bilingual/multilingual students?

   - What will this look like in your classroom?

   - What will it sound like?

2. **Make a plan.** While keeping your students' voices in mind, work out a plan to make your dreams/goals a reality. Consider:

- What (if any) supports (materials, texts, mentors, colleagues, funding, or time, for example) do you already have that will help you to reach your goal? How useful are those supports?

- What (if any) supports do you still need?

  - Where can you get the support you need?

  - Who can help you to get the support you need?

- What steps do you need to take to reach your goal?

3. **Put the plan to work.** Create a visual representation of these goals to keep yourself motivated and focused. Challenge yourself to find a way to work toward these goals each day.

For instance, a goal might be to grow your classroom library so that it includes a wider bilingual and Latinx representation. You might make a plan to work toward that goal by considering:

- **What supports do I already have?**
  I can assess my current library (classroom or school) by asking myself:

  - Are there characters from different minoritized Latinx groups, and are they authentically represented (avoiding stereotypes)?

  - Do the characters use bilingual/multilingual Latinx language practices that accurately reflect the language practices of minoritized groups?

  - Do the stories encourage appreciation and respect for differences between people and their ways of being?

  - Do the stories remind students that they are important, that their voice matters, and that they can make a difference in their family, their community, and their world?

We also recommend that you dig deeper and seek books that support the many other intersecting identities from family structures to abilities, especially since the Latinx experience is not limited to language or culture. As you seek to build your library, keep the following in mind:

- Do the stories have a wide range of family structures (single parent, foster or adoptive parents, families with two moms or two dads, families with an incarcerated parent, etc.)?

- Do the characters in the story represent a variety of jobs and careers (farmworkers, artists, professionals, service workers, etc.)?

- Do the stories have a variety of able and differently abled characters from all racial/ethnic groups, genders, and socioeconomic classes, and do they play an important role in the story?

- Do the characters represent varied gender identities and expressions (avoiding stereotypical gender roles)?

(Adapted from "Creating an Anti-Bias Library" by Social Justice Books [2016])

- **What supports do I need?**

  - I need new texts.

  - I need a list of the texts I want to add to the classroom collection. I may find ideas in this book: many of the lessons in the earlier chapters reference age-appropriate texts by Latinx authors and illustrators and focusing on authentic representations of Latinx characters and people.

  - I may need funding to pay for these texts.

- **Where can I get these supports?**

  - School library: Your school library may already have some of these titles. Otherwise, suggest that your school purchase these book titles for your school library, if not your classroom library; that way the entire school can have access to these books.

  - Local library: Your local library may already have some of these titles as well; if they don't have them at that branch, some libraries can request an interlibrary loan from a different branch in the same system. Otherwise, you could also suggest that they purchase specific book titles. Also, some libraries have book club sets or class sets of texts available for educators to borrow. Ask your local librarian about educator privileges and systems (online borrowing with books mailed to your school).

- **Who can help me to get these supports?**

  - School administration and school librarian: You can request to meet with your administration and/or school librarian (if your school has one) to ask about book orders. Ask key questions to help you plan accordingly with your colleagues: How much is allocated for books, per grade, per class, and so on? When are book orders placed? When is the deadline to submit book lists? Who is the point person for book orders? Are there books somewhere in the building that are not being used? You'd be surprised to find out how many school closets and basements both Carla and Luz have been through after asking these questions!

  - Families and community members through class wish lists: You can create wish lists on an online platform or make an arrangement with your local bookstore and create a book wish list there. Ask families/school community members to purchase a book for the class, whenever possible. It may not be feasible for every caretaker to contribute in this way, but some might, and if they ask what you need, you can have a list ready to go and they can choose to purchase a book from there.

  - Donors through crowdfunding: There are a variety of platforms specifically designed to secure funding for a variety of educators' projects, such as DonorsChoose, which was founded by Charles Best, a former public school teacher in the Bronx. Organizations like this encourage educators to put together a very short proposal describing a classroom need and the amount that can help fulfill that need. Anyone can browse and choose to fund your project. Some projects have multiple donors at a time, which is encouraging because a little amount across several people can result in a project getting fully funded. Browse their website to get some ideas on what kinds of projects educators post. Some teachers get class book club sets funded while others request support for listening libraries for their Emergent Bilingual Learners.

Grow a Coalition of Edu-Activists

You are not alone in this work. As you consider your goals and develop your action plan in your teaching journal, consider joining a coalition of edu-activists to share ideas, to learn with and from, and to support you as you work toward your goal:

- Who will be your thought partner(s)? Consider people you know in your own life as well as educational leaders and online communities.

- Who can you visit to see what some of these goals look like in action? How might you start a study group that meets regularly to strategize, implement ideas, and reflect?

Look around you. Start with your school—who is already engaging in powerful teaching? Consider the schools in your district and create opportunities for in-person visitations or online communication. Also, if you already engage in social media at some level, explore the possibility of becoming involved with an online community. There are many conversations already happening in these virtual spaces. You can follow other educators discussing topics that matter to your students and your school community; look for hashtags like #EduColor or #DisruptTexts. Continue listening to, learning from, and centering the experiences of minoritized children and educators.

Recommended Thought Partners

The groups and individuals described next continuously engage in this work in ways that extend beyond the classroom. They have inspired us, and we hope that you connect with them, read their work, and share your own as we grow our community of bilingual advocates. They each have different approaches to their work with language-minoritized students. Their creativity, drive, and nonnegotiable stance on building up our students encourage us to be better versions of ourselves, inside and outside of the classroom. Their antiracist stance aligns with our approach that supports students' counter-narratives so these stories, their experiences, their writing, and their language practices can move further and further away from the margins, toward the center of curriculum. Each profile provides a brief biography, ways we have been impacted by their work, and places where you can connect with these educators. May these profiles help grow your own professional learning community and help clarify your educator-activist path!

#DisruptTexts

#DisruptTexts is an interactive movement that seeks teacher participation in disrupting traditional reading lists. They take an antiracist approach and center the experiences of minoritized voices. The founders of #DisruptTexts are all about this work: Tricia Ebarvia (@triciaebarvia), English teacher at Conestoga High School, near Philadelphia; Lorena Germán (@nenagerman), teacher at Headwaters School in Austin and author of *The Anti-Racist Teacher Reading Instruction Workbook* (2019); Dr. Kimberly N. Parker (@TchKimPossible), the assistant director of teacher training at the Shady Hill School in Cambridge, Massachusetts; and Julia Torres (@juliaerin80), a teacher and librarian in Denver Public Schools. Their expertise regarding culturally and linguistically sustaining texts means so much to educators who engage with their #DisruptTexts Twitter chats, blog posts, and presentations both online and at national conferences.

Dr. Debbie Reese

Dr. Debbie Reese, a tribally enrolled member of Nambé Pueblo, shares her critiques of children's literature on her blog *American Indians in Children's Literature* and on Twitter (@debreese). When Carla was supporting elementary school teachers in El Barrio, New York City, she sought Dr. Reese's expertise when creating book lists for the bilingual and monolingual teachers. One of her recommendations, *Jingle Dancer* (2000) by Cynthia Leitich Smith, became the teachers' favorite text! The interview with Dr. Reese on *The Children's Book Podcast* episode "'Don't Miss' Books of 2018 Part 2" is a valuable resource when considering how to revise reading lists to include texts by Native authors. Her Ed Collab Gathering keynote address (2017) (video can be found online) outlines all-too-common issues related to the depiction of Native peoples in books for young people.

CUNY-NYSIEB

The City University of New York–New York State Initiative on Emergent Bilinguals (CUNY-NYSIEB) is a research project funded by the New York State Education Department. It aims to improve the educational outcomes of Emergent Bilingual Learners across the state by developing the school's multilingual ecology, so that the students and the community feel welcomed and represented, and by seeing students' bilingualism as a resource. This initiative is led by Drs. Ricardo Otheguy, Ofelia Garcia, and Kate Menken. Luz was a part of the CUNY-NYSIEB research team and currently serves as an advisor. We have used the translanguaging guides and video resources from CUNY-NYSIEB in professional learning sessions with teachers to develop bilingual curriculum and bilingual programming.

Raciolinguistic ideologies and pedagogies with Dr. Nelson Flores and Dr. Jonathan Rosa

In 2015, Drs. Flores and Rosa's (2015) *Harvard Educational Review* article, "Undoing Appropriateness: Raciolinguistic Ideologies and Language Diversity in Education," took the "drop the mic" memes in our education field to another level. For too long, the discourse around Emergent Bilingual Learners or the teaching of language-minoritized students was framed along deficit lines. It was not unusual to hear "Those children need to learn the academic language," and "Oh, their Spanish isn't the 'correct' Spanish." Comments like these placed students on the lowest levels in this manufactured language hierarchy, where the monolingual English teachers' or bilingual teachers' language practices were deemed superior. In their work, Flores and Rosa ask us to question the ways that we think about language in relationship with the societal power structure, specifically the person who is listening and judging bilingual Latinx language practices. These ideologies can be perpetuated by white, monolingual teachers, but also by teachers of color who have internalized a racialized hierarchy of language practices that deems language and literacy practices of students of color as deficient. Dr. Flores continues this work at the University of Pennsylvania, on his blog *The Educational Linguist,* across the nation in his talks, and on Twitter @NelsonFlores. Dr. Rosa's book, *Looking Like a Language, Sounding Like a Race: Raciolinguistic Ideologies and the Learning of Latinidad* (2019), in addition to his social media presence (@DrJonathanRosa), are great reads for teacher and administration book clubs. Several teachers on social media have also shared how they use Dr. Flores and Dr. Rosa's #raciolx (raciolinguistics) tweets as texts of analysis with their students!

Texts as Thinking Partners

Sometimes, a text can be so helpful that it feels like having a thinking partner there with you. Here are a few that we hope will be as helpful to you as they have been to us.

Rethinking Ethnic Studies, edited by R. Tolteka Cuauhtin et al. (2019)

Carla assigned this text in her Multicultural Education course as soon as it was published! First-year bilingual teachers were impacted by the frameworks for ethnic studies, the focus on indigeneity, and the examples of teaching. The examples included a range of activities across elementary, middle, and secondary levels. These examples help readers rethink curriculum that has for so long centered on whiteness.

Biliteracy from the Start: Literacy Squared in Action by Kathy Escamilla and Members of the Literacy Squared Team (2013)

A key text in Carla's Bilingual Literacy courses with preservice and inservice bilingual teachers, *Biliteracy from the Start* cultivates an approach to literacy instruction that has one end goal: biliteracy. This is not a "teach your ELLs these strategies" or "ways to get your ELLs to transition to English" book. This book includes programming examples to support bilingual teaching (great for Bilingual Dual Language programs), reading and writing assessments that authentically assess students' literacy in Spanish and in English, and reading and writing activities that have been used in authentic learning settings in Spanish (not strategies that have been translated from English to Spanish). The activities and lessons (including entire unit examples from kindergarten and fifth grade) are all research based.

"Translanguaging Literacies: Children's Literature and Literacy Instruction" by us—Carla and Luz (forthcoming)
This chapter in the forthcoming book *Translanguaging and Transformative Teaching for Emergent Bilingual Students: Lessons from the CUNY-NYSIEB Project,* edited by Ofelia García and the CUNY-NYSIEB Team, examines how translanguaging is enacted in children's literature. We review several of the books that we also recommend in this book, such as *Dreamers* by Yuyi Morales (2018), and we discuss how teachers can use translanguaging books like this in their literacy instruction.

This book has centered the experiences of bilingual Latinx students and developed lessons, questions, and texts that can be implemented in classrooms, emphasizing the importance of critical literacies where we welcome the experiences and voices of these students. Yet texts that center these bilingual Latinx voices are often unheard of in students' assigned readings or independent reading choices. As you grow a coalition of edu-activists and as you share texts that highlight varied experiences across the Latinx community with each other and with your students, you are helping to disrupt harmful narratives and instead be a part of a more humanizing way to teach and build relationships with bilingual Latinx students.

Build a Community of Practice to Reflect and Revise

Lastly, we encourage you to build a community of practice to have a dedicated space to constantly reflect and revise. In your teaching journal, jot down responses to the following questions:

- What might your community of practice look like?

- When would you meet?

- What artifacts would you need to have with you during these meetings?

- How might you include students, families, and community members in these reflection times?

A community of practice works toward goals but understands that learning and progress comes not from a single attempt but from a long-term commitment to a cycle of learning and action.

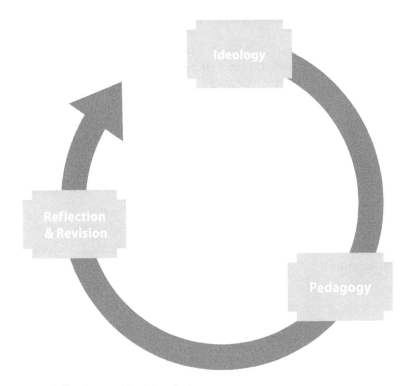

Figure 7.1 Reflecting and Revising Cycle

- *Ideology*: Start with the theories that guide your teaching or your pedagogical stance. What are your beliefs and your approach to teaching bilingual/multilingual students? Refer to Chapter 1 in this book for further support.

- *Pedagogy*: Implement transformative pedagogy that reflects an ideology that centers students' lives. Refer to Chapters 2 through 6 for examples.

- *Reflection and Revision*: Reflect on the implementation, and make revisions considering the students' artifacts and feedback. Repeat this cycle. Refer to the recommended thought partners in this chapter. Revisit their writing for support on revisions in your teaching.

If you are looking for a place to begin your work with your community of practice, consider using the lessons in this book with the community. Luz's work with translanguaging in texts has extended from middle-grade teaching to her teacher education courses with preservice and inservice K–12 teachers. Together, they have read culturally and linguistically sustaining texts, created lessons based on these, and shared "literature guides" (handouts where candidates design learning activities based on the texts). In Carla's curriculum development workshops with literacy teachers, developing book lists, addressing translanguaging objectives in interactive read-alouds, and integrating work on dominant narratives and counter-narratives have been key moves to set the teachers up for continued learning at their schools. Also, during school visits, engaging students in texts sets and analyzing their bilingual/multilingual participation with teachers has been a moving part of Carla's work. What started as "My students can't do that" or "We only teach in English here" turns into "Wow, the children really loved reading and translating" or "We really need to do more of this." Whether it's the shared reading poetry plans across the week that teachers found super accessible and life changing or the lessons that helped students think about their own bilingual identities and language practices, they end the planning and coteaching sessions by really considering how to keep this going.

This work is life work. The work of seeking justice for children who are relegated to the margins is not something we can resolve with one single book—whether it's a mentor text for your class or even our own book for teacher study—or a library makeover. As we've shared in previous chapters, we are constantly learning more about ourselves, our histories, what we need to unlearn, and what needs to be reimagined to create inclusive and sustaining learning spaces. We are also constantly learning more about our students as we center their experiences. Doing all of this in community helps keep us accountable to our mission and humbled by the reality that it isn't about being the superhero teacher. We aren't the ones we are centering. The teacher as savior narrative is toxic and to dismantle it we must emphasize the growth that happens when we grow together, en comunidad.

Conclusion

It is our hope that you take the pedagogical approaches presented in this book and apply them to other topics and texts that elevate your students and classroom community, amplify the voices of minoritized youth, and engage them in critical thinking about the world around them.

Chapters 1 and 2 focused on developing our En Comunidad pedagogical approach by framing it around three focal areas: topics, texts, and translanguaging.

These three areas are the basis of the pedagogy as we seek to facilitate powerful learning opportunities and experiences on meaningful topics anchored in transformative texts while engaging your students' linguistic repertoires through translanguaging and forging spaces for your students to be their full, authentic selves.

These introductory chapters focused on creating a collaborative learning community to grow your stance and commitment to teaching in this way. As García, Ibarra Johnson, and Seltzer (2017) remind us, having a translanguaging stance takes a specific type of teacher: a co-learner. They describe a teacher who "believes that the classroom space must be used creatively to promote language collaboration. . . . A translanguaging stance always sees the bilingual child's complex language repertoire as a resource, never as a deficit" (García, Ibarra Johnson, and Seltzer 2017, 27). We hope that this En Comunidad approach captures the essence of this stance as we seek to engage children and youth in learning content that is powerful and meaningful while welcoming and encouraging their entire linguistic repertoire to shine through.

Chapter 3 considered writing mentors and how stories that center bilingual Latinx experiences can inspire children to tell their own stories and interview their family members. Chapter 4 focused on unlearning—on critically tackling problematic historical and current narratives while examining and elevating the counter-narratives to challenge any attempts to normalize the exclusion of marginalized people.

Chapter 5 guided you through a teaching approach that you can apply to studying movements, social justice issues, or other events that dominate the news cycle with which your students are grappling. Our work lies not only in making some connections to these events, but in realizing we are active change agents; we have multiple means to amplify children and youth's voices.

Finally, Chapter 6 captures the ways that you can facilitate your students' access to the power of poetry and can enable your students to engage meaningfully with relevant spoken word art while creating a space for them to develop their own. Even through mandated, monolingual, often rigid curricula, we can and must forge these spaces for our children.

When we apply the frameworks of translanguaging, critical literacies, counter-narratives, and raciolinguistic ideologies to not only our text selections but also our pedagogy, transformative teaching practices take root and allow our students to grow and be their full selves. In other words, we are purposeful in our text selection, but our work doesn't end there. Texts are a starting point to consider representation, especially learning more about the varied Latinx experiences and language practices. We take these texts and our lived experiences as inspiration to craft teaching and learning moments where bilingual Latinx students' lives are centered. With this, we reveal how thoughtful topics, texts, and translanguaging practices all come together to grow together en comunidad.

REFERENCES

Abramson, Michael, and the Young Lords Party. *Palante: Voices and Photographs of the Young Lords, 1969–1971*. Chicago, IL: Haymarket Books.

Acevedo, Elizabeth. 2014. "Hair." SlamFindTV. Last modified July 2014. www.youtube.com/watch?v=0svS78Nw_yY.

———. 2018. *The Poet X*. New York: Harper Teen.

Acevedo, Sylvia. 2018. *Path to the Stars: My Journey from Girl Scout to Rocket Scientist*. New York: Clarion Books.

Acuña, Rodolfo F. 2014. *Occupied America: A History of Chicanos*. New York: Pearson.

Ada, Alma Flor. 1998. *Under the Royal Palms: A Childhood in Cuba*. New York: Atheneum Books for Young Readers.

———. 2009. *Bajo las palmas reales: una infancia cubana*. Madrid, Spain: Alfaguara.

———. 2015. "Bilingual"/"Bilingüe." In *The Poetry Friday Anthology for Celebrations: Holiday Poems for the Whole Year in English and Spanish*, edited by Sylvia Vardell and Janet Wong. Princeton, NJ: Pomelo Books.

Ada, Alma Flor, and F. Isabel Campoy. 2013. *Yes! We Are Latinos: Poems and Prose About the Latino Experience*. Watertown, MA: Charlesbridge.

———. 2014. *¡Sí! Somos Latinos*. Madrid, Spain: Alfaguara.

Adler, David A. 1991. *A Picture Book of Christopher Columbus*. New York: Holiday House.

Alarcón, Francisco X. 1997. *Laughing Tomatoes: And Other Spring Poems/Jitomates risueños: y otros poemas de primavera*. San Francisco: Children's Book Press.

———. 1998. *From the Bellybutton of the Moon and Other Summer Poems/Del ombligo de la luna: y otros poemas de verano*. San Francisco: Children's Book Press.

———. 1999. *Angels Ride Bikes: And Other Fall Poems/Los ángeles andan en bicicleta: y otros poemas de otoño*. San Francisco: Children's Book Press.

———. 2001. *Iguana in the Snow: And Other Winter Poems/Iguanas en la nieve: y otros poemas de invierno*. San Francisco: Children's Book Press.

———. 2002. *From the Other Side of Night/Del otro lado de la noche: New and Selected Poems*. Tucson, AZ: University of Arizona Press.

———. 2005. *Poems to Dream Together/Poemas para soñar juntos*. New York: Lee & Low Books.

———. 2015 "Family Day"/"Día Familiar." In *The Poetry Friday Anthology for Celebrations: Holiday Poems for the Whole Year in English and Spanish*, edited by Sylvia Vardell and Janet Wong. Princeton, NJ: Pomelo Books.

Alexander, Kwame. 2014. *The Crossover*. New York: Houghton Mifflin Harcourt.

———. 2019. *El crossover*. New York: Houghton Mifflin Harcourt Books for Young Readers.

Alim, H. Samy, and Geneva Smitherman. 2012. *Articulate While Black: Barack Obama, Language, and Race in the U.S.* New York: Oxford University Press.

Allende, Isabel. 2003. *My Invented Country: A Nostalgic Journey Through Chile*. New York: HarperCollins.

———. 2004. *Mi país inventado: un paseo nostálgico por Chile*. New York: HarperCollins Español.

Alvarez, Julia. 1991. *How the García Girls Lost Their Accents*. Chapel Hill, NC: Algonquin Books.

———. 1994. *In the Time of the Butterflies*. Chapel Hill, NC: Algonquin Books.

———. 1995. "Bilingual Sestina" in *The Other Side/El otro lado*. Boston: E.P. Dutton.

———. 2000. *The Secret Footprints*. New York: Knopf Books for Young Readers.

———. 2002. *Antes de ser libres*. New York: Knopf Books for Young Readers.

———. 2002. *Before We Were Free*. New York: Knopf Books for Young Readers.

———. 2002. *Las huellas secretas*. New York: Knopf Books for Young Readers.

———. 2005. *En el tiempo de las mariposas*. New York: Plume Press.

———. 2007. *De cómo las muchachas García perdieron el acento*. New York: Vintage Español.

Alvarez, Julia, and Bill Eichner. 2001. *A Cafecito Story/El cuento del cafecito*. Hartford, VT: Chelsea Green Publishing Company.

American Immigration Council. 2019. "An Overview of U.S. Refugee Law and Policy." www.americanimmigrationcouncil.org/research/overview-us-refugee-law-and-policy.

Amnesty International. n.d. "I Welcome: Protecting the Rights of Refugees and Asylum-Seekers." www.amnestyusa.org/campaigns/refugee-and-migrant-rights/.

———. n.d. "USA: 'You Don't Have Any Rights Here.'" www.amnesty.org/en/latest/research/2018/10/usa-treatment-of-asylum-seekers-southern-border/.

Anaya, Rudolfo. 1994. *Bless Me, Ultima*. Berkeley, CA: Quinto Sol Publications.

———. 2011. *La Llorona/The Crying Woman*. Albuquerque, NM: University of New Mexico Press.

Anderson-Lopez, Kristen, and Robert Lopez. 2017. "Remember Me (Dúo)" Performed by Miguel feat. Natalia Lafourcade. *Coco* (Original Motion Picture Soundtrack), Walt Disney Records, Pixar.

Anzaldúa, Gloria. 1987. *Borderlands/La frontera: The New Mestiza*. San Francisco: Aunt Lute Books.

———. 1997. *Friends from the Other Side/Amigos del otro lado*. San Francisco: Children's Book Press.

———. 1997. *Prietita and the Ghost Woman/Prietita y la Llorona*. San Francisco: Children's Book Press.

Argueta, Jorge. 2001. *A Movie in My Pillow/Una película en mi almohada*. San Francisco: Children's Book Press.

———. 2006. *Talking with Mother Earth/Hablando con Madre Tierra*. Toronto, ON: Groundwood Books.

———. 2016. *Somos como las nubes/We Are Like the Clouds*. Toronto, ON: Groundwood Books.

Au, Wayne. 2011. *Critical Curriculum Studies: Education, Consciousness, and the Politics of Knowing*. New York: Routledge.

Augenbraum, Harold, and Ilan Stavans, eds. 1993. *Growing Up Latino: Memoirs and Stories—Reflections on Life in the United States*. Boston: Houghton Mifflin.

Barraza, Jesus, and Melanie Cervantes. 2016. *Solidarity with Standing Rock*. PDF, 8.5" x 11". San Leandro, CA.

———. 2018. *Viva la Mujer*. 6-Color Handmade Screen Print, 9" x 12". San Leandro, CA.

Bigelow, Bill, and Bob Peterson. 2003. *Rethinking Columbus: The Next 500 Years*. Milwaukee, WI: Rethinking Schools.

Blackstock, Cindy. 2011. "The Emergence of the Breath of Life Theory." *Journal of Social Work Values and Ethics* 8 (1). http://jswve.org/download/2011-1/spr11-blackstock-Emergence-breath-of-life-theory.pdf.

Blakemore, Erin. 2018. "The Brutal History of Anti-Latino Discrimination in America." History.com. Updated August 29. www.history.com/news/the-brutal-history-of-anti-latino-discrimination-in-america.

Blanco, Richard. 1998. *City of a Hundred Fires*. Pittsburgh, PA: University of Pittsburgh Press.

———. 2005. *Directions to the Beach of the Dead*. Tucson, AZ: University of Arizona Press.

———. 2013. "One Today: A Poem for Barack Obama's Presidential Inauguration, January 21, 2013." Pittsburgh, PA: University of Pittsburgh Press.

Bomba Estéreo. 2015. "Soy yo." *Amanecer*. Sony Music Entertainment U.S. Latin LLC.

Bowles, David. 2013. *Flower, Song, Dance: Aztec and Mayan Poetry*. Beaumont, TX: Lamar University Press.

———. 2015. "Losing My Accent." http://davidbowles.us/poetry/.

———. 2018. *Feathered Serpent, Dark Heart of Sky: Myths of Mexico*. El Paso, TX: Cinco Puntos Press.

———. 2018. *They Call Me Güero: A Border Kid's Poems*. El Paso, TX: Cinco Puntos Press.

Bratt, Peter, dir. 2017. "Dolores." Arlington, VA: PBS.

Brown, Monica. 2004. *My Name Is Celia: The Life of Celia Cruz/Mi nombre es Celia: La vida de Celia Cruz*. Flagstaff, AZ: Northland Publishing.

———. 2005. *My Name Is Gabriela: The Life of Gabriela Mistral/Mi nombre es Gabriela: La vida de Gabriela Mistral*. Flagstaff, AZ: Luna Rising Books.

———. 2009. *Side by Side: The Story of Dolores Huerta and Cesar Chavez/Lado a lado: La historia de Dolores Huerta y César Chávez*. New York: HarperCollins Children's Books.

———. 2011. *Marisol McDonald Doesn't Match/Marisol McDonald no combina*. New York: Children's Book Press.

———. 2011. *Pablo Neruda: Poet of the People*. New York: Henry Holt and Company.

———. 2013. *Marisol McDonald and the Clash Bash/Marisol McDonald y la fiesta sin igual*. New York: Children's Book Press.

Bruchac, Joseph. 1995. *The Earth Under Sky Bear's Feet: Native American Poems of the Land*. New York: PaperStar.

Burgos, Hilda Eunice. 2018. *Ana María Reyes Does Not Live in a Castle*. New York: Lee and Low Books.

Burton, LeVar. 2017. "'The Paper Menagerie' by Ken Liu." *LeVar Burton Reads*. https://art19.com/shows /levar-burton-reads/episodes/639de627-e0e7-47da-936c-b97949b8b30e

Calderón, Margarita, Diego Fuenzalida, and Elizabeth Simonsen. 2018. *Mapuche nütram: Historias y voces de educadores tradicionales*. Santiago, Chile: Universidad de Chile. www.libros.uchile.cl/710.

Callender, Kheryn. 2018. *Hurricane Child*. New York: Scholastic.

Campoy, F. Isabel, and Alma Flor Ada. 2006. *Tales Our Abuelitas Told: A Hispanic Folktale Collection*. New York: Atheneum Books for Young Readers.

Candlewick Press. 2018. "Una entrevista con Juana Martinez-Neal, la creadora de Alma." YouTube. www .youtube.com/watch?v=5mv2rKP6A94&feature=youtu.be.

Cardoza, Melissa. 2016. *13 Colors of the Honduran Resistance/13 colores de la resistencia hondureña*. Scotts Valley, CA: CreateSpace Independent Publishing.

Carlson, Lori Marie, ed. 1994. *Cool Salsa: Bilingual Poems on Growing Up Latino in the United States*. New York: Henry Holt & Co.

———, ed. 2005. *Red Hot Salsa: Bilingual Poems on Being Young and Latino in the United States*. New York: Henry Holt & Co.

Carrigan, Ana, and Juliet Weber, dirs. 2011. "Monseñor: The Last Journey of Oscar Romero." Notre Dame, IN: Kellogg Institute at the University of Notre Dame. DVD, ITunes.

Cartaya, Pablo. 2017. *The Epic Fail of Arturo Zamora*. New York: Puffin Books.

———. 2018. *Marcus Vega Doesn't Speak Spanish*. New York: Puffin Books.

———. 2019. *Each Tiny Spark*. New York: Kokila.

Castañeda, Omar S. 1993. *Abuela's Weave*. New York: Lee & Low Books.

———. 1994. *El tapiz de abuela*. New York: Lee & Low Books.

Celic, Christina, and Kate Seltzer. 2013. *Translanguaging: A CUNY-NYSIEB Guide for Educators*. CUNY-NYSIEB. www.cuny-nysieb.org/wp-content/uploads/2016/04/Translanguaging-Guide-March-2013.pdf.

Center for Puerto Rican Studies–Centro. 2012. "Pura Belpré, a Storyteller (Trailer)." YouTube. www.youtube .com/watch?v=375vw6lS4-Y.

———. 2012. "Pura Belpré, Storyteller." DVD.

Cepeda, Raquel. 2013. *Birds of Paradise: How I Became Latina*. New York: Atria.

Cervantes, J. C. 2018. *The Storm Runner*. New York: Disney Hyperion.

———. 2019. *The Fire Keeper*. New York: Disney Hyperion.

Cervantes, Melanie. 2012. *Tumbling Down the Steps of the Temple*. Screen Print. 30h x 22w. San Leandro, CA.

The Children's Book Podcast. 2018. "Our 'Don't Miss' Books of 2018 Part 2 with Dr. Debbie Reese and Traci Sorell (American Indians in Children's Literature & Cynsations)." http://lgbpodcast.libsyn.com /our-dont-miss-books-of-2018-part2-with-dr-debbie-reese-and-traci-sorell-american-indians-in -childrens-literature-cynsations.

———. 2018. "Yuyi Morales." http://lgbpodcast.libsyn.com/yuyi-morales.

Cisneros, Sandra. 1991. *The House on Mango Street*. New York: Vintage.

———. 1991. *Woman Hollering Creek and Other Stories*. New York: Random House.

———. 1994. *Hairs/Pelitos*. New York: Alfred A. Knopf.

———. 1994. *La casa en Mango Street*. New York: Vintage Español.

———. 2015. "Dear Sixth-Grade Students of Ms. Jill Faison, Hogan Middle School, Vallejo, California." Letter. www.sandracisneros.com/2015_05/.

CNN. 2009. *Latino in America* (documentary series).

Colato Laínez, René. 2017. *Telegramas al cielo: La infancia de monseñor Óscar Arnulfo Romero/Telegrams to Heaven: The Childhood of Archbishop Oscar Arnulfo Romero.* Lyndhurst, NJ: Lectorum Publications.

Colorín Colorado. 2016a. "A Family of Storytellers." YouTube. www.youtube.com/watch?v=YF8vMeYxBYM&feature=youtu.be.

———. 2016b. "Growing Up in Queens." YouTube. https://youtu.be/kx5PoN1ppmE.

———. 2016c. "Learning to Read in Spanish." YouTube. www.youtube.com/watch?v=6hv3nsuYWaA&feature=youtu.be.

Congressional Resolution. 2018. "Juneteenth Independence Day." S. Res. 547—115th Congress (2017–2018). www.congress.gov/bill/115th-congress/senate-resolution/547/text.

Cooper, Floyd. 2015. *Juneteenth for Mazie.* Mankato, MN: Capstone for Young Readers.

Crenshaw, Kimberlé. 1991. "Mapping the Margins: Intersectionality, Identity Politics, and Violence Against Women of Color." *Stanford Law Review* 43 (6): 1241–99.

———. 2016. "The Urgency of Intersectionality." TEDWomen 2016. Last modified October 2016. www.ted.com/talks/kimberle_crenshaw_the_urgency_of_intersectionality?language=en.

Cross, Terry. 2007. "Through Indigenous Eyes: Rethinking Theory and Practice." Paper presented at the 2007 Conference of the Secretariat of Aboriginal and Islander Child Care in Adelaide, Australia.

Cruz, Angie. 2001. *Soledad.* New York: Simon & Schuster.

———. 2019. *Dominicana: A Novel.* New York: Flatiron Books.

Cuauhtin, R. Tolteka, Miguel Zavala, Wayne Au, and Christine E. Sleeter, eds. 2019. *Rethinking Ethnic Studies.* Milwaukee, WI: Rethinking Schools.

Dalton, Roque. 2000. "Como tú." In *Poetry Like Bread: Poets of the Political Imagination*, edited by Martín Espada, 128. Evanston, IL: Curbstone Press.

———. 2000. "Like You." In *Poetry Like Bread: Poets of the Political Imagination*, edited by Martín Espada, 129. Evanston, IL: Curbstone Press.

Danticat, Edwidge. 2015. *Mama's Nightingale: A Story of Immigration and Separation.* New York: Dial Books for Young Readers.

Delacre, Lulu. 2017. *Us, in Progress: Short Stories About Young Latinos.* New York: HarperCollins.

de la Peña, Matt. 2015. *Last Stop on Market Street.* New York: G.P. Putnam's Sons.

———. 2016. *Última parada de la calle Market.* Barcelona, Spain: Corimbo.

———. 2018. *Carmela Full of Wishes.* New York: Penguin Random House.

———. 2018. *Los deseos de Carmela.* New York: Penguin Random House

del Valle, Mayda. 2009. "A Faith Like Yours." Mayda del Valle at the White House Poetry Jam. The Obama White House. Last modified May 2009. www.youtube.com/watch?v=WCZTlXb4w3Y.

———. 2010. "Descendancy." Def Poetry – Mayda de Valle – Descendancy. Urbanrenewalprogram. Last modified August 2010. www.youtube.com/watch?v=paM03zurPQw.

Denise, Anika Aldamuy. 2019. *Planting Stories: The Life of Librarian and Storyteller Pura Belpré.* New York: HarperCollins Children's Books.

———. 2019. *Sembrando historias: Pura Belpré: bibliotecaria y narradora de cuentos.* New York: HarperCollins Children's Books.

Dias, Marley. 2018. *Marley Dias Gets It Done: And So Can You!* New York: Scholastic.

Diaz, Alexandra. 2016. *The Only Road.* New York: Simon & Schuster Books for Young Readers.

Dominguez, Angela. 2018. *Stella Diaz Has Something to Say.* New York: Roaring Brook Press.

———. 2018. *Stella Diaz tiene algo que decir.* New York: Scholastic.

Echevarri, Fernanda, and Marlon Bishop. 2017. "'No Mexicans Allowed': School Segregation in the Southwest." NPR *Latino USA*. www.latinousa.org/2016/03/11/no-mexicans-allowed-school-segregation-in-the-southwest/.

elvecindariocalle13. "Calle 13—Latinoamérica." 2011. YouTube. September 27. Accessed October 27, 2018. www.youtube.com/watch?v=DkFJE8ZdeG8.

Engle, Margarita. 2006. *The Poet Slave of Cuba: A Biography of Juan Francisco Manzano*. New York: Henry Holt and Co.

———. 2015. *Drum Dream Girl: How One Girl's Courage Changed Music*. New York: HMH Books for Young Readers.

———. 2015. *Enchanted Air: Two Cultures, Two Wings: A Memoir*. New York: Atheneum Books for Young Readers.

———. 2016. *Lion Island: Cuba's Warrior of Words*. New York: Atheneum Books for Young Readers.

———. 2017. *Aire encantado: Dos culturas, dos alas: una memoria*. New York: Atheneum Books for Young Readers.

———. 2017. *¡Bravo! Poemas sobre hispanos extraordinarios*. New York: Henry Holt and Co.

———. 2017. *Bravo! Poems About Amazing Hispanics*. New York: Henry Holt and Co.

———. 2017. *Forest World*. New York: Atheneum Books for Young Readers.

———. 2018. *Jazz Owls*. New York: Atheneum Books for Young Readers.

———. 2019. *Isla de leones: El guerrero cubano de las palabras*. New York: Atheneum Books for Young Readers.

———. 2019. *La selva*. New York: Atheneum Books for Young Readers.

———. 2019. *Soaring Earth: A Companion Memoir to Enchanted Air*. New York: Atheneum Books for Young Readers.

Escamilla, Kathy, Susan Hopewell, Sandra Butvilofsky, Wendy Sparrow, Lucinda Soltero-González, Olivia Ruiz-Figueroa, and Manuel Escamilla. 2013. *Biliteracy from the Start: Literacy Squared in Action*. Philadelphia, PA: Caslon.

Espada, Martín, ed. 2000. *Poetry Like Bread: Poets of the Political Imagination from Curbstone Press*. Evanston, IL: Curbstone Press.

———. 2002. *Alabanza: New and Selected Poems 1982–2002*. New York: W. W. Norton & Company.

España, Carla. 2019. *The Moon Within: Discussion Guide for Ages 8–12: Honoring Our Bodies, Connections with Our Ancestors, and Healing Through Arts and Community*. New York: Scholastic, www.aidasalazar.com/teachers-guide.html.

España, Carla, and Luz Yadira Herrera. Forthcoming. "Translanguaging Literacies: Translanguaging in Children's Literature and Literacy Instruction." In *Supporting, Teaching, and Translanguaging with Emergent Bilingual Students: Lessons from the CUNY-NYSIEB Project,* edited by Ofelia García and the CUNY-NYSIEB Team. New York: Routledge.

Fajardo, Kat. Forthcoming. *Miss Quinces*. New York: Scholastic/Graphix.

Fernández, Anita E. 2019. "Counter-Storytelling and Decolonizing Pedagogy: The Xicanx Institute for Teaching and Organizing." In *Rethinking Ethnic Studies,* edited by R. Tolteka Cuautin, Miguel Zavala, Christine Sleeter, and Wayne Au, 33–37. Milwaukee: Rethinking Schools.

Fernandez-Armesto, Felipe. 2014. *Our America: A Hispanic History of the United States*. New York: W. W. Norton & Company.

Flecha, Dulce-Marie. 2018. "Literacy on the Move: Supporting Your Highly Mobile Students." Presentation at National Council of Teachers of English Convention, November 21–24, Houston, TX. Accessed January 10, 2019. https://docs.google.com/presentation/d/1wFlQGsWDwBQ2fg_ccmiviAD9ZOI7pUMfRZxSn_eABIE/mobilepresent?slide=idg4708cef7db_1_21.

Flores, Nelson (@NelsonFlores). 2019. "In grad school I switched from the use of language minority to language minoritized to emphasize the institutional process of minoritization. I am now switching . . ." Twitter, September 14, 2019, 11:12 am. https://twitter.com/nelsonlflores/status/1172890922557857792.

Flores, Nelson, and Jonathan Rosa. 2015. "Undoing Appropriateness: Raciolinguistic Ideologies and Language Diversity in Education." *Harvard Educational Review* 85 (2): 149–71. www.hepgjournals.org/doi/abs/10.17763/0017-8055.85.2.149.

Freire, Paulo. 1970. *Pedagogy of the Oppressed*. New York: Herder and Herder.

Fryman, Pamela, dir. 2019. *One Day at a Time*. Season 3, episode 2. "Outside." February 8, Netflix.

García, Cristina. 1992. *Dreaming in Cuban*. New York: Penguin Random House.

García, Ofelia. 2009. *Bilingual Education in the 21st Century: A Global Perspective*. Malden, MA: Wiley-Blackwell.

———. 2016. "Language." In *The Wiley Blackwell Encyclopedia of Race, Ethnicity, and Nationalism,* edited by John Stone, Rutledge M. Dennis, Polly S. Rizova, Anthony D. Smith, and Xiaoshuo Hou, 1–4. John Wiley & Sons, Ltd. DOI: 10.1002/9781118663202.wberen459.

———. 2018. "When in New York City . . . : Bilingual Education Programs, Practices and Contexts." O. Garcia (Discussant). American Educational Research Association Annual Meeting, April 13.

García, Ofelia, and the CUNY-NYSIEB Team, eds. Forthcoming. *Supporting, Teaching, and Translanguaging with Emergent Bilingual Students: Lessons from the CUNY-NYSIEB Project.* New York: Routledge.

García, Ofelia, Susana Ibarra Johnson, and Kate Seltzer. 2017. *The Translanguaging Classroom: Leveraging Student Bilingualism for Learning.* Philadelphia: Caslon.

García, Ofelia, and Camila Leiva. 2014. "Theorizing and Enacting Translanguaging for Social Justice." In *Heteroglossia as Practice and Pedagogy*, edited by Angela Creese and Adrian Blackledge, 199–216. New York and London: Springer.

Gates, Henry Louis, Jr. 2011. *Black in Latin America* (documentary series). Directed by Ricardo Pollack. United States: Inkwell Films, Wall to Wall Media LTD, and Thirteen in association with WNET.org.

———. 2011. "Haiti and the Dominican Republic: An Island Divided." *Black in Latin America* (documentary series). Directed by Ricardo Pollack. United States: Inkwell Films, Wall to Wall Media LTD, and Thirteen in association with WNET.org.

Gay, Geneva. 2000. *Culturally Responsive Teaching: Theory, Research, and Practice.* New York: Teachers College Press.

German, Lorena. 2019. *The Anti-Racist Teacher Reading Instruction Workbook.* http://multiculturalclassroom consulting.com/the-anti-racist-teacher/.

Giovanni, Nikki, ed. 2008. *Hip Hop Speaks to Children: A Celebration of Poetry with a Beat.* Naperville, IL: Sourcebooks Jabberwocky.

Girl Scouts of the USA. 2016. "Meet Sylvia Acevedo." YouTube. www.youtube.com/watch?v=jeTZTaNBqNw& feature=youtu.be.

Gonzalez, Juan. 2011. *Harvest of Empire: A History of Latinos in America.* New York: Penguin Random House.

González, Lucía. 2008. *The Storyteller's Candle/La velita de los cuentos.* San Francisco: Children's Book Press.

Gonzalez, Maya Christina. 2017. *Coloring the Revolution.* San Francisco: Reflection Press.

———. 2018. *The Gender Wheel: A Story About Bodies and Gender for Everybody.* San Francisco: Reflection Press.

Gonzalez, Maya Christina, and Matthew SG. 2017. *They She He Me: Free to Be!* San Francisco: Reflection Press.

Gonzalez, Nathalie. 2018. *Women's History Month* series for MAKERS. http://nathaliegonzalez.com /womens-history-month-series.

Gorena Morales, Patty, and Joshua Barajas. 2018. "What Happens When a Child Arrives at the U.S. Border?" *PBS NewsHour.* www.pbs.org/newshour/politics/what-happens-when-a-child-arrives-at-the-u-s-border.

Grande, Reyna. 2016. *The Distance Between Us* (Young Readers Edition). New York: Aladdin Paperbacks.

Grimes, Nikki. 2017. *One Last Word: Wisdom from the Harlem Renaissance.* New York: Bloomsbury Press.

Guerrero, Diane, and Erica Moroz. 2018. *My Family Divided: One Girl's Journey of Home, Loss, and Hope.* New York: Henry Holt and Co.

Hamer, Dean, and Joe Wilson. 2014. *A Place in the Middle.* ProRes Quicktime, DVD, Blue-Ray. Running time: 24 minutes. https://vimeo.com/121840165.

Hanault, Caitlin. 2018. "From Girl Scout to Rocket Scientist—Sylvia Acevedo's Story." www.hmhco.com /blog/podcast-from-girl-scout-to-rocket-scientist.

Hernandez, Jaime. 2018. *The Dragon Slayer: Folktales from Latin America.* New York: Toon Books.

———. 2018. *La matadragones: Cuentos de Latinoamérica.* New York: Toon Books.

Herrera, Juan Felipe. 2015. "Borderbus." In *Notes on the Assemblage.* San Francisco: City Lights Books.

———. 2016. *Cinnamon Girl: Letters Found Inside a Cereal Box.* New York: Harper Teen.

Hinojosa, Maria. 2017. "Yes She Did: Dolores Huerta." NPR *Latino USA.* www.latinousa.org/2017/09/29 /yes-dolores-huerta/.

Holiday House. 2018. "Dreamer's Video." YouTube. www.youtube.com/watch?v=CAiTFJaNiD8&feature= youtu.be.

Huenún Villa, Jaime Luís. 2011. *Rayengey ti dungun: Pichikeche ñi Mapuche kumwirin/La palabra es la flor: Poesía mapuche para niños*. Concepción, Chile: Trama Impresores, S.A. http://plandelectura.gob.cl/wp-content/uploads/2015/08/La-palabra-es-la-Flor.pdf.

Hughes, Langston. 1990, 1987, 1959. *Selected Poems of Langston Hughes: A Classic Collection of Poems by a Master of American Verse*. New York: Vintage Books.

———. 1994. *The Collected Poems of Langston Hughes*. New York: Vintage Books.

International Rescue Committee. 2019. "Fact Check: What Is the National Emergency? Do We Need a Wall?" www.rescue.org/article/fact-check-what-national-emergency-do-we-need-wall.

Jesse & Joy. 2015. "Un besito más (feat. Juan Luis Guerra)." *Un Besito Más*. Warner Music Mexico S.A. de C.V.

Jiménez, Francisco. 1998. *La Mariposa*. New York: Houghton Mifflin.

———. 2002. *Cajas de cartón: relatos de la vida peregrina de un niño campesino*. New York: Houghton Mifflin.

———. 2002. *The Circuit: Stories from the Life of a Migrant Child*. New York: Houghton Mifflin.

Joseph, Lynn. 2001. *The Color of My Words*. New York: HarperCollins.

———. 2004. *El color de mis palabras*. Lyndhurst, NJ: Lectorum.

Kavilanz, Parija. 2017. "Conoce a Sylvia Acevedo, la científica espacial de origen latino a cargo de las 'Girl Scouts.'" CNN Espanõl. https://cnnespanol.cnn.com/2017/05/22/conoce-a-sylvia-acevedo-la-cientifica-espacial-de-origen-latino-a-cargo-de-las-girl-scouts/.

Kazi 88.7FM. 2017. "Vanessa Valdés Discusses Biography of Arturo Schomburg." *KAZI Book Review with Hopeton Hay, Kazi 88.7FM, Austin TX*. https://kazibookreview.wordpress.com/2017/09/17/podcast-vanessa-valdes-discusses-biography-of-arturo-schomberg/.

KidLit. n.d. "Diverse Voices in Latinx Children's Literature LIVE STREAM!" https://kidlit.tv/2019/03/diverse-voices-in-latinx-childrens-literature-live-stream/.

King, Thomas. 1992. *A Coyote Columbus Story*. Toronto, ON: Groundwood Books.

Kirkland, David E. 2008. "The Rose That Grew from Concrete: Postmodern Blackness and New English Education." *English Journal* 97 (5): 69–75.

Krensky, Stephen. 1991. *Christopher Columbus*. New York: Random House.

Ladson-Billings, Gloria. 1995. "Toward a Theory of Culturally Relevant Pedagogy." *American Educational Research Journal* 32 (3): 465–91.

Latin American Youth Center. 2018. *Voces sin fronteras: Our Stories, Our Truth*. Washington, D.C.: Shout Mouse Press.

Latino Rebels. 2018. "The Canonization of Archbishop Oscar Romero." www.latinorebels.com/2018/09/01/oscarromero/.

Lázaro, Georgina. 2007. *Cuando los grandes eran pequeños: José Martí*. Lyndhurst, NJ: Lectorum Publications.

Lê, Minh. 2018. *Drawn Together*. New York: Disney Hyperion.

Lee, Spike, dir. 1992. *Malcolm X*. Brooklyn, NY: 40 Acres and a Mule Filmworks, DVD.

Lehman, Christopher, and Kate Roberts. 2014. *Falling in Love with Close Reading: Lessons for Analyzing Texts and Life*. Portsmouth, NH: Heinemann.

Levien, Richard. 2009. *Immersion*. Media That Matters. https://youtu.be/I6Y0HAjLKYI.

Levins Morales, Ricardo. 2010. *Peace Is a Product of Justice*. Digital Print. 11" x 17." RLM World Headquarters.

———. 2014. *My Hands/Mis Manos – Victor Jara*. Digital Print. 11" x 17." RLM World Headquarters.

Library of Congress. 2018. "Sylvia Acevedo: 2018 National Book Festival." YouTube. www.youtube.com/watch?v=bdMNst2hwsk&feature=youtu.be.

López, Gustavo, and Ana Gonzalez-Barrera. 2016. "Afro-Latino: A Deeply Rooted Identity Among U.S. Hispanics." Pew Research Center. www.pewresearch.org/fact-tank/2016/03/01/afro-latino-a-deeply-rooted-identity-among-u-s-hispanics/.

Lopez, Mark Hugo, Jens Manuel Kronstad, and Antonio Flores. 2018. "Key Facts About Young Latinos, One of the Nation's Fastest-Growing Populations." Pew Research Center. www.pewresearch.org/fact-tank/2018/09/13/key-facts-about-young-latinos/.

Lyiscott, Jamila. 2014. "3 Ways to Speak English." TedSalon NY. www.ted.com/talks/jamila_lyiscott_3_ways_to_speak_english/transcript.

MAKERS. n.d. "Dolores Huerta, Co-Founder, United Farm Workers." www.makers.com/profiles/591f27805bf6236c3464b1b8.

———. n.d. "Sandra Cisneros, Pioneering Latina Writer." www.makers.com/profiles/591f277e5bf6236c34 64b1a2.

Maldonado, Torrey. 2018. *Tight.* New York: Nancy Paulsen Books.

Manzano, Sonia. 2012. *The Revolution of Evelyn Serrano.* New York: Scholastic.

Mark, Michelle. 2017. "A Trump Adviser Told DACA Recipients to 'Get in Line' to Immigrate to the US—Here's Why They Can't." *Business Insider.* www.businessinsider.in/A-Trump-adviser-told-DACA-recipients -to-get-in-line-to-immigrate-to-the-US-heres-why-they-cant/articleshow/60383521.cms.

Martinez, Reuben. 2010. *Once Upon a Time: Traditional Latin American Tales/Había una vez: Cuentos tradicionales latinoamericanos.* New York: HarperCollins.

Martinez, Xiuhtezcatl. 2017. *We Rise: The Earth Guardians Guide to Building a Movement That Restores the Planet.* Emmaus, PA: Rodale Books.

Martinez-Neal, Juana. 2018. *Alma and How She Got Her Name.* Somerville, MA: Candlewick.

———. 2018. *Alma y cómo obtuvo su nombre.* Somerville, MA: Candlewick.

Maxwell, Lesli A. 2014. "Sylvia Mendez and California's School Desegregation Story." *Education Week.* http: //blogs.edweek.org/edweek/learning-the-language/2014/05/sylvia_mendez_and_californias_.html.

Mayeno, Laurin. 2016. *One of a Kind Like Me/Único como yo.* Oakland, CA: Blood Orange Press.

Mayers, Steven, and Jonathan Freedman. 2018. "From Solito to Solidarity." Voice of Witness. http: //voiceofwitness.org/solito-to-solidarity/.

———, eds. 2019. *Solito, Solita: Crossing Borders with Youth Refugees from Central America.* Chicago, IL: Haymarket Books.

McCall, Guadalupe García. 2011. *Under the Mesquite.* New York: Lee & Low Books.

———. 2016. *Shame the Stars.* New York: Lee & Low Books.

———. 2018. *All the Stars Denied.* New York: Lee & Low Books.

Medina, Juana. 2016. *Juana & Lucas.* Somerville, MA: Candlewick.

Medina, Meg. 2015. *Mango, Abuela, and Me.* Somerville, MA: Candlewick.

———. 2015. *Mango, abuela y yo.* Somerville, MA: Candlewick.

———. 2018. *Merci Suárez Changes Gears.* Somerville, MA: Candlewick

———. 2018. National Council of Teachers of English (NCTE) Annual Meeting.

Menchú, Rigoberta, and Dante Liano. 2006. *The Honey Jar.* Toronto, ON: Groundwood Books.

Méndez, Yamile Saied. 2019. *¿De dónde eres?* New York: HarperCollins Español.

———. 2019. *Where Are You From?* New York: HarperCollins Children's Books.

Mendez v. Westminster, 161F.2d 774, 11310 (9th Cir. 1947).

Mohr, Nicholasa. 1993. *El Bronx Remembered.* New York: HarperCollins Children's Books.

———. 1996. *Nilda.* Houston, TX: Arte Público Press.

Moll, Luis, C., Cathy Amanti, Deborah Neff, and Norma Gonzalez. 1992. "Funds of Knowledge for Teaching: Using a Qualitative Approach to Connect Homes and Classrooms." *Theory into Practice* 31 (2): 132–41.

Montilla, Yesenia. n.d. "Poetry, Interviews & Reviews." Accessed September 15, 2019. www.yeseniamontilla .com/poetry.

Mora, Pat. 2000. *My Own True Name: New and Selected Poems for Young Adults.* Houston, TX: Piñata Books for Young Adults.

Moraga, Cherríe L. 2011. *A Xicana Codex of Changing Consciousness: Writings, 2000–2010.* Durham, NC: Duke University Press.

Morales, Iris. 1996. "Palante, Siempre Palante! The Young Lords." New York: Third World Newsreel. https: //vimeo.com/ondemand/palantesiempreprepalante/.

———. 2016. *Through the Eyes of Rebel Women: The Young Lords 1969–1976.* New York: Red Sugarcane Press.

Morales, Yuyi. 2017. "Dreamers." YouTube. www.youtube.com/watch?v=B5XbU7H5OM8&feature=youtu.be.

———. 2018. *Dreamers.* New York: Neal Porter Books.

———. 2018. *Soñadores.* New York: Neal Porter Books.

Morales Almada, J. 2014. "Testimonio: Hermanitos migrantes relatan su trauma por 'la hielera.'" *La Opinión.* August 23. https://laopinion.com/2014/08/23/testimonio-hermanitos-migrantes-relatan -su-trauma-por-la-hielera/.

Morrell, Ernest. 2007. *Critical Literacy and Urban Youth: Pedagogies of Access, Dissent, and Liberation.* New York: Routledge.

———. 2015. "The 2014 NCTE Presidential Address: Powerful English at NCTE Yesterday, Today, and Tomorrow: Toward the Next Movement." *Research in the Teaching of English* 49 (3): 307–27.

Muñoz Ryan, Pam. 2000. *Esperanza Rising.* New York: Scholastic.

———. 2002. *Esperanza renace.* New York: Scholastic.

———. 2010. *The Dreamer.* New York: Scholastic.

———. 2010. *El soñador.* New York: Scholastic en español.

———. 2015. *Echo.* New York: Scholastic.

My Immigration Story. n.d. "My Immigration Story: The Story of U.S. Immigrants in Their Own Words." https://myimmigrationstory.com.

National Immigration Forum. 2019. "Fact Sheet: U.S. Asylum Process." https://immigrationforum.org/article/fact-sheet-u-s-asylum-process/.

National Museum of American History. n.d. "Latino History." https://americanhistory.si.edu/topics/latino-history.

Nava, Pedro E. 2017. "Abuelita Storytelling: From Pain to Possibility and Implications for Higher Education." *Storytelling, Self, Society* 13 (2).

NBC News. n.d. "U.S. System for Refugee, Asylum Seekers Explained." www.nbcnews.com/id/43442030/ns/us_news-life/t/us-system-refugee-asylum-seekers-explained/#.XWroVpNKjOQ.

Nebehay, Stephanie. 2018. "U.N. Reaffirms Refugees' Right to Seek Asylum in U.S." Reuters. www.reuters.com/article/us-usa-immigration-un/un-reaffirms-refugees-right-to-seek-asylum-in-us-idUSKCN1NW1OD.

Nieto, Sonia. 1994. "Affirmation, Solidarity, and Critique: Moving Beyond Tolerance in Multicultural Education." *Multicultural Education* 1 (4): 9–12, 35–38.

NPR. 2009. "'House on Mango Street' Celebrates 25 Years." NPR *Morning Edition.* www.npr.org/templates/story/story.php?storyId=102900929.

———. 2017. "Recién llegados/Newly Arrived." *Radio Ambulante.* http://radioambulante.org/en/audio-en/newlyarrived.

———. 2019. "Portrait of: Sylvia Acevedo." NPR *Latino USA.* www.nprorg/2019/01/23/687951333/portrait-of-former-nasa-engineer-sylvia-acevedo-on-being-the-only-woman-in-the-r.

Nuñez, Victoria. 2012. "Centro Teaching Guide," Teaching Guide for Documentary. Center for Puerto Rican Studies. https://centropr.hunter.cuny.edu/sites/default/files/edu/Pura%20Belpre%CC%81%2Teaching%20Guide-2016.pdf.

Nye, Naomi Shihab, ed. 1995. *The Tree Is Older Than You Are: A Bilingual Gathering of Poems and Stories from Mexico with Paintings by Mexican Artists.* New York: Simon Schuster Books for Young Readers.

O'Brien, Soledad. 2009. *Latino in America.* New York: New American Library.

Older, Daniel José. 2018. *Dactyl Hill Squad.* New York: Arthur A Levine.

Olivarez, José. 2018. "(Citizen) (Illegal)" in *Citizen Illegal.* Chicago, IL: Haymarket Books.

———. n.d. "Poems." https://joseolivarez.com.

Orellana, Marjorie Faulstich. 2009. *Translating Childhoods: Immigrant Youth, Language, and Culture.* New Brunswick, NJ: Rutgers University Press.

Ortiz, Paul. 2018. *An African American and Latinx History of the United States.* Boston: Beacon Press.

Ortiz, Simon J. 2017. *El pueblo seguirá.* New York: Lee & Low Books.

———. 2017. *The People Shall Continue.* New York: Lee & Low Books.

Otheguy, Emma. 2017. *Martí's Song for Freedom/Martí y sus versos por la libertad.* New York: Lee & Low Books.

———. 2019. *Silver Meadows Summer.* New York: Alfred A. Knopf.

Paliza-Carre, Sophia. 2018. "Dolores Huerta and Her Daughter Talk Gender and Power." NPR *Latino USA.* www.latinousa.org/2018/11/06/doloreshuerta/.

Palmer, Deborah, Ramón Antonio Martínez, Suzanne G. Mateus, and Kathryn Henderson. 2014. "Reframing the Debate on Language Separation: Toward a Vision for Translanguaging Pedagogies in the Dual Language Classroom." *The Modern Language Journal* 98 (3): 757–72.

Paris, Django, and Samy H. Alim. 2017. *Culturally Sustaining Pedagogy: Teaching and Learning for Justice in a Changing World*. New York: Teachers College Press.

Parras, Bryan. 2012. "Sandra Cisneros Reads at the Librotraficante Caravan Banned Book Bash in San Antonio." YouTube. https://youtu.be/vJWsHoAb57g.

PBS. 2012. "Yuyi's Story." YouTube. www.youtube.com/watch?v=RQdI5r-Ac3w&feature=youtu.be.

———. 2013. "Latino Americans: Timeline of Important Dates." www.pbs.org/latino-americans/en/timeline/.

———. n.d. *"Mendez v. Westminster:* Desegregating California's Schools." PBS Learning Media. https://witf.pbslearningmedia.org/resource/osi04.soc.ush.civil.mendez/mendez-v-westminster-desegregating-californias-schools/.

Pelaez Lopez, Alan. 2018. "The X in Latinx Is a Wound, Not a Trend." *Color Bloq*. http://efniks.com/the-deep-dive-pages/2018/9/11/the-x-in-latinx-is-a-wound-not-a-trend.

Penguin Random House. n.d. "Sandra Cisneros." www.penguinrandomhouseaudio.com/narrator/4977/sandra-cisneros/.

Perdomo, Willie. 1996. *Where a Nickel Costs a Dime: Poems*. New York: W. W. Norton & Company.

Pérez, Ashley Hope. 2019. *Out of Darkness*. York, PA: Holiday House.

Pérez, Celia C. 2017. *The First Rule of Punk*. New York: Puffin Books.

———. 2019. *Strange Birds: A Field Guide to Ruffling Feathers*. New York: Kokila.

Persichetti, Bob, Peter Ramsey, and Rodney Rothman, dirs. 2018. *Spider-Man: Into the Spider-Verse*. Sony Pictures Releasing.

Pietri, Pedro. 2008. "Love Poem for My People." In *Hip Hop Speaks to Children: A Celebration of Poetry with a Beat*, edited by Nikki Giovanni. Naperville, IL: Sourcebooks Jabberwocky.

———. 2015. *Pedro Pietri: Selected Poetry*. San Francisco: City Lights Books.

Pimentel, Miguel Jontel. 2017a. "102 Earthworks: Miguel: Mexico Chapter 1." YouTube. June 9. Accessed October 27, 2018. www.youtube.com/watch?v=08vbGWfYFFI.

———. 2017b. "102 Earthworks: Miguel: Mexico Chapter 3." YouTube. June 9. Accessed October 27, 2018. www.youtube.com/watch?v=rT-GJtTpcFA.

Quintero, Isabel. 2019. *Mi papi tiene una moto*. New York: Kokila.

———. 2019. *My Papi Has a Motorcycle*. New York: Kokila.

Radford, Jynnah, and Luis Noe-Bustamante. 2019. "Facts on U.S. Immigrants, 2017: Statistical Portrait of the Foreign-Born Population in the United States." Pew Research Center. June 3. www.pewhispanic.org/2019/06/03/facts-on-u-s-immigrants/.

Ramos, Jorge. 2016. "The Many Homes of Sandra Cisneros." Interview with Sandra Cisneros. August 24. https://jorgeramos.com/en/many-homes-sandra-cisneros/.

Reading Rockets. n.d. "A Video Interview with Meg Medina." www.readingrockets.org/books/interviews/medina.

Reese, Debbie. 2017. "Opening Keynote #TheEdCollabGathering Fall 2017." The Educator Collaborative, LLC [YouTube]. September 23. www.youtube.com/watch?v=K776U3n8mU8.

———. 2018. "My Response to 'Can You Recommend a Book About Columbus?'" *American Indians in Children's Literature* [blog]. October 13. https://americanindiansinchildrensliterature.blogspot.com/2018/10/my-response-to-can-you-recommend-book.html.

Reynolds, Jason. 2017. "How Poetry Can Help Kids Turn a Fear of Literature into Love." *PBS NewsHour*. www.pbs.org/newshour/show/how-poetry-can-help-kids-turn-a-fear-of-literature-into-love.

———. 2018. *For Every One*. New York: Atheneum Books for Young Readers.

Riojas, Yocelyn. 2018. *My Dreams Are Not Illegal*. Poster. Austin, TX. https://bastatexas.org/resistance-art/yocelynriojas_posters-2_page_1/.

Riojas Clark, Ellen, Belinda Bustos Flores, Howard L. Smith, and Daniel Alejandro González. 2015. *Multicultural Literature for Latino Bilingual Children: Their Words, Their Worlds*. New York: Rowman & Littlefield.

Riordan Seville, Lisa, and Hannah Rappleye. 2014. "Border Children Tell Their Stories: Why We Came to the US." NBC News. www.nbcnews.com/news/investigations/border-children-tell-their-stories-why-we-came-us-n129646.

Rodriguez, Favianna. 2013. *No Human Being Is Illegal*. Digital Print, 13 x 13 inches. Oakland, CA.

———. 2017. *You Are Welcome Here*. Offset Poster, 24 x 18 inches. Oakland, CA.

Rodríguez, Luis, J. 1993. *Always Running: La Vida Loca: Gang Days in L.A.* New York: Touchstone.

———. 1998. *América Is Her Name.* Evanston, IL: Curbstone Books.

Rogow, Faith, Dean Hamer, and Adam Chang. n.d. *A Place in the Middle: A Strength-Based Approach to Gender Diversity & Inclusion. Discussion and Activity Guide.* https://aplaceinthemiddle.org/uploads/websites/675files/56b47f0ab53b5.pdf.

Rosa, Jonathan. 2019. *Looking Like a Language, Sounding Like a Race: Raciolinguistic Ideologies and the Learning of Latinidad.* New York: Oxford University Press.

Russo, Anthony, dir. 2018. *Avengers: Infinity War.* Burbank, CA: Marvel Studios.

Salazar, Aida. 2019. *The Moon Within.* New York: Arthur A. Levine Books.

Salgado, Julio. 2015. *Undocumented, Unafraid and Unapologetic.* Digital Print, 17 x 11 inches.

———. 2016. *No LGBTQ Exclusion!* Digital Print, 17 x 11 inches.

Sanchez, Mary Louise. 2018. *The Wind Called My Name.* New York: Tu Books.

Santiago, Esmeralda. 1993. *When I Was Puerto Rican.* Boston: Da Capo Press.

———. 1994. *Cuando era Puertorriqueña.* New York: Vintage Español.

Scholastic. n.d. "Meet Young Immigrants." *Scholastic's Immigration: Stories of Yesterday and Today.* http://teacher.scholastic.com/activities/immigration/young_immigrants/.

Schomburg Center. 2015. "The 2015 Puerto Rican Day Parade Honors Arturo Schomburg." YouTube. www.youtube.com/watch?v=angdbBG-GMQ&feature=youtu.be.

———. n.d. "Arturo Schomburg Lecture." Vimeo. https://livestream.com/accounts/7326672/events/4655068/videos/110525479.

Smith, Cynthia Leitich. 2000. *Jingle Dancer.* New York: HarperCollins.

Social Justice Books: A Teaching for Change Project. 2016. "Creating an Anti-Bias Library." https://socialjusticebooks.org/creating-an-anti-bias-library/.

Sotomayor, Sonia. 2018. *The Beloved World of Sonia Sotomayor* (Young Readers Edition). New York: Delacorte Press.

———. 2018. *El mundo adorado de Sonia Sotomayor* (adaptado para jovenes mayores). New York: Vintage Español.

———. 2018. *Pasando páginas: La historia de mi vida.* New York: Philomel Books.

———. 2018. *Turning Pages: My Life Story.* New York: Philomel Books.

Stavans, Ilan, and Lalo Alcaraz. 2000. *Latino USA: A Cartoon History.* New York: Philip Lief Group.

Tafolla, Carmen. 2008. *That's Not Fair! Emma Tenayuca's Struggle for Justice/¡No es justo! La lucha de Emma Tenayuca por la justicia.* San Antonio, TX: Wings Press.

Thomas, Piri. 1967. *Down These Mean Streets.* New York: Alfred A Knopf.

Tijoux, Ana. 2015. "Antipatriarca." YouTube. May 29. Accessed August 30, 2019. www.youtube.com/watch?v=RoKoj8bFg2E.

Tintiangco-Cubales, Allyson, Rita Kohli, Jocyl Sacramento, Nick Henning, Ruching Agarwal-Rangnath, and Christine Sleeter. 2019. "What Is Ethnic Studies Pedagogy?" In *Rethinking Ethnic Studies,* edited by R. Tolteka Cuautin, Miguel Zavala, Christine Sleeter, and Wayne Au, 20–25. Milwaukee: Rethinking Schools.

Tonatiuh, Duncan. 2010. *Dear Primo: A Letter to My Cousin.* New York: Abrams Books for Young Readers.

———. 2010. *Querido primo: Una carta a mi primo.* New York: Scholastic.

———. 2013. *Pancho Rabbit and the Coyote.* New York: Abrams Books for Young Readers.

———. 2014. *Separate Is Never Equal: Sylvia Mendez and Her Family's Fight for Desegregation.* New York: Abrams Books for Young Readers.

———. 2017. *Separados no somos iguales: Sylvia Mendez y la lucha de su familia por la integración.* Distrito Federal, Mexico: SITESA.

———. 2018. *Undocumented: A Worker's Fight.* New York: Abrams Books for Young Readers.

Ulaby, Neda. 2016. "How NYC's First Puerto Rican Librarian Brought Spanish to the Shelves." *Boundbreakers: People Who Make a Difference.* www.npr.org/2016/09/08/492957864how-nycs-first-puerto-rican-librarian-brought-spanish-to-the-shelves.

United States Citizenship and Immigration Services. 2015. "Refugees & Asylum." https://www.uscis.gov/humanitarian/refugees-asylum.

Universidad de Chile. n.d. "Mapüche Nutram." www.libros.uchile.cl/files/presses/1/monographs/710 /submission/proof/index.html.

Valenzuela, Angela. 1999. *Subtractive Schooling: U.S. Mexican Youth and the Politics of Caring.* Albany: SUNY Press.

Valle Sentíes, Raquel. 2005. "Soy como soy y qué." In *Red Hot Salsa: Bilingual Poems on Being Young and Latino in the United States*, edited by Lori Marie Carlson. New York: Henry Holt & Co.

Vardell, Sylvia, and Janet Wong. 2017. *Here We Go: A Poetry Friday Power Book.* Princeton, NJ: Pomelo Books.

Vega, E. J. 1994. "Translating My Grandfather's House." In *Cool Salsa: Bilingual Poems on Growing Up Latino in the United States,* edited by Lori Marie Carlson. New York: Henry Holt & Co.

Weatherford, Carole Boston. 1995. *Juneteenth Jamboree.* New York: Lee & Low Books.

———. 2017. *Schomburg: The Man Who Built a Library.* Somerville, MA: Candlewick.

———. 2019. *Schomburg: El hombre que creó una biblioteca.* Somerville, MA: Candlewick.

Weaver, Lila Quintero. 2012. *Darkroom: A Memoir in Black and White.* Tuscaloosa, AL: The University of Alabama Press.

———. 2018. *My Year in the Middle.* Somerville, MA: Candlewick.

Wikipedia. 2019. "Refugee Act." https://en.wikipedia.org/wiki/Refugee_Act.

Winter, Jonah. 2009. *Sonia Sotomayor: A Judge Grows in the Bronx/La juez que creció en el Bronx.* New York: Atheneum Books for Young Readers.

Woodson, Jacqueline. 2014. *Brown Girl Dreaming.* New York: Nancy Paulsen Books.

———. 2018. *The Day You Begin.* New York: Nancy Paulsen Books.

———. 2018. *El día en que descubres quién eres.* New York: Nancy Paulsen Books.

Zehtabchi, Rayka, dir. 2019. "Period. End of Sentence." 2019. United States: Netflix.

Zinn Education Project. n.d. "The People vs. Columbus, et al." www.zinnedproject.org/materials /people-vs-columbus/.

INDEX

emotional responses in students, 7, 35, 116–117, 134. *See also* classrooms

En Comunidad pedagogical approach, summary, 167–169

Engle, Margarita, 146, 150

English language classrooms, 45–46

Escamilla, Kathy, 164–165

Espada, Martín, 150

España, Carla
   family journey, story of, 4–5
   impact of Lee's *Malcolm X* movie on, 96
   influence of government policies on, 13
   language practices, traditions, 6–8, 11–12
   sharing personal stories with students, 86, 120
   teachings on colonialism and resistance, 77
   "Translanguaging Literacies: Translanguaging in Children's Literature and Literacy Instruction," 165

exemplar texts. *See also* digital media/texts
   about immigration experiences, 124
   choosing, factors to consider, 82
   for countering harmful narratives, 131, 134
   for exploring folklore and mythology, 80–82
   for identifying personal language practices, 29
   identifying themes and topics in, 68–70, 72–73
   on immigration experiences, 124
   on immigration policy, 130
   interviews with authors of, 67
   for lesson on master and counter-narratives, 95, 99
   for poetry, 140–141, 143–144, 148–152
   for reading in community, 51–52
   stories from Latinx authors, 47–50
   for supporting translanguaging, 27
   for understanding relationship of language and power, 36–37

exploring language, identity, and power
   curating poems, building text sets, 148–152
   discussions on language, power, and identity, 153
   and the power of poetry, 147–148
   renaming text sets, 153

F

families/caretakers. *See also* translanguaging
   connecting classroom experience with, 35
   engaging in support and advocacy activities, 161
   interviewing, 67–68, 73–74, 120–123
   as language partners, 22

"A Family of Storytellers," 68

Feathered Serpent, Dark Heart of Sky: Myths of Mexico (Bowles), 83 87

Fernández, Anita, 111

Flores, Nelson, 18, 111, 164

folklore and mythology lesson
   mentor texts, 80–83
   partner and group research, 86–88
   purpose, value, 80

   shared reading, 83–86
   sharing research findings, 87–88
   time for personal reflections, 88

Fourth of July events, narratives about, 92

Freire, Paulo, 18

G

gallery walk, 87–88

García, Ofelia, 18, 163

García, Yaritza, 1–2

Gay, Geneva, 18

gender diverse cultures, 86–87

Germán, Lorena, 163

globalization, 78

government policies, understanding, 13–14. *See also* immigration policies; dominant narratives

Grimes, Nikki, 146

H

"Hair" (Acevedo), 148

Hairs/Pelitos (Cisneros), 77–78

"Haiti and the Dominican Republic: An Island Divided" (documentary), 77

hate speech, 117

Herrera, Juan Felipe, 150

Herrera, Luz Yadira
   family journey, 5–6
   immigration story, 120
   influence of government policies on, 14, 78
   language practices, traditions, 7–9, 12
   standing against injustice, 112–113
   "Translanguaging Literacies: Translanguaging in Children's Literature and Literacy Instruction," 165

Hip Hop Speaks to Children (Giovanni, ed.), 146

historical events. *See also* counter-narratives; Latinx history, culture; dominant narratives
   choosing for lesson focus, 97–98
   partnership and group discussions, 100
   rethinking, 97–98

"How Do You Tame a Wild Tongue?" (Anzaldúa), 36–44

"How Poetry Can Help Kids Turn a Fear of Literature into Love" (Reynolds), 140

Huerta, Dolores, 105

Hughes, Langston, 146

hybridity concept, 17–18

I

identity
   bilingual, importance of validating, 45–46
   as inmigrante/immigrant, 112–113
   as multi-leveled, complex, 32, 35
   and self-image, 116–117

immigration policies
   Business Insider infographic, 128
   discussion topics/counter-narratives, 131

about migrant youths' experiences, 125–126
for reading counter-narratives, 132
for recognizing bilingual practices, 33, 42
for recognizing identities, 16
about research, 87–88
about students' journeys, 6
for understanding language practices, 8

R

raciolinguistic ideologies, 18, 164
racism, internalized, 77, 111
read-alouds. *See* reading in community
reading in community
  *Alma and How She Got Her Name/Alma y cómo
    obtuvo su nombre* (Martinez-Neal), 56–57
  approaches to, 51–53
  class discussion, 62
  considering themes and lessons, 61
  folklore and mythology studies, 84
  introducing the exemplar books, 61
  and learning communities, 51–52
  Mango, abuela y yo/Mango, Abuela, and Me
    (Medina), 58–60
  process, 62
  Soñadores/Dreamers (Morales), 54–55
  teacher or student reading/sharing ideas, 61–62
reading materials. *See* digital media/texts; exemplar
  texts
Reese, Debbie, 163
reflection time
  about colonization, 94
  about folklore and mythology, 88
  approaches to, 127, 166–167
  importance, 22, 52
Reimagining Migration Project (UCLA), 126
research skills, 86–88, 128–132
resistance. *See also* social movements
  introducing term to students, 90
  poetry as tool for, 139
  as theme, 39
Rethinking Ethnic Studies (ed. Cuauhtin), 164
Rethinking Schools and Teaching Tolerance, 77
The Revolution of Evelyn Serrano (Manzano), 108
Reynolds, Jason, 134, 140, 146
Roberts, Kate, 26
Romero, Óscar Arnulfo, xiv, 106
Rosa, Jonathan, 18, 164

S

safe classrooms. *See* classrooms
Salazar, Aida. *See The Moon Within* (Salazar)
Schomburg, Arturo, xiv, 106
Sentíes, Raquel Valle, 15
setting, as focus for personal stories, 64
shared reading
  example poems for, 143–144
  of firsthand accounts of migrant experience, 125

folklore and mythology lesson, 84–86
  of writings on immigration policy, 130
sharing poetry reading across the week
  example poems and topics, 144
  example schedules, 145–146
  starting the lesson, 142–144
Silk Road Connect Partnership, 137–138
slave trade, introducing to students, 90
small-groups
  for facilitating discussion, 85 145
  for rehearsing poetry performances, 154
  for research, 100
  supporting translanguaging during, 2, 27, 50, 75
Smith, Cynthia Leitich, 163
social movements. *See also* standing against injustice sequence
  examples of Latinx activism, 113–114
  as form of counter-narratives, 108–109
  and publishing messages opposing harmful
    narratives, 135
  social action, activism guidelines, 134
  and social justice issues, 114–115
Soñadores/Dreamers (Morales)
  interview questions inspired by, 72
  overview, 51
  reading in community, 54–55
  themes and topics from, 69–70
Sotomayor, Sonia, 106
spoken word poetry, watching, 154
standing against injustice. *See also* immigration
  policy; social movements; support and
  advocacy
  and countering harmful dominant narratives,
    112–113, 133–136
  forms of resistance, 89–90
  goal, 117
  hearing and sharing personal narratives/
    mi origen, 119–123
  lesson sequence, 113–114
  researching policies, 128–132
  using primary and secondary sources, 124–127
storytelling. *See also* counter-narratives
  counter-storytellers, 102–110
  as a craft, and writing personal stories, 63–66
  intergenerational, 67–71
  Latinx classics, 106–107
  and reading in community, 51–62
  as a skill, 46–47
subtractive schooling, 12
support and advocacy
  clarifying focus, 158
  creating and implementing plans for, 159–162
  edu-activism, 162–163
  implementing plans, 158–162
  importance, 158
  raciolinguistic ideologies, 164
  texts for, 164–165

Supporting, Teaching, and Translanguaging with Emergent Bilingual Students: Lessons from the CUNY-NYSIEB Project (ed. García and CUNY-NYSIEB Team), 165

sustaining community through poetry
    exploring language, identity, and power, 147–153
    and integrating poetry into students' lives, 146
    lesson sequence, 140
    performing poetry for resistance, healing, and teaching, 154–156
    power of bilingual poems, 137–139
    sharing poetry reading across the week, 142–146
    translanguaging and, 141

T

teaching, lessons about, 35, 42–43. *See also* classrooms; communities of practice; questions, guiding/starter

telling our stories
    complexity and depth of stories to be told, 75
    creating safe spaces for, 46–47
    and the importance of validating bilingual identities, 45–47
    interviewing others, learning others' personal stories, 67–71
    lesson sequence, 47
    and reading in community, 51–54
    supporting translanguaging, 50
    and writing our own stories, 63–66

text sets for poetry, 152–153. *See also* exemplar texts

Thanksgiving/Columbus Day holidays, counter-narratives, 90

themes and topics
    and close reading, 31
    as focus for personal stories, 64
    in mentor texts, identifying, 68–70

They Call Me Güero: A Border Kid's Poems (Bowles), 139

"3 Ways to Speak English" (Lyiscott), 148

Torres, Julia, 163

translanguaging
    approaches to supporting, 118
    and bilingual Latinx students, 21–22

Bilingual/Multilingual Concept Guide on colonization, 91
    characteristics and benefits, 20–21
    and the depth and complexity of personal stories, 75
    and the goal of counter-storytelling, 111
    and the impact of circumstances on language choice, 147
    non-Spanish speakers, 21–22
    and opposing harmful narratives, 136
    poetry for, 156
    supporting, role of classroom or school in supporting, 33–34
    supporting using paired lessons, 27
    supporting while telling our stories, 50
    through poetry, 141
    using, value of, xviii–xix
    and using all available linguistic resources, 134
    and the value of creating personal stories, 75
    and white middle-class language norms, 18

"Translating My Grandfather's House" (Vega), 147

U

undocumented students/undocumented status, 5, 14, 71, 113, 129. *See also* immigration policy; migration experiences

"Undoing Appropriateness: Raciolinguistic Ideologies and Language Diversity in Education" (Flores and Rosa), 164

United Farm Workers Union, 108–109

unlearning bad practices, 42–43

V

Valenzuela, Angela, 12, 17

Valerie (teacher), multilingual classroom, 2

Vega, E. J., 147

W

Woetzel, Damian, 138–139

Woodson, Jacqueline, 146

writing personal stories
    identifying a focus, 64
    making connecting with mentor texts, 63
    mentor texts as models for, 64